I HAVE THIS NIFTY IDEA
...*Now what do I do with it?*

This book contains the outlines for science fiction and fantasy novels which real authors (new and old) used to sell their books to major publishing companies. These outlines are actual examples drawn from the authors' files, not idealized versions prepared just for textbooks.

Whether you're a beginning writer looking to break into novels, an experienced professional looking for new tools and techniques to sell books, or a fan curious about the remarkable thought-processes of some of the great genre writers of our time, you will find something here which enlightens, educates, and entertains you.

Editor Mike Resnick has drawn together an impressive lineup, ranging from masters like Robert Silverberg *(Lord Valentine's Castle)* and Joe Haldeman *(Forever Peace)*, and cutting-edge talents like Robert Sawyer *(Starplex)* and Kevin J. Anderson *(The Saga of Seven Suns)*, to newer writers like Susan R. Matthews, Laura Resnick, and Kathleen Ann Goonan, with a wide range in between.

I Have This Nifty Idea... is the perfect addition to every library of books on writing.

I HAVE THIS NIFTY IDEA
...Now what do I do with it?

Selected and edited by

Mike Resnick

WILDSIDE PRESS
PENNSYLVANIA • CALIFORNIA • OHIO • NEW YORK

I HAVE THIS NIFTY IDEA

Published by:

Wildside Press
PO Box 301
Holicong, PA 18928
www.wildsidepress.com

Contents

Introduction

ASK ANY SCIENCE FICTION writer what question he hears the most often, and the odds are that he'll tell you it's "Where do you get your crazy ideas?"

But ask that same writer what question he hears most often at conventions and workshops, and in e-mail from fans, and it's "I've got this nifty idea for a novel. How do I write a synopsis or proposal to send to a book editor?"

I heard that almost hourly when I taught Clarion. I hear (or read) it daily as the author of the *Ask Bwana* column. It comes up at least twice a week on the Resnick Listserv.

And I'm not alone. Every pro who has led a workshop or lectured beginning writers hears the same question: how do you write an outline or a synopsis for a book editor? And then, almost in the same breath: how long should it be? How short? How thorough? How vague? What do you cover? What do you leave out? How impersonal should it be? How formal?

So, after a couple of decades of answering one questioner at a time, I thought it might be useful to put together a book of outlines, synopses and proposals.

You'll find all types here. One-pagers. Forty-pagers. Formal proposals. Informal letters to friendly editors. Trilogy synopses. Movie synopses. You name it, we've got it.

In closing, I want tell you a little something about the contributors. We've got some unquestioned giants of the field here. We've got some bestsellers, some award winners, some first novelists. Every single one of them contributed their pieces free of charge. Why? Because in the science fiction community, we take seriously the notion that you can't pay back and therefore you must pay forward. I don't know of any other community of artists in any field that is so unfailingly generous with its time and possessions. I salute them, and I am proud to be included in their fraternity.

–Mike Resnick
www.mikeresnick.com

ROBERT SILVERBERG

ROBERT SILVERBERG IS one of the true giants of science fiction. He has quite a few Hugo awards, even more Nebulas, he was probably the youngest Worldcon Guest of Honor in history, he is an accomplished editor, he was the second President of SFWA (the Science Fiction Writers of America), and his writing excels at all lengths. More than one critic has called him our finest practitioner.

In the late 1960s and early 1970s, he produced such classics as *Thorns, Nightwings, Son of Man, Born With the Dead*, and my personal favorite, *Dying Inside*. Then he retired from writing for a few years.

Lord Valentine's Castle was his "comeback" book. It sold for an advance of $127,500, which was a record back in 1980. This is the outline that got him the contract.

LORD VALENTINE'S CASTLE

by Robert Silverberg

THIS LONG PICARESQUE adventure—the manuscript will probably run 600 pages—takes place on the huge world of Majipoor, a planet enormously bigger than Earth, but lacking most of the heavier elements, so that the gravity is only about three-fourths that of Earth. All is airy and light on Majipoor: it is a cheerful and playful place in general, although highly urbanized, bearing a population of many billions. Food is abundant, the air is fresh, the streams and oceans are clean. Majipoor was settled by colonists from Earth some fourteen thousand years ago, but also is occupied peacefully by representatives of six or seven of the galaxy's other intelligent species, as well as the descendants of Majipoor's own native race, humanoid in form, capable of physical changes of shape. These last beings are regarded with some uneasiness by the others, and this uneasiness is reciprocated.

Across the vastness of Majipoor's three colossal continents is spread an incredible diversity of cities, glittering and majestic, separated by parks, agricultural territories, forest preserves, wastelands kept deliberately barren as boundaries, and holy districts occupied by religious devotees. Such a gigantic cosmos of a planet hardly be efficiently governed by one central authority, and yet a central authority does exist, to which all local governors do indeed lip-service and on occasion direct homage. This central authority is the Pontifex, an imperial figure, aloof and virtually unknowable, who has no direct contact with those he rules. Surrounded by a great entourage, the Pontifex moves his court constantly from city to city according to a randomly determined pattern, retreating occasionally into a labyrinthine palace where he lives in total seclusion for part the years The arrival of the court procession is dreaded by all Majipoorans, for it is a great expense and inconvenience to be host to the entourage of the Pontifex, and his presence generally means an acceleration of the processes of justice in the neighborhood, a remedying of old abuses and leveling of privileges that no one but the victims appreciates.

Although the authority of the Pontifex is absolute, in practice he rules through three subordinates. These are:

—The Coronal. He is the heir apparent to the pontificate, and is generally a man of young or early middle years. The Coronal is the chief administrative officer of the realm, a combination field marshal and prime minister, a person of vigor and decisiveness. He is considered to be the adoptive son of the reigning Pontifex, and is chosen by him from a cadre of specially trained candidates, The genetic children of the Pontifex, if he has any, are prohibited by the constitution from attaining the rank of Coronal. Upon the death of the Pontifex, the Coronal succeeds him and adopts a new Coronal. At the time of the story this post is held by a dashing young prince known as Lord Valentine.

—The Lady of the Isle of Sleep. She is high priestess of the realm, virtually a mother-goddess figure as well. From her island sanctuary she presides over the spiritual life of the planet, appearing in dreams to citizens and guiding them toward higher aspiration—a process made possible through technological means. She is more often invoked as a symbol of virtue than actually in volved in direct political activity. The Lady of the Isle of Sleep is normally the mother of the Coronal, and when he succeeds to the Pontificate she customarily retires in favor of the mother of the new Coronal, although she may retain her post should he be motherless. Any vacancy in the Ladyship can also be filled from among her associated priestesses.

—The King of Dreams. This dark and powerful figure occupies an ambiguous role in the hierarchy, often opposing the decrees of the Pontifex and thwarting the actions of the Coronal. His power, which is only about a thousand years old, derives from his control of thought-amplifying apparatus more potent than that used by the Lady of the Isle of Sleep. While she can make suggestions that guide and direct, his machinery is capable of controlling.

Customarily he serves as the executive arm of the Pontifex-Coronal administration, but when he chooses to defy them he can cause considerable trouble, and this often is the case. The office of King of Dreams is hereditary and has remained within the family of the Barjazids since its establishment.

These three functionaries govern from widely separated points on the giant planet. The King of Dreams holds his power from the heart of the southern continent, hot and dry, a desert territory swept by cruel winds; but his apparatus can reach to any part of Majipoor. The Lady of the Isle of Sleep presides over a holy island of almost continental size that lies in the great sea dividing the two northern continents; there she is surrounded by thousands of priestesses and devotees. As for the Coronal, he holds the most imposing place of all, for the planet of Majipoor is geomorphically deformed, and out of the center of its northeastern continent rises a tremendous plateau that tapers into a single enormous mountain, thirty miles above sea level. On the slopes of this mountain are hundreds of cities of great majesty and wealth—the population of the foothills alone is well over a billion—and near the summit, in a zone controlled climatically so that the air is balmy and the breezes ever gentle, lies Lord Valentine's Castle, an incredible sprawling city of a building, a structure eight thousand years old with at least five rooms for every year of its existence, a thing of towers and prismatic battlements and mysterious underpassages and subdwellings. Lord Valentine's Castle is the summit of Majipoor, literally and metaphysically, and from this gigantic edifice governing decrees of the Coronal flow.

THE PROTAGONIST, though not the novel's only viewpoint character, is Lord Valentine, the Coronal. He is a surprisingly young man who has held his post only two years, although the reigning Pontifex, Tyeveras, has had the throne for forty. Valentine is in fact Tyeveras' third Coronal, the first two having met accidental deaths; Valentine's predecessor was his elder brother, so that the Ladyship did not change hands when he assumed power.

But Lord Valentine has recently been deposed—and is not even aware of it, Several months before the opening of the story, Valentine was drugged and seized by Dominin Barjazid, younger son of the King of Dreams. Though afraid to kill the Coronal, young Barjazid caused him to be surgically altered beyond recognition and to be supplied with an implanted identity completely obliterating his own. Then he was turned loose in a remote part of the northwestern continent, where he lives now as a member of a wandering troupe of jugglers, completely unknowing that he is in truth Coronal of Majipoor. Dominin Barjazid has had himself physically altered to assume the appearance of Lord Valentine, and currently rules at the Castle. For the first time, two of the great offices of Majipoor are in the hands of the Barjazid family. The scheme of old Simonan Barjazid, the King of Dreams, is to have his son Domitin eventually become Pontifex, his first son Minax to succeed him as King of Dreams, and his third son Cristoph to be named Coronal under Domitin, thereby concentrating virtually all the power of the realm under the Barjazids.

The form of the novel is a gigantic odyssey, divided into five "books" of 35,000-40,000 words each, during which the deposed Lord Valentine learns of his true identity, gradually and at first reluctantly resolves to regain his power, seeks successfully to obtain access to his original personality and memories and crosses all of immense Majipoor, enlisting allies as he goes, engaging in strange and colorful adventures, finally to confront the usurper at the Castle.

BOOK ONE:
THE BOOK OF THE KING OF DREAMS

WE ARE IN the city of Pidruid, a provincial capital near the western coast of the northwestern continent. The city is in great excitement, for Lord Valentine the Coronal is making a grand administrative procession through this part of Majipoor—the visit of the Coronal is traditionally as welcome as that of the Pontifex is unwelcome—and vast entertainments are being organized for his amusement.

The Coronal who will shortly arrive is actually Dominin Barjazid, the usurper, but of course no one knows this. The true Valentine is also in Pidruid, where he was dumped by Barjazid's agents after undergoing alterations. In his present identity he is an amiable, good-natured young man, sunny and open of spirit; people are naturally drawn toward him, though most tend to think he is simpler than he really is. The innate intelligence and of the fallen Coronal are still there, but far beneath the surface; now he seems no more than an easy-going wanderer, but this seeming simplicity is in reality an effect of the identity change. Stripped of his power, his functions, and all significant intellectual challenge, he has no focus for his mental energies and, for the moment, is content to take each moment as it comes.

What comes, at this moment, is a troupe of jugglers of the humanoid Skandar species. Skandars are tall six-limbed beings of formidable strength and coordination, and they are jugglers beyond compare. This troupe, led by the giant Zalzan Gibor, has been hired to perform in the parade honoring Lord Valentine. But under a recent decree of the Pontifex Tyeveras, all entertainment troupes on Majipoor must be composed at least one-third of human Majipoori citizens, and the six Skandar jugglers find themselves obliged to hire three very much less talented humans. This infuriates Zalzan Gibor and his comrades, but the penalties for non-compliance are severe. In Pidruid they manage to find two professionals of at least reasonable competence, a lithe, forceful young woman named Carabella and a scarfaced whitebearded veteran named Sleet. But the law requires a third, and jugglers of human birth are hard to find in Pidruid. Valentine (he continues to go by this name, which is a common one on Majipoor, even after being deposed) observes the jugglers at their practice in the courtyard of a tavern where he is staying. He is amused by their antics and falls into a flirtation with Carabella as the practice session proceeds. to him; he catches it and tosses it back; Teasingly she tosses a club; she tosses him two; the game goes on until finally he is handling more clubs than he can manage, and drops them all.

But Zalzan Gibor has noticed his fine reflexes and intuitive skills. Obviously he is no juggler, but doubtless he can learn; and he is, after all, a human. The foolish new law must be obeyed. Zalzan Gibor offers to take him on as a juggler-apprentice. They will find something for him to do in the grand parade; the law does not, Zalzan Gibor reasons, require all members of the troupe to have equal responsibilities or skills.

Under the tutelage of Carabella and Sleet, Valentine receives three intense days of training as a juggler and learns the basics with astonishing swiftness. In their different ways, the shrewd cynical Sleet and the jaunty irreverent Carabella are fascinated by Valentine, by the apparent strength and depth of character that lies beneath his simple, cheerful exterior.

The grand parade takes place. Through the streets of Pidruid comes the ornate chariot of the Coronal; amid the cheers of millions, the false Lord Valentine gestures his greetings and bestows honors on the leaders of the community. The Skandar jugglers performl splendidly, but their work goes virtually unnoticed in the circus atmosphere of the gigantic festival.

That night Valentine dreams, as he lies in Carabella's arms for the first time, that he is duelling with his brother, who is at the point of slaying him.

It is a terrifying dream, and several times he cries out, but like all Majiporans he is trained to experience dreams to the fullest, never to allow himself to wake in the midst of one. Dream analysis is central to the Majipooran philosophy, Majipoorans believe that dreams are no mere expression of the irrational unconscious, but actually are manifestations of the deepest truth. Dreams are socially important messages; they guide behavior and demonstrate ethical precepts, Much waking activity in Majipoor is devoted to the understanding of dreams, and no one lightly ignores the messages they bring.

Valentine persists in the dream, and a reversal occurs: at the point of death, he finds new strength, rises from the ground, and slays his brother. It is a mystifying dream, for Valentine has no brother of whom he knows, and, indeed, as he discusses the dream with Carabella both of them observe an odd vacancy of experience surfacing; Valentine has no very convincing context of autobiography against which to interpret his dream. His family, his childhood, his education, everything has an improvised, insubstantial feel to it, as though either his memory is faulty or his mind is dim.

Carabella suggests that he seek guidance, One must take responsibility for one's dreams. If you dream that you have injured someone, you must make atonement in waking life. If you dream that someone has injured you, you are entitled to seek reparation. The violence of Valentine's dream is unnatural on peaceful Majipoor. Sleet, hearing the story, suggests that Valentine has somehow drawn the attention of the King of Dreams, who perhaps is sending him nightmares for some obscure political motive. But this seems implausible to Valentine.

The troupe moves on. Valentine continues to have disturbing dreams. The Pontifex and the Coronal begin to figure in them. At Carabella's repeated urging he seeks the therapeutic aid of a wise old priestess in an inland village. He spends the night (chastely) with her and she shares his dreams. In the morning she tells him that he has fallen from a high place and must begin to climb back to it. He laughs. A high place? The highest place is Castle Mountain, he says. Shall I climb it, then?

Yes, Lord Valentine, you should, she replies.

He is amused by her use of the title. Not Lord Valentine, he says. Only Valentine. Valentine the juggler, is all. He pays her and leaves.

But in the days ahead he rescues from the wrath of Zalzan Gibor a small wizened sorcerer, Autifon Deliamber, who nudges him further toward discovery of his identity. Deliamber has perceived instantly who Valentine really is, and will play the role of tutor/guide in the adventures ahead. Valentine's suppressed real identity is attempting to break through; Deliamber encourages this process through dream analysis, telepathic communion, and out-and-out wizardry. When bluntly confronted with the awareness that he is Lord Valentine turned into a changeling and magicked out of his imperial powers, he resists the concept, again saying that he is only Valentine the juggler and prefers to remain that way. It only lightly troubles him to shrug off the high responsibility, for his mind still tells him that he is no one but a wanderer, and it seems reasonable to regard the Lord Valentine notion as an unhealthy delusion. Besides, in his changed condition it seems madness to him for anyone to want to be a Coronal or other high official; power is only a burden, government a chore; he prefers to be a free man and a juggler. He will throughout the novel never display lust for power for its own sake, but will gradually come to accept the necessity of exercising the responsibilities he once had held.

Deliamber, subtly and persistently, moves him away from frivolity. After a vivid dream in which he goes to the far-off palace of the King of Dreams, is taunted by him for cowardice and laziness, and beholds Dominin Barjazid in the robes of the Coronal, Valentine awakens with.the knowledge that he may very well be the true Lord Valentine and that if so, he must go forth, for the sake of stability of the commonwealth, to overthrow the tyrant and reclaim his rightful position.

BOOK TWO:
THE BOOK OF THE METAMORPHS

NOW HE SETS OUT on his adventures. His first goal is to find his way to the Isle of Sleep ahd gain the confidence of his putative mother, the Lady of the Isle. Even though his outward appearance is no longer that of Lord Valentine, she should be able through her arts and through her knowledge of his soul to confirm his identity and help him in his quest.

But the Isle of Sleep is halfway across giant Majipoor and Valentine is a penniless juggler. All he can do is travel eastward with the troupe, saving his coins and biding his time. And so they go, from city to city, into territories often wild and perilous and into some exploits sometimes heroic and sometimes absurd. Much of this book is told through the viewpoint of Carabella, who at this point is shrewder and more dynamic than Valentine and who will be a powerful force in his life as he struggles to regain his own completeness of spirit.

The jugglers pass through the territory of the Metamorphs, the native race of Majipoor, a folk that has the power of shapeshifting and, sullen and resentful, practices all sorts of trickery; it is dangerous business to enter their domain, but profitable for the jugglers, and Zalzan Gibor will not be dissuaded from entering the area. Along the way Valentine acquires two new companions, Falstaffian Lisamon Holtin, a huge hard- drinking warrior-woman down on her luck, and Khun, a stranded spacefarer of an alien species, who by nature is a classic malcontent, filled with cynical despair and an almost demonic anger. They form symmetrical complements to Valentine's personality, for Khun is as dark and bitter as Valentine is sunny, and Lisamon's raw earthiness balances a certain fastidiousness on Valentine's part. Both are given good reason for intense loyalty to him—as, in fact, is almost everyone he encounters.

He does not regard it as good tactics to reveal his true identity yet, partly because he still feels like an impostor. But in dreams his past begins to break into his consciousness; he feels more and more certain that he is the Coronal, remembering episodes when he did wield the princely authority; and he continues to shed his reluctance to reclaim his office, as he recognizes that it would be a betrayal of all Majipoor for him to, in effect, abdicate by remaining a juggler and leaving power in the hands of the Barjazids. Gradually he takes the others into his confidence. (Some, like Carabella, have already learned the truth from Deliamber.) The jugglers are last to know, for Zalzan Gibor is a rough, crude sort with whom Valentine is not really comfortable. In the end it is the

Metamorphs that reveal the truth, staging a bizarre panto-mime in which they flicker between the appearance of Valentine the juggler and Lord Valentine the Coronal. Ultimately the Skandar jugglers guess the truth and pledge their aid to Valentine,

The basic cast is now complete; Valentine is surrounded by an odd and raffish crew who have had reason to develop strong loyalty to him. Onward they go. Trouble develops near the eastern edge of the Metamorph territory; several of the jugglers are killed in an ambush and the band is scattered. Valentine, alone, stumbles toward the sea.

BOOK THREE:
THE BOOK OF THE ISLE OF SLEEP

DELIAMBER FINDS HIM camped miserably on the beach, and together they collect the survivors of the troupe, a project that takes some time. Now they set forth on the sea journey to the Isle of Sleep, renting passage aboard a dilapidated whaling ship. They pass through stormy waters infested by monstrous sea-beasts bigger than ocean liners; the ship is wrecked; Valentine is swallowed whole by one of the beasts, from which he is rescued by Lisamon Holtin in gory fashion; with the aid of dreams and sorcery the bedraggled voyagers collect themselves once again and raft onward, through kinder and ever more tropic waters, to the Isle of Sleep. Here they must observe the elaborate forms of pilgrimage, for visitors cannot simply approach the sanctuary directly but must undergo a spiritual ascent, a kind of Masonic initiation, that can conceivably take years. Valentine finds sly methods of abbreviating this process and eventually penetrates the inner temple, coming face to face with his mother, the Lady of the isle. (He is brought to her as a prisoner, but of course she recognizes him from his aura alone.)

In a long intense scene she heals him of the last of his amnesia, explains to him the meaning of much of what he has undergone and arms him with the only weapon at her command: the power to transmit meaningful dreams. He can use this to guide and perhaps to control others, and to build his army. His next objective, she tells him, is the labyrinth within which the Pontifex has lately immured himself; it will be an almost hopeless task, but he must try to make Pontifex understand what has happened and gain his support in defeat of the usurper.

BOOK FOUR:
THE BOOK OF THE LABYRINTH

VALENTINE AND HIS BAND, constantly growing in number, cross now to the western continent in ships supplied by the Lady of the Isle, and seek the labyrinth. It is a colossal, intricate underground structure, and entering it is a kind of descent into hell. Through circle after circle they gow, taxed to their limits at every stage; Valentine lies, bribes, begs, seduces, and fights his way downward and downward, and at last reaches the ministers of the Pontifex, who, after he convinces them of his true identity, take him to the emperor. But the Pontifex is senile, a weird and quavering creature who

makes sense only intermittently. Valentine discovers the ultimate meaninglessness of supreme rank: to be Coronal is to
live in the world of deeds and moral responsibility, to succeed to the Pontificate means eventually to vanish into crazy
tyranny at the end. He sees now why the system separates the
doer and the ruler: every emperor must decay into this sort of
madness, but at least the Coronal is a functional being.

Yet the Pontifex does offer a blessing of sorts and puts
an army at Valentine's disposal. Now it remains for him only
to go after Dominin Barjazid and undergo the final confrontation.

BOOK FIVE:
THE BOOK OF THE CASTLE

DOMININ BARJAZID HAS, of course, become aware of Valentine's progress across Majipoor and throughout the second
half of the book, as it has become apparent that Valentine is
bent on regaining power, the false Coronal's agents have
made various attempts to thwart his advance—a series of
sub-plots to be made manifest in Books Three and Four as
they are written. Now that Valentine is openly marching on
the Castle the confrontation between Coronal and usurper
becomes more direct.

But which is the usurper? Barjazid wears Lord Valentine's countenance and holds the seals of power. Making use
of all the force the King of Dreams can supply, Dominin
Bariazid rallies the people to his side, accusing Valentine of
subversion and rebellion, and formidable forces gather to

defend the false Coronal. Valentine and his army press forward, nonetheless.

Now begins the ascent of Castle Mountain, the great set-piece that forms the climax of the novel. Castle Mountain is no mere steep peak, but rather an enormous looming jagged plateau covering thousands of square miles, so that the climb is a gradual process. The army of Valentine moves through city after city on the crowded slopes of Castle Mountain, now hailed as liberators, now met with stiff resistance. As they approach the higher elevations they are opposed not by the citizen-militia but by the first troops of the Coronal's own army; and since these are soldiers once loyal to Valentine, and known to him from his time in office, he feels dismay at the need to make war on them. For a dark moment he wavers and nearly decides to abandon power to Barjazid rather than plunge the world into this final convulsion of violence; but then, hearing tales of the atrocities of the false Coronal, he regains his resolve. In a fierce battle many of the Coronal's soldiers are slain, and Valentine, meeting with surviving officers, is able to convince them that he is the rightful Coronal. A confused situation of cascading loyalty switches develops; several of the most influential officers have recognized Valentine's manner of speech and give him their allegiance, but many of the defenders fail to comprehend what is going on, and the army fights against itself in a muddled way while Valentine's smaller but more coherent force pushes relentlessly onward to the perimeter of the Castle itself.

And now the Castle is reached, and now the war proceeds into its thousands of rooms. Dominin Barjazid is somewhere within, but where? The Castle is a city in itself, and a labyrinth more intricate than the one within which the Pontifex hides, Although the end now is inevitable, Valentine must find Barjazid, and this he finally does, with the aid of Carabella and the sorcerer Deliamber. He is barricaded within the innermost and highest circle of chambers. The juggler Zalzan Gibor and the warrior-woman Lisamon argue for flooding the area with poison gas, but Valentine will have none of that. Through the device given him by his mother he sends the hidden Barjazid a dream of love and friendship. Barjazid projects a retaliatory dream of fury and defiance. Valentine responds more firmly with a dream of pardon, to which Barjazid replies with hatred. The duel of dreams continues; meanwhile the jugglers have found ways to infiltrate the inner chambers and are busily opening a path to the usurper,

At last Valentine, alone, confronts the sinister Barjazid across the vast space of the Coronal's judgment-room. Barjazid accuses Valentine of being too mild, too naive to rule, and invites him to return to juggling. Valentine admits lightly that that is a powerful temptation; nevertheless destiny requires him to carry the burdens of government. Barjazid hurls weapons at Valentine, who catches them neatly in mid-air and juggles them, enraging the usurper still further. Barjazid is almost incoherent with frustration. Valentine, sensing that the end is near, rushes toward his adversary, only to be hit by a barrage of dream-commands that, even though he is awake, nearly knocks him to the ground. Somehow he struggles onward, lunges at Barjazid, almost catches him. The usurper pulls free, but Valentine has him cornered. Suddenly, in terror, Barjazid dives into a curtained alcove at the far side of the room.

Valentine rips away the curtain and beholds an astonishing sight: Barjazid, a trembling heap huddling at the knees of another figure , the King of Dreams himself, old Simonan Barjazid, who clutches the controls of his dream-machinery in one hand. But as Barjazid hysterically begs his father for help, an even more amazing thing occurs. The face and form of the King of Dreams waver, and for a moment, under the pressure of the chaotic events, the King of Dreams vanishes and a Metamorph is visible. Barjazid collapses in horror; Valentine is frozen in confusion and disbelief; the Metamorph flings his device at Valentine and, rushing past him, throws himself to his death from a window.

The world is redeemed; order is restored; the threat of tyranny is averted. Dominin Barjazid, at the verge of insanity, is taken into custody. Valentine is able now to piece together the story. The King of Dreams ostensibly had fallen ill some months before, but, aided by a new physician, had made a miraculous recovery. It was then that he had goaded his son Dominin into trapping and displacing Lord Valentine. What had happened, in truth, is that the King of Dreams had died, and the physician a Metamorph, had masqueraded as him ever since—the first step in an intended secret coup d'etat by which Metamorphs would regain control of Majipoor. One by one, the key figures of the realm would be replaced by Metamorphs, until the usurpation was complete. What had seemed—even to Dominin Barjazid—to be a seizure of power by the Barjazid family was actually the beginning of a rebellion by the planet's aborigines.

Much now must be done. The injustices of the usurpation period have to be corrected, and, Valentine realizes, some kind of rapprochement with the embittered Metamorphs is necessary lest Majipoor be thrown into endless war. But first comes celebration. Lord Valentine, with his consort Carabella beside him, throws a grand banquet for his comrades in the feasting-hall of the Castle, and celebrates the victory with a grand exhibition of juggling, in which he takes part with great skill—although for the final number, the most dazzling of all, he becomes a mere spectator, watching the intricate maneuvers in a curiously ambivalent way. He knows that his time as a juggler, the freest and in some ways most happy time of his life, is ended now, and the responsibilities of power are descending on him once more.

KATHARINE KERR

KATHARINE KERR IS one of those rare authors who sells every bit as well in England as she does here, which is very well indeed.

This is the proposal she sent to her agent, Elizabeth Pomada, for her forthcoming novel, *The Snare*, which may or may not be out when this appears. It will be published by Tor in the United States and HarperCollins in England.

COVER LETTER

April 24, 1998
Elizabeth Pomada
[address deleted]

Dear Elizabeth,

Enclosed is the proposal for *The Snare*, a work of science fantasy or as I prefer to call it, a fantasy of the future. I'm planning it as a substantial adventure story. Since a good bit of it is already written, I should be able to finish it within a year after signing the contract. First of course I have to finish *The Black Raven*.

In a nutshell, here's what it's about:

From early childhood Ammadin has trained to serve her people, the nomadic Tribes, as a Spirit Rider: a healer, a guardian of the sacred figures of the gods, a magician who can guide her people through the dangers of life on a planet where humans were never meant to live. Now, however, doubt is eating her faith in the gods, and without their support, her magic will fail her and her people both—or she has always been told. In hopes of finding the truth, she journeys to the war-torn lands east of her own country, only to find herself embroiled in a political intrigue that could destroy the very things she's trying to save.

I've printed out the proposal with British spelling, since it will be going to HarperCollins UK.

Anyway, as a first step I hope you like it.

THE SNARE

*A stand-alone novel of the far future, by Katharine Kerr,
approximately 800 standard manuscript pages in length,
to be delivered by December, 2000.*

QUICK SUMMARY

A STARFLEET OF COLONISTS, gone irrevocably off-course
on their way to a paradisal planet, found refuge on a world
never meant to be theirs. Now, some thousand years later,
their descendants grapple with problems that the original
colonists never could have imagined, and thanks to that lack
of imagination, the human beings trapped on Snare have
woefully inadequate tools in the struggle to survive. Here
and there a few individuals, like Ammadin, a shaman trained
in the magic of the nomadic Tribes, realize that the only
thing that will save their people is learning the truth about
themselves, no matter how threatening that truth may be to
those in power.

From early childhood Ammadin has trained to serve her
people as a Spirit Rider: a healer, a guardian of the sacred
figures of the gods, a magician who can guide her people
through the dangers of life on a planet where humans were
never meant to live. Now, however, doubt is eating her faith
in the gods, and without their support, her magic will fail her
and her people both—or she has always been told.

At a horse fair on the border of the Kazrak Empire she

takes in an outcast, Zain, a cashiered cavalry officer—or so she thinks. In reality Zain is a member of The Chosen, a secret group of spies and assassins who have sworn personal allegiance to the Great Khan of the civilized Kazrak empire. He needs to travel with the Tribes for reasons of his own, in particular, to find the truth about the mysterious sorcerer, Yarl Soutan, who came to the Kazraki lands with a letter of introduction from a member of the royal family that everyone thought was dead.

The man who received the letter, Idres Warkannan, is a retired cavalry officer, a devout follower of Islam who has lost his faith in the current ruler of the Islamic empire. In the news that Khan Jezro is still alive, in exile in the war-torn country far to the east of the empire, Warkannan sees hope for a revolution. He travels with Yarl across the tribal plains to bring the khan home only to find out that Yarl has been telling him only half of a very complicated story involving ancient technology and the sapient species native to the planet, the Chiri Michi.

Snare, the planet itself, is based on my reading in the sciences of paleogeology and paleobotany. What the characters think of as "magic" is in fact remnants of the biotechnology known to the original colonists, presented in a coherent and, I hope, sound way. As always in my books, I've thought out the history lying behind the characters' time to provide depth and a logical rationale for the peculiar situation in which they find themselves.

BACKGROUND

SOME THOUSAND OF YEARS in our future, humanity spread to the stars and planted colonies on suitable worlds in the area of the galactic rim near Earth. There, together with other sapient races they built an enlightened, democratic civilization, fueling their high ideals with an abundance of natural resources. What made this expansion possible, however—the jumpshunt irregularities in the structure of Space-Time—were as dangerous as they are essential, and there were terrible losses of entire colony fleets. Some were destroyed during the jumps; others found themselves far from their original destination only to perish between the stars. A lucky few found previously unknown habitable worlds to give them refuge.

But no lost colonists ended up as far from home as the group that settled Snare, a planet orbiting one of the "remnant stars" that drift alone through intergalactic space, where the enormous gravitational forces of colliding galaxies dragged and scattered them. Here, where the colonists faced an intractable world and a hostile sapient race under a sky devoid of stars, the deep differences between them added to their troubles. One group of colonists were devout followers of Islam, migrating in hopes of restoring the laws of the Prophet in a simpler life away from the intricate technology of the Rim civilization. Others were hard-headed settlers desperate for a better life away from their overcrowded home worlds. A significant few came for adventure and a freedom denied them in a highly regulated society.

Snare is a young planet, and life there arose fairly recently compared to Earth's timeline. Without vast ages of life and the attendant mass extinctions, there are no deposits of coal and oil, no seed-bearing plants, no mammals to speak of. That an intelligent species evolved here at all is a tribute to the universe's drive toward consciousness, but the amphibian Chiri Michi have developed only the most primitive technologies. Most of their short lives are devoted to a complex reproductive cycle that evolved in response to the planet's dangers.

Snare has one large landmass, (on the model of Earth's Pangea), which tectonic shifts are tearing into continents. In the centre of this supercontinent lie huge deserts, cut off from the moisture of the low-salinity ocean. All round its edges, in fertile terrain, earthquakes and volcanoes abound. Some of the smaller changes to the land are happening so fast that they can be observed within the compass of human memory, but of course the forming of continents is a thing of millions of years, and no one on Snare currently understands what's happening to the planet. Everyone knows how rare good land for sapients is, though. The Chiri Michi bitterly resent the human interlopers who have stolen some of it.

For a number of reasons, the leaders of the colony realized from the first that their settlements would never be able to maintain the high level of technology that they'd brought with them from the Rim civilization. As good citizens of their idealistic culture, they were all committed to preserving the Chiri Michi and their way of life "unspoiled". Thus they decided to bow to the inevitable while providing their descendants with as much security as possible. Rather than exterminate the Chiri Michi, they bargained with them for territory and promised to respect their natural environment. In their ships they carried the scientific equipment of their day, which they devoted to making genetic alterations in the colonists and the first generation of children. Dark skins made it possible for humans to survive the radiation from Snare's bluish sun. Since the alien plant and animal life was based on a different biochemistry than that of the home planets, they changed the basic digestive chemistry of the humans and their Earth-type animals to allow them to eat the food Snare offered.

Tinkering with DNA, however, amounted to gilding the lily in most cases, because in the Rim civilizations biotechnology had for a thousand years been producing highly specialized types of human beings. The colonists could only hope that this internal technology, as it were, would allow their descendants to hold their own on Snare. The basis metabolic changes did take hold; any throwbacks starved as infants or died of melanomas as children, and only the new genes got passed on. The specialized traits, however, proved unstable. Just as double roses will revert to their simple ancestors if allowed to go wild, in most populations the normal human DNA reasserted itself over the centuries. Genetic sports remain, however, when the ancient recessive traits come together in individuals to give them some peculiar traits.

Beyond this genetic fine-tuning, there was little the colonists could do for their future descendants, except hope that someday they might be rescued by the civilization left so far behind. Yet they knew that it would take a miracle for the Rim planets to trace the lost ships. A thousand years later, no help has ever come.

When the original generations of colonists died out, some of their ideals died with them. Among the followers of Islam a new prophet rose up, and in the grand tradition of Mohammed he preached jihad and conquest. Even among the infidels he found plenty of supporters when the time came to drive the Chiri Michi back and take more land for humanity. Now the original inhabitants of the planet cling to marginal territory and nurse their resentments, waiting for a time to strike back.

JACK DANN

JACK DANN WAS NOMINATED for ten Nebulas before he finally won one—and he won it for a novella-length excerpt from *The Memory Cathedral*, which was a bestseller in Australia, where Jack has lived since leaving New York a few years back.

Prior to *The Memory Cathedral*'s breakthrough, Jack was known as a writer's writer, an exquisite craftsman who was more appreciated within the field than without. Here's the informal outline to the book that made him appreciated everywhere he goes.

This proposal takes the form of an informal letter that Jack wrote to his editor, pitching the novel.

THE MEMORY CATHEDRAL

by Jack Dann

WHEN I'M WRITING A BOOK or a story, there's a magical transitional moment when it suddenly comes alive, when the characters reveal their true and secret motivations and begin to move along their own certain paths; and I become a mere peephole observer tapping away at the keys, listening to their convesations, watching their most intimate moments. When that happens, it's wonderful, it's joyous, it's downright right-brained mystical—of course, it also always involves going back and rewriting in light of what the characters have told me. But an outline ... it's such a dead thing. He went here and she went there and it takes place in such and such a time. So, since you asked me for an outline, and since I know these things must be done, I'll do it; but I'll circle around it like Indians around Custer, and perhaps in my own circular way I can bring some of the luminous light that I envision to the page.

On to *The Memory Cathedral.* This novel has been generating a lot of excitement; and it has all been sight- unseen. (An oxymoron of a word if I ever saw one!) The idea is, I think, one of those very few precious gems that a writer gets over a lifetime.

This is ostensibly the story of Leonardo da Vinci's finest invention. We've discovered that he had had invented workable submarines, machine guns, grenades (much of this is

explicitly detailed in his letter to Lodovico Sforza), para-
chutes, and even tanks, but his most sublime invention was
not recorded in any of the known notebooks (and now you
must suspend your disbelief) for I intend to weave the skein
of reality and fantasy together into a Renaissance version of
magical realism).

That was, of course, the modern airplane.

We know that Leonardo was fascinated with flight from
the time he was a child, as witnessed by his dream of the
great bird, which I'll go into more detail later on. Leonardo
was an acute and astute observer, perhaps the finest to have
graced our history, and he studied birds for some twenty-five
years (e.g., his notes in *Manuscript B*, begun in 1488 and
Codice Sul Volo degli Ucelli [*Manuscript on the Flight of
Birds*] written sometime around 1505). It was said that he
would buy caged birds from vendors in the street only to let
them fly, to give them their freedom. Actually, it was to study
them. Leonardo has written that "The genius of man may
make various inventions, encompassing with various instruments one and the same end; but it will never discover a
more beautiful, a more economical, or a more direct one than
nature's, since in her inventions nothing is wanting and
nothing is superfluous." It is because of this reasoning—and a
few other errors of observation, which I won't bore you with
here, for after all this is only an outline—that he was loath to
look for the other mode of flight, that of the fixed-wing. He
literally wanted to fly like a bird, and he was fascinated with
the concept of ornithopters until his last years (although, of
course, he did make drawings of a machine that is the fore-

runner of the helicopter). It is even thought, and this is merely legend, that he even attempted it again in his last years, having laid aside his fixed wing version of flight, which would have indeed worked. (Leonardo had, in fact, done a series of sketches, which can be found in the *Codex Atlanticus*, 381 v.a., that experts agree to be the first European conception of gliding flight.)

My story is about this fixed wing aircraft of Leonardo's, and how he came to invent it, but that would be like saying that *Remembrance of Things Past* by Proust is about smell. This expansive, multi-layered novel is also about Leonardo's trip to the fabled East, which was commissioned by the Devatdar of Syria, Lieutenant of the Sacred Sultan of Babylon; and there how Leonardo and the adventurer and traveler Benedetto Dei, Zoroastro de Pertola (the charlatan painter who combined his genius for mechanical devices with all the pretensions of being a great sorcerer and magician), Lorenzo di Credi—a brilliant technical artist, who was an imitator of Leonardo and one of the students in Verrocchio's studio—and Niccolo Machiavelli (yes, the same one who wrote *The Prince*) witnessed and recorded the terrifying earthquake near Mt. Maurue and its wholesale destruction; how Leonardo and his comrades fought for the Sultan Kait Bey who was resisting the encroachments of Alaeddoulet, the Asian prince who threatened Syria and Asia minor; and how he utilized his submarines and airplanes and other engines of war to fight by sea and land.

As an aside, Machiavelli was but a lad of eighteen when this adventure takes place; and how he comes to go with Leonardo to the far reaches of the then-known world is another interesting story, which is also part of the book. (It is also one of my many be so authentic, that the reader will accept my little historical revisions.) You see, although Niccolo came of a very ancient family, which had been counted as one of the principle houses of Florence since the 13th Century, Niccolo's father, Bernardo, Doctor of Laws, was poor by comparison with the other branches of the family; and as it happened, Niccolo had much in common with Leonardo, for like Leonardo, he did not have the formal education he should have had, was also deficient in Latin (a major stumbling block during the classicism of the Renaissance when Green and Roman culture was worshipped and Cicero and Virgil were quoted matter-of-factly in cultured conversation, all spoken in Latin), and he, Michiavelli, hungered to be an artist. Another fiction, but what an interesting one! But it is through the Machiavelli family that Leonardo gets his commission to go to the east, with the proviso that young Niccolo be taken along to become seasoned in life and the arts of warfare and diplomacy, which he would make good use of later when, at the age of twenty-nine, he would be made head of the *concelleria* of Florence.

Much of my story is based on letters Leonardo wrote to the Devatdar, but which historians have only recently begun to take seriously. Let me digress for a moment, for what else have I been doing? Here is what Rachel Annand Taylor writes in her version of Leonardo, a book entitled *Leonardo the Florentine*: "It is impossible to believe that Leonardo could have gone to serve a Sultan, and wandered in the Orient, without some Eastern episode appearing in his legend ... Vasari would have heard of Leonardo, in Phygian cap and Asian robes, seducing barbaric princes, bridging the awful chasm of Afriet-haunted mountains, watching the immortal motion of these great waters, the Tigris and the Euphrates, pausing dreamingly over fabulous buried cities, wandering lost amid the tremendous pillars of ancient sun-temples, received as an enchanter by Mazdean priests, becoming a kind of solar myth in the savage heights and lost waters of the ranges of Taurus."

But, indeed, it is possible. Jean Paul Richter, who compiled the definitive two volume set, *The Notebooks of Leonardo da Vinci*, writes: "We have no information as to Leonardo's history between 1482 and 1486; it cannot be proved that he was either in Milan or in Florence. On the other hand, the tenor of this letter [the letter to the Devatdar] does not require us to assume a longer absence than a year or two. For, even if his appointment (*offitio*) as Engineer in Syrua had been a permanent one, it might have become untenable—by the death of perhaps the Devatdar, his patron, or by his removal from office—and Leonardo on his return home may have kept silent on the subject of an episode which probably had ended in failure and disappointment."

Actually, that was *not* what happened. Leonardo's aircraft, Renaissance flying machines powered by an engine of Leonardo's invention (which I've worked out with a top IBM engineer) and born aloft by great balloons, a sight both beautiful and awe-inspiring, Alaeddoulet, with the help of his other inventions of war: armored cars, transportable siege bridges, beams for overturning scaling ladders, an instrument similar to the modern flame-thrower, spherical projectiles filled with gunpowder and metal shot, the diversion of streams to an enemy's disadvantage (the first known use of waterpower for destruction), bombs made of hemp and fish glue that would throw out sheaves of fire six ells long, sulfur filled gas projectiles in "pruduce stupor," and I could go on and on. But all of these inventions, which were put to use to cause death and destruction on as large a scale as the earthquake Leonardo had witnessed, took their toll on him psychologically. He saw what his inventions, the indiscriminate products of his mind could do, and he destroyed them and swore his companions to secrecy. Of course, there were problems, as Zoroastro de Pertola and Benedetto Dei saw what use such weapons could be made of in the west. And it is Machiavelli, without Leonardo's knowledge, who hires his father's men to assassinate them.

A pause for some background on Leonardo. While he was writing his famous memorandum to Lodovico Sforza, Leonardo drew many sketches of his machineries of death, with victims being cut to pieces, writhing in agony, yet when one looks at these sketches, one feels almost at peace, for, as the author Antonina Vallentin (who wrote the lucid and brilliant *Leonardo da Vinci: the Tragic Pursuit of Perfection* writes, "Yet there is such an atmosphere of peace and harmony in the sketch that it seems as if the artist cannot for a moment have been conscious of what the scene he was drawing meant in reality." It is apparent from what I have read that Leonardo was quite neutral, or more specifically, amoral, when it came to his machines of destruction. It was as if they did not exist in any real world, for when one looks as his bombs bursting and people dying, the sketches are drawn so quietly and beautifully that although they depict violence, they are almost Platonic in nature. And so when Leonardo finally fits his 'Platonic ideas' to reality, sees and smells the blood and putrefaction, hears the screams and agonies, he comes to a moral revelation, one that he will carry throughout the rest of his life. Even though he will continue to be an armament expert for princes, he will never again permit himself to be associated with the kind of wholesale destruction he had engineered in Persia.

And the aircraft, soaring and drifting like great winged Chinese kites, made of colored silk and balsa, casting shadows on the desert hills, as they dropped fire on burning children and women and villages; the beautiful conception of the flying machine left unwritten and—Leonardo hoped—forever hidden from the world. Only the ornithopter, the machine that could make a man fly like a bird, in the image of the creator's creation, would Leonardo permit himself to try to bring to life. For it would be difficult, if not impossible, to put such a machine to the uses of war. Here is the classic theme: put succinctly (and to quote Damon Knight), it is the story of the boy who learned better.

So Leonardo will encounter all that Taylor said he could not, for although Taylor yearned for Leonardo to have had an adventure such as this, she could not bring herself to believe what Leonardo had himself written. It is that kind of magical time and situation about which I will write, a magical reality, if you will; a world of satin and silk, of mages and intrigues, of wealth and perversity, of color, as alien and enchanting as any fantasy or science fiction drama, yet this was all real. It is the coloratura of history, of executions and conspiracy, or the great Pazzi conspiracy that started a war between the Medici and pope, when Giuliano de'Medici was knifed in the Duomo Cathedral during the Sabbath celebration of high mass when the congregation sang, and Giuliano's brother, Lorenzo the Great, who became the great ruler of the Republic of Florence, escaped only by climbing the bell tower and locking the door . . . with the help of Leonardo—another episode that never came to light, for Lorenzo was quaking with fear, and although Leonardo helped to save his life, he never forgave the artist for seeing him in such condition. (Don't ask Dave Hartwell, the historian, about this, for he'll look at you dumbfounded; I'm writing what John Crowley would call 'the secret history'.) How to convey to you the wonder of Leonardo's age and surroundings? Of Florence, which was lambent with tints of translucent bright light that could only captured by Leonardo, his enemy Michaelangelo, and the other great artists of Renaissance: Raphael, Mantagna, Ghirlandajo, Botticelli, Filippino Lippi, Fra Bartolommeo—for Florience was like no other city, and Leonardo, to the end, considered himself a Florentine above all. Florence: her courts and red lilies, the Florence of Brunellesco, Michelozzo, Alberti, Ghiberti, Donatello, Florence surrounded by hills, her palaces and keeps and towers and domes, the street life and danger, and the breathtaking extravaganzas masterminded by Leonardo for the Medici and later the Sforza family, for the festivals where he would create forests in the center of the city with paint and paper, and construct machines that would make the sun seem to appear at midnight. It was a time of spectacular luxury and agonizing poverty; and it is through the streets and botegas, through the bars and slums and florious palaces that Leonardo travels. Here, in this book, we see the west and the dreaming, opulent east through the eyes of the fifteenth century, as we travel with Leonardo and his retinue of dangerous, brilliant and fascinating followers.

This book is about the unknown life of Leonardo, not the Leonardo that we think we know, in that way we think we know any historical personage, but a flesh and blood man who will come through the pages of my book as if magicked from yesterday's photographs. Leonardo exists as a legend, a puzzle, with various historians and schools claiming one piece or another, yet we don't really have a coherent picture of him, except as a brilliant genius who was a homosexual. But that view is probably wrong; there is at least enough evidence pointing toward Leonardo being a bisexual. And he *might* have been heterosexual. It is also probable that he became chaste, or nearly so, after the period with which my novel will focus on, i.e., from the time he was leaving his master Verrocchio's bottega until he left Florence for imagined greener pastures in the stolid, fortressed Milan of Lodovico Sforza. The latter is what *I* consider to be the true history of his later psycho sexuality.

It's become common belief that Leonardo was a homosexual, mostly, or at least in part due to Sigmund Freud's work on his psychosexuality. And in that work, Freud was projecting his own mind-set upon Leonardo. The book begins with Leonardo's famous dream of the great bird, in which a kite (a kind of bird, not a 'kite' kite) swoops out of the sky and slaps him upon the face with its tail. (I'm not going to make the obvious connection of this, his first remembered dream, and his lifelong fascination and preoccupation with flight.) But Freud read Leonardo's notes in translation, not a very good translation, and confused the word 'kite' with vulture, which he went on to detail how the vulture stood for Mut, the Egyptian mother goddess, a feminine symbol, and the tail was symbolic of the nipple, etc., but in fact kite, *nibbio* in Italian, was a masculine symbol, like a hawk or an eagle.

However, there is evidence that Leonardo fell in love with the beautiful Ginevra de' Benci, the daughter of Amerigo de' Benci, a Florentine merchant of considerable wealth. That is entirely possible, for Leonardo was a long-time friend of the de' Benci family, for when he left Florence for Milan in 1481, he left his unfinished panel of the Adoration of the Magi with them for safekeeping.

Ginevra was to marry an older man, the widower Luigi di Bernardo Nicolini; and we have an absolutely sublime painting of her, done by Leonardo; it has been said to be the equal of his famous Mona Lisa in technique, although it is not as mature a work. But to look at Leonardo's portrait of her is to fall in love with her: her heavy lidded eyes, her mouth held in almost a pout, her oval face of seemingly perfect complexion, childlike yet sensual and womanly; to look at the painting is like looking through a pane of glass; it is to see Leonardo's lovely vision of her; it is almost a definition of young love. And in my story, Leonardo does indeed fall in love with her. But it was during that time, in 1476, that the seventeen-year-old Jacopo Saltarelli, an artists' model, accused four young Florentines of sodomia by dropping his written denunciation into the tamburo-a box situated outside the Palazzo Vecchio. Leonardo was one of the accused, and the humiliation and trial changed his life. Although he was found innocent, he was humiliated and had lost everything. It was after Leonardo's accusation that Ginevra broke the news to him that she was going to marry someone else, which was her father's wish and command; and so Leonardo lost her, as he did most of his friends. Even his father broke off communications with him, horrified by the scandal. In one smashing blow, Leonardo fell from grace, for he was gliding on the shoulders of the scions of Florentine society, his work was lauded, until an accusation by a peasant boy brought him down. Only his Uncle Francesco and his Master Verrocchio stood by him. After this personal cataclysm, Leonardo reigned in his sexuality, repressing it deep into the recesses of himself—for it was a strong part of his very nature; hadn't his father married three times, siring some sixteen children, the later when he was well into old age? And suddenly, in a trice, the very fiber of Leonardo's sexuality had become inextricably linked with scandal and humiliation, and the subsequent loss of his beautiful Ginevra. He had lost her to a man as old as his father, and in Leonardo's mind, it might as well have been his father: one of his char-coal-sketched caricatures of lechery.

Leonardo had to begin life again at twenty-six, agonized and cynical and worldly-wise, throwing himself into his work, drawing his famous caricatures as he learned the ways of the streets and their people; writing, sketching, painting, experimenting, inventing model ornithopters that could fly-and the tiny things did fly! As he had said, "There is no lack of ways and means of dividing and measuring these wretched days of ours, which we should try not to live in vain and squander without leaving any fame, any lasting memory of us in the minds of mortals. So that our poor passage through life shall not be in vain."

But it is now that his greatest adventure begins: his journey to the east, which is to change his life and yet never appear in his notebooks . . . or in the myriad books about him.

The time I have chosen in Leonardo's life will show great change in his attitudes and personality—even his sexuality; it will describe and delineate how he came to be the legend begun by Vasari and continued to the present. Here the reader will find a man fighting for control of himself, his emotions, his drives, and his genius, a man who can create objects as beautiful as the Mona Lisa and weapons as deadly as anything invented centuries later. We will see a Leonardo never before described, a man in love who loses everything, a pawn in the dangerous political machinations of the Medici, a man soured by the world yet in love with it, who sees it through 'modern' eyes, and yet it is his sight and genius that take him to pellucid heights and damn him to the depths of his soul.

So, this is a big book, the mainstream novel of the fantastic, a historic novel, an epic adventure, a novel based on fact, yet with the magical touches of the fantastic, a novel that can be accepted in and out of genre.

Now I ask you . . . what the hell else could you ask for?

JACK CHALKER

SAYS JACK L. CHALKER, prolific author of a shelf of best-sellers:

"My second novel was my career-maker. Although it was unpublicized and appeared in midsummer after a lackluster first novel sale, it somehow hit just as students were going back to high school and college and word of mouth turned it into a major bestseller. That kind of success breeds many sequels, but the first one in that series, never intended as anything more than a single stand-alone novel, is unique."

This is the synopsis to the book he's referring to, *Midnight at the Well of Souls.*

MIDNIGHT AT THE WELL
OF SOULS (1977)

AFTER HUMANITY HAS BECOME a spacefaring species they keep finding the remains of an ancient civilization on world after world. What's unusual is that the worlds they find their ancient cities on do not seem to have ever had atmospheres, water, etc., and while the structural designs of what are clearly cities remain, not one single artifact, not one piece of art, writing, tools, ANYTHING, has ever been found. Named the Markovians after the man who first discovered the ruins, they remain an ancient enigma. On one of their dead worlds, students from several human colonies have set up a camp for study, and their professor discovers that the core of the world is actually some sort of synthetic organism and that it is dormant but still "alive." Theorizing that this is some kind of ancient Markovian computer that, energized by pure thought, could create whatever was desired and that this was how the Markovians lived, the professor is close to accessing the "brain" through an active energy "doorway" when a student stumbles over his discovery. The professor, obsessed with potential godhood, murders all the students save the one who discovered his work. The student tries to beat the professor to the "doorway," they meet, struggle, the doorway opens, and both vanish.

A freighter with some passengers intercepts a distress call from the Markovian world, heads there, and discovers the murders. When instruments show the doorway, the captain, Nathan Brazil, and his passengers, a drug dealer and his addicted female companion, and a diplomatic courier, all are caught up when the door opens and transported to a great entrance station. There they are met by a six-armed creature with the face of a walrus and the body of a snake who, upon seeing them, exclaims "Well I'll be damned! If it ain't Nathan Brazil!" He goes on to explain that many disappearances have wound up here, and "here" is the Well World, a gigantic Markovian laboratory where 1560 very different biomes, each with its own race, climate, atmospheric properties, and, in some cases, limits on technology, are maintained as they were when the last Markovian left. It is theorized that the Markovians attained godhood, had a good time with it for eons, but ultimately found it empty and decided that somewhere along the line they must have made a wrong turn in evolution. The race then decided to repursue perfection, using the labs of the artificially created Well World to run small scale live experiments to allow development of new forms of life. If successful, a world that matched the characteristics would be prepared and populated and let run free. Virtually all the races of the universe are products of this system. To enter, you must become one of the creatures of one of the biomes. Thus Serge Ortega, the six armed walrus-snake, was once human but was changed by the Well. Now they, and the two that came before them, also must be changed.

But, while the courier becomes a plant-like creature, the

drug dealer a great insect, his companion a centaur, and so on, Nathan Brazil changes not one bit. Now the murderous professor teams up with the drug dealer and others to see if the professor can get into the Well World's depths and thus be a god in control of all the races of the universe, while Nathan Brazil, who may just be a real Markovian left to guard against just such an eventuality, leads a second team in a race across the hexagonal shaped biomes towards the entrance to the Well of Souls, with other local powers manipulating things unseen from the sidelines. In the end, all find a measure of justice and all but Brazil find peace.

Kathleen Ann Goonan

WHEN I HEAR new writers moan that the deck is stacked against them, I just point to Kathleen Ann Goonan, a lady so skilled that who stacks the deck and who deals the cards is of absolutely no importance. If the game is science fiction, she's going to win.

Her first novel, *Queen City Jazz*, made her A Newcomer To Watch. These days she's A Star To Read, and this is the outline for her latest.

CRESCENT CITY RHAPSODY

Two Novels by Kathleen Ann Goonan

CRESCENT CITY RHAPSODY and a second novel, presently untitled, will form the first and last books of my Nanotech Cycle, completing it as a quartet dealing with the development of nanotech from personal, national, international, and interstellar perspectives.

Crescent City Rhapsody is a far-ranging international thriller which prequels the world of *Queen City Jazz*. Spanning a century, *CCR* details the genesis and results of a developing nanotechnology, not only from scientific, legal, intelligence, and military points of view but from the pov of ordinary people. It begins with the First Wave of nanotech development and continues through a worldwide socioeconomic upheaval to a powerful, transformational conclusion well into nanotech's Fourth Wave. During this century radio fails, nanotech thrives, and extraterrestrials play a pivotal role in the fate of humanity. Most of the characters survive this time span because of new developments in nanotechnology.

The book begins in the near-future. MARIE LEVEAU, a new-style mob boss in New Orleans, is the victim of a hit. Marie has made cryonan arrangements and is resurrected secretly after her ornate funeral. However, her child, living in Paris for protection, is also killed; her resurrection is not successful. Grieving, Marie vanishes into the Caribbean for a time with her bodyguard HUGO, an African-American dwarf, and absorbs Afro- Caribbe culture, including music, voodoo, and dance. During this time, the first period of radio failure occurs, stoking the fires of superstition worldwide, but Marie is not superstitious by nature—she is pragmatic and scientifically oriented. Finally healed, Marie returns to New Orleans in triumph. Her money has allowed her to be so far ahead of the curve that her resurrection is seen as a miracle—or the triumph of forces of darkness for those so inclined. She has a flair for the dramatic, and allows the city to catch glimpses of her occasionally; soon her legend as a Voodoo Queen knows no bounds. Bionan developments take the concepts of the zombie or the idea that bits of one's body can give power to one's enemies to new levels. Marie knows the city and its inhabitants intimately. She's the Boss.

Tempered by loss, Marie does what she can to dismantle the mob machinery in New Orleans, which makes her more enemies. Her money comes from shrewd investments in the new, growing field of nanotechnology. She finds that her killers were actually part of an international intelligence operation trying to prevent nanotechnology from falling into the hands of the public. She keeps abreast of all developments and is a major player in the events to come, including the eventual development of the floating city of Norleans.

A fan of Duke Ellington, Marie studies his methods of composition. She compares his process of writing music to suit his carefully chosen musicians and meld them into a single strong musical vision to her own goal of choosing those

singular people who will best be able to learn what has be-
fallen Earth and to lead humanity to the heart of this mystery
and beyond, to an exploration of other galaxies. She thinks
of this entire intellectual and emotional composition, comprised of that which is highest and best in humanity, as an
Ellingtonian-style rhapsody—not random evolution any
more, but a plan designed and played out by those at the top
of their game, each person's style contributing to the whole.

ZEB is a professor of astronomy at a university in
Southwest Virginia. Divorced, he has no close relatives,
other than a sister, and her family. He is monitoring his student's dipole antenna, a very basic sensing device which
gathers signals from space, on Thanksgiving Eve when the
first radio blackout occurs, thereby becoming privy to information which immediately becomes classified. From his recorded data, which a mysterious intruder steals, he draws his
own conclusion—that the interruption must have been
caused by an intelligent source—but when he tries to go public he is forcefully warned to keep quiet. Because most forms
of getting signals from space depend on the use of computers, which were knocked out during the blackout, the data he
has is quite rare. He makes contact with SETI, but its members are mysteriously disappearing, as have others who directly observed the radio data of the incident. He works out
mathematical predictions of when other blackouts will occur,
and when the blackout will become permanent. He knows
that his predictions are correct, but falls prey to the international conspiracy to silence this information and keep the
world from knowing that an intelligent extraterrestrial

source is responsible. Always unstable, he completely disassociates under this pressure and becomes a bum in Washington D.C.

His niece, Annie, in college when this begins, suspects the truth, because she takes Zeb seriously. While a government employee, she begins working with a secret organization dedicated to forming a complete picture of what has happened by stealing information from various governments and exploiting all possible informational vectors. Annie tries to get Zeb to live in a small apartment she rents in downtown D.C. but Zeb is always leaving. He thinks entirely in abstract terms and scribbles equations on scraps of paper which Annie salvages and passes on to her cohorts.

Two-thirds of the way through the book, Zeb blunders into a a Church of Nanotechnology, where through a nan communion service his original intelligence and personality are restored.

He is one of the few surviving people who know what really happened, inasmuch as can be speculated from Earth. Much time has passed. He goes to New Orleans, where Marie is assembling what is left of the scientific community and planning to build a floating city in the Gulf of Mexico.

JARDIN joins the narrative several years after Marie. He is a twenty-five-year old Tibetan refugee living in Kathmandu. He repairs bicycles but finds that new nan-based novelties for tourists bring in more money, so he becomes a street magician. A Buddhist, he has taken on a sick eight-year-old girl; she reminds him of the sister he lost in Tibet. The local clinic can only determine that she has a rare disease, and that she ought to go to a research center in Munich. Jardin raises enough money to send her there. After several months he has enough money to follow, but at the research center he is told that the girl is dead. Jardin believes this, though the girl is not dead; she surfaces later. Angry and bitter, Jardin discovers that the research center is investigating an obscure genetic anamoly on a worldwide basis. He thinks the girl died during the course of an experiment.

He is at a loss, and his journey back to Nepal stalls in Bangkok. There he meets a young woman who disguises herself as a man and calls herself the General. Via an ever-growing army of young girls, she tracks down and liberates girls sold into prostitution. This generally involves some violence. Jardin joins her terrorist cause, and thereby enters the international terrorist community. Eventually he becomes a feared international nanotech terrorist.

Two-thirds of the way through the book, a cataclysmic event causes him to embrace Buddhism once again. The world has changed dramatically since his days in Kathmandu, and he reassess his life. He becomes a part of Marie's network, an Asian operant.

KITA is a US-educated Japanese woman living in Osaka. She works for a top-secret company which is developing various nanotech products, including crucial Flower-City technology. In the SECOND WAVE section, Marie, with whom Kita attended college, contacts her via her bodyguard, Hugo. Reluctantly, Kita becomes a nanotech spy, which is quite perilous. She and Hugo become lovers. Kita is instrumental in helping Marie assimilate the information and prototypes she needs to carry out her long-term plans, and provides a window on events in Japan.

JULIA PEABODY is twenty-three, lives in Sedona, Arizona, and embraces every weird philosophy that comes down the pike. She makes a living by doing internet psychic predictions, working in a health-food restaurant, and giving tours for Vortex, Inc. In Sedona, "vortexes" are understood to be geologic locales which concentrate cosmic energies. Julia is at the famous and potent Airport Vortex giving a talk when the initial blackout occurs. Julia, newly pregnant, immediately changes her name to that of a distant star system. She is convinced that during the blackout an event of cosmic magnitude has taken place. Such sentiments are Sedona's bread and butter, where so-called events of cosmic magnitude are fodder for commercial development.

But this time Julia is right. During the initial blackout, alien genetic material enters the atmosphere, and when it comes in contact with pregnant women during the next forty-eight hours, becomes a part of the genetic makeup of the embryo. This has to be during a very specific stage of fetal development or else the melding does not take place; hence, the number of people in the world who are thus affected is not great. Julia knows that something is different about Jason from the very beginning. He grows up to be Peabody in *Mississippi Blues*, and we see his young life here.

Some of the fetuses thus affected are miscarried, and of those brought to term some are developmentally flawed. But the development of some of them goes as planned, as best as could be foreseen by the desperate time and resource limited aliens.

The ALIENS, whom we never see directly, are on their way from somewhere to somewhere when they become aware that they are in the first stages of being destroyed by something analogous to a virus. Earth is not their destination, but it is convenient. Knowing that they will all die, they park nearby, blocking detection of their craft, and comprehend the DNA composition of humanity via radio and television broadcasts.

They have no desire to take over this planet. But they work out a plan to transmute their essence into the form of DNA, which will lie dormant in the humans it enters until triggered by various combinations of radio signals. They block radio communication as a pod shoots this material into the earth's atmosphere. The alien ship, locked into a holding pattern, will remain until the new alien/humans return. The aliens cleanse the ship of the virus and jettison themselves. Their only hope for continuity lies in the success of their hastily contrived plan. They hope that their history and learning and arts will be expressed in some form through the humans they will become, and that their decedents will eventually use this stored knowledge to find the ship, assume their ancestor's form, and resume the interrupted journey. A signal is set to kick in at a predetermined time to guide them back, and they clear away the earth-generated radio garbage that has filled the pureness of space for the past century in order to facilitate their continued evolution at predetermined times via signals transmitted by the waiting ship.

This information emerges gradually. The characters who have the alien-enhanced DNA are different, but feel this only vaguely at first—they don't know why. Only in stages which take place over a long maturation period do they get even a glimmering of who and what they are. The young girl Jardin tries to help is such a person. The information-gathering abilities that would enable those capable of pinpointing these anomalous children become crippled early in the book, so the existence of these children is known by only a few.

Other characters will be woven into the tapestry during each section to illustrate the vast social upheaval accompanying each new wave. ARTAUD, a former art critic, commands the Eiffel Tower in a Flower-City Paris. A Chinese scientist stranded on the abandoned Moon Colony goes mad, and leaves information behind about the nature of the aliens which is eventually transmitted to earth, though it is only picked up by a few lone operators and recognized for what it is. An Argentinean cattle rancher copes as best she can with changes which render her ancestral mode of making a living obsolete. THE GAIANS believe that humans are destroying a living earth, and become a terrorist force. The MILLENNIALISTS develop the plans for a floating city, revising them in the face of each new technological development.

The following historic continuum is followed through the book. The characters advance through the narrative in a jazz-based progression, each illuminating the others in a composition of dissonance and harmony.

The book opens a few years before the beginning of the First Nanotech Wave, though no one of course recognizes it as such. Limited nanotech applications become available to the public. Some are spinoffs of laboratories interested in financing further research, while others are the direct result of targeted development. Nanotech is not taken very seriously. But new developments in the fields of medicine, manufacturing, and the invention of entirely new applications take place every day. In this milieu, Marie is killed and resurrected. It would seem a miracle to most people, but repairs of medical trauma, paired with new, albeit undependable, methods of storing the information which makes us individuals, is at this time possible for those who can afford it, and who dare to make the leap.

A year or so before the first wave begins in earnest, the first radio blackout occurs. In the wake of disasters and a brief chaos which doesn't last long enough to develop into anything serious, two international summits take place. One is public, designed to quell rising uproar and speculation. Soothing lies are broadcast, stories of a solar flare. The other summit is top secret, and a pact is made to stonewall the world until more information is gathered. But it is the contention of several scientists that the interruption must have been the result of some sort of deliberately manufactured radio blackout from somewhere in space. Almost all those involved or in a position to speculate in an educated fashion agree to keep silent in the face of this shattering possibility, fearing the widespread chaos which might result should everyone believe that aliens are on the way.

The second communication break takes place three months later. This time, they are prepared. The story of the quasar is spun and takes hold. There are, in fact, very few as-tronomers or cosmologists who are independent of universi-ties, and though speculation rages among this community, a Manhattan project-like silence is maintained in the face of the public. Whatever is causing this, whether alien or natu-ral, the fact is that communication alternatives must be de-veloped. And if aliens are the cause, chaos must still be avoided. Those who try and tell the world the truth are si-lenced by the intelligence community. Space-oriented re-search is stepped up.

Finally, what everyone has desired, but also feared, oc-curs. Self-replicating molecules enter the world via small se-cret labs and the vaults of prestigious international consortiums. Some are legal. Most violate the international laws and treaties set up in haste. The world is catapulted into the Second Wave.

A fully functioning moon colony is established, com-plete with tourist facilities, an international cooperative. Mars is settled by a few hardy pioneers operating privately, a maverick operation condemned but not thwarted by various governments, which eventually piggy-back onto this foot-hold. Nanotechnology allows many kinds of architectural and structural breakthroughs, which are put to use not only to renovate the infrastructure of cities but to develop new designs for space-related endeavors. Many consumer goods become theoretically cheap, but like pharmaceuticals today this savings is not passed on to the consumers, but used to repay the cost of research and development.

The disaffected of the world suddenly have access to immense power, though of course it is withheld as much as possible. Nanotechnology does not require rare elements such as uranium.

Religious fundamentalists from Christians to Muslims realize that one way to return the world to a more acceptable state is to destroy technology, which is becoming ever more frightening and out of control. The US Government has developed several top-secret nanotech devices which eat fiberoptic cable, others which render copper wire useless for carrying information. These are all sought by terrorists.

The efforts of all governments and the intelligentsia of the world focus on the problem of developing alternate means of communication before radio is completely gone. Biological alternatives to encoding and transporting information are feverishly developed. The concept of using pheromones to enable humans to receive and send information is unveiled at an international conference. A growing number of proponents herald this as a promising breakthrough; another faction works instead on the possibility of downloading the contents of the human mind into a less destructible medium, which eventually evolve to become the domes glimpsed in *Mississippi Blues*. All is in disarray during this time. Communications are often reduced to printed documents transported by couriers; energy alternatives such as solar generation of electricity and using grain by-products to fuel engines and generators are frantically refined in the face of quickly approaching cusp of complete radio blackout.

The developers of the flower cities know that there are flaws, but there is little time for refinement.

As one city after another worldwide votes to convert to the new system—and others are converted without a vote—radio blackout becomes almost complete, with only a few holes now and then.

Many humans modify themselves to receive and transmit precise information. Within the cities, information can be accessed or sent from any room. Glowing interstices filled with fluid transport information to rooftop collectors. These evolve via nanotechnological breakthroughs into huge flowerlike entities. Those who do not accept the changes are left behind in primitive communities. Those who are changed experienced terror and wonder; enslavement, and release into utterly new ways of knowing.

Denver, New York, San Francisco, the eastern seaboard from Boston to Washington, Seattle, Houston, New Orleans all become part of a vast network of new, almost utopian cities, linked by the powerfully swift maglev train line known as NAMS, the North American Magline System, running on a switching amalgamation of solar power, steam, and electricity. Jets are unusable, since so many components of their operations are now undependable, but NAMS is almost as swift, and much more convenient, delivering travelers within blocks of their destination. During the heyday of the Flower cities, pouches of business-imbued metapheromones are swiftly transported by NAMS; literature hypertexed metapheromonally fills users with emotional intensity and immersion in author's visions an infinity beyond clumsy old-fashioned virtual reality.

But the Information Wars put an end to this brief magnificence. Entire cities can be easily sabotaged and nanotechnologists work in top secret laboratories and think tanks to find defenses. Some of these defenses turn out to be lethal. Airborne plagues can kill quickly, or change the neuronal patterns of the plagued to fill them with any thoughts the creator of the plague might desire. Plagues of thought—viruslike, airborne informational nan—released during the Information Wars are so compelling that those unwilling to be drawn into the strangeness can only isolate themselves and hope for favorable winds. The Third Wave begins.

The Third Wave isolates the flower cities, turning the world into an unstable collection of independent, individual human frontiers. Cumulative tampering with ancient genetic programs governing aspects of human function and behavior including the ability to survive famine results in a precipitous worldwide drop in population. Yet at the same time, for those so privileged, the old dream of human immortality becomes a reality.

Against this backdrop, Marie strives to overcome the rising darkness, and seeks those who can help. New Orleans becomes a worldwide beacon, an oasis of sanity, a promise of salvation—and, for many, just a rumor. Jardin, Kita, and other characters make their way there after playing important roles in creating the new possibilities envisioned by Marie. Eventually New Orleans is perceived as a threat to what is left of the US government, and is successfully destroyed.

But the international band Marie has assembled triumphs over the many odds against them, manage to build their floating city, and escape New Orleans before it is destroyed. Though *Crescent City Rhapsody* takes place in the world of *Queen City Jazz* and *Mississippi Blues*, it will be a stand alone novel with complete closure. Though reading the first two books is not necessary in order to understand *CCR*, it will nonetheless be of interest to readers of *Queen City Jazz* and *Mississippi Blues*.

UNTITLED SECOND BOOK

THE SECOND NOVEL begins not long after the conclusion of *Mississippi Blues*. The characters from *Queen City Jazz* have joined those in the floating city of Norleans. Some of them try to find remedies for the disasters that have overtaken the earth. Others prepare to put into play the last stage of Marie's plan—to go into space, track down the source of the Signal, and discover the secrets of interstellar travel. They also discover what has happened to the Moon and Mars Colonies, where survivors have set up their own forms of government.

At the end, radio communication is restored to the Earth, and people are charged with the responsibility of deciding what to do with this second chance at civilization. And in a transcendent finale, those who are part human and part alien have to make decisions generated from who and what they really are, and how they will deal with their starfaring past, their devastating effect on the Earth, and their future.

(I reserve the right to use CCR as a title for either book, depending on the appropriateness of other titles I may generate as the books progress.)

WALTER JON WILLIAMS

HERE ARE A PAIR of proposals from Walter Jon Williams, one of our better sellers, who has been falsely accused of writing cyberpunk, New Wave, and hard science fiction. What he writes are Walter Jon Williams books.

Metropolitan became a bit of a *cause celebre* when a misguided New York publisher tried to back out of a contract for it. All's well that ends well, and *Metropolitan* sold to a rival New York house for even more money, and certainly got better handling and promotion.

The Rift lacks such a dramatic history, but that's about all it lacks.

THE RIFT

by Walter Jon Williams

Prologue: Last Chant of the Sun Man

WE OPEN WITH THE SUN MAN atop his ancestral mound above the Mississippi River. Below him is the settlement where he and his people spend their days, fields and homes set in a wide bend of the river. Other tall pyramid-shaped mounds are visible on both sides of the river, marking the sites of other towns. The Sun Man's great ancestor, the founder of his clan, is buried in the mound beneath his feet, an eternal guardian who guarantees his descendents harmony and prosperity.

The Sun Man chants as the sun rises, welcoming the renewal of life and the return of warmth and light to the world. Filling his heart is a sensation of utter tranquility and peace.

And then the tranquility is abruptly shattered as the entire world seems to give a violent lurch to one side. Sun Man is flung to the ground, and before his horrified eyes the ancestral mound splits open. Trees in the surrounding forest topple. Flocks of panicked birds rise into the sky.

The Sun Man gazes down at the crack at his feet, and to his utter horror he sees the sightless eyes of his ancestor looking back at him from the crack in his earthen grave.

Screams and cries for help rise up from the town. The Sun Man staggers to the edge of the mound to look down at his people. The sturdy houses have all fallen flat. Some are on fire. A strange white mist is rising from the ground, and there is a hideous sulphurous stench in the morning air.

And the Mississippi is gone! The silty bed of the great river is empty, as if a giant drain had opened in the riverbed and all the water poured out. The Sun Man stares in disbelief. Fear fills his heart for the fate of his wife and family, but he knows his duty.

As the religious leader of his people, his job is to stay on the mound and pray. He begins to chant with a fervor he has never known before.

Within *seconds*, the strange white mist has filled the world below, leaving the Sun Man isolated on a floating island of earth. From the invisible village below come the eerie cries of the injured and bewildered. Within *minutes*, the clear blue sky has turned black as midnight. Lightning begins to rain down on the world below, *hundreds* of bolts within minutes. The air fills with ozone as a bolt rips into the temple built on the mound, but the Sun Man, out in the open, is miraculously hurt.

And then the world fills with a terrible rumbling, like a thousand giants roaring their war cries. The white mist parts like a curtain before an oncoming horror. The Sun Man stares helplessly, forgetting to chant.

The river is coming back! And it's running *backwards*, south to north, coming in a huge flooding mass, a churning wall of water fifty feet high. Trees are going down before it like pinecones.

With an overwhelming roar the wall of water falls on the town, sweeping away the flattened houses, the terrified people, the fields, the fires, all trace that they were ever there. Spray drenches the Sun Man as he huddles in speechless terror at the top of his mound.

After the water levels fall, the Sun Man looks out at his new world. As far as he can see there is nothing but a tangled mass of shattered timber, fetid swamp, and the endless fields and rivers of mud into which the lightning bolts continue to fall.

The only indications that a prosperous, thriving people once clustered along the banks of the Mississippi are the lonely mounds that stand mute above the landscape filled with oozing wreckage.

Geology: The Rift

FOURTEEN MILLION YEARS AGO the North American continent was pulling apart, creating a great rift that is now the valley of the Mississippi. Though North America was not quite torn in two, the powerful movements of the earth's tectonic plates left behind cracks and faults below the surface of the continent.

One of these is the New Madrid fault, running across the Mississippi near New Madrid, Missouri, halfway between St. Louis and Memphis. Unlike the better-known San Andreas fault in California, which slips gradually, causing many

small earthquakes every year along with the occasional localized catastrophe, the New Madrid fault builds tension
gradually over the years and then suddenly *SNAPS* in a
powerful, catastrophic sideways lurch.

And there is another crucial difference between the New
Madrid and San Andreas faults. Whereas the San Andreas
fault produces localized quakes that shake up and down, the
New Madrid fault produces "continental channel waves,"
which spread *sideways* over vast distances. Continental
channel waves can travel hundreds of miles without significant reduction in their power.

The last time the New Madrid fault snapped was in the
winter of 1811, totally destroying the then-insignificant settlement of New Madrid. There were three major earthquakes
and over 1800 aftershocks. The area of total destruction was
40,000 square miles. Continental channel waves carried the
shocks thousands of miles, setting church bells ringing in
Boston and Charleston. The Missouri River ran backwards
for a day. Chimneys were shaken down in Cincinatti. Glass
shattered in New York City. In Baltimore, panicked people
ran into the streets at the force of the tremors.

In Missouri, there wasn't a single farmer's field that
wasn't torn by fractures. Not a single road remained intact.
Solid land turned into swamps, lakes, or rivers, while
riverbeds and swamps rose to became dry land. In one area
150 miles by 40 miles, the ground sank from three to nine
feet and the entire area was inundated. In Natchez, people
assumed New Orleans had been destroyed. The inhabitants of
New Orleans believed that everything north of Natchez had

ceased to exist. The three major quakes were the largest anywhere in the world in the 19th Century.

Because no reliable records existed of earth tremors prior to the arrival of the Europeans, geologists have only pieced together the history of the New Madrid fault in the last decade. The evidence was so *huge* that geologists simply hadn't noticed it, hadn't connected it to earthquakes. The thirty-foot-high fracture lines running across Missouri, eroded into gentler shapes, had been mistaken for rolling prairie hills. The evidence of tidal waves on the Mississippi, Ohio, and Missouri had been mistaken for periodic flooding, but it seems clear now that tidal waves have come as far up the Ohio as Cincinatti.

Since 1811, New Madrid has been rebuilt. North America's great rift valley has been settled by tens of millions of newcomers. Cities have sprung up on the river and on the prairies, along with a complex support structure of bridges, dams, reservoirs, power transmission lines, highways, levees, and the occasional nuclear power plant.

None of these structures have been built with earthquakes in mind.

The New Madrid Fault snaps, on average, every 150 years. The last time was in 1811.

It's now overdue. And the longer the strain builds without relief, the worse the result will be.

Prelude to the Catastrophe

SIX HUNDRED YEARS after the earthquake that wiped out the Sun Man's civilization, the sound of chanting and drums once again rings out from the top of the old overgrown mound. Below, in the new town of Cabell's Mound, the inhabitants look up and shake their heads. The New Age Lady is at it again.

The lady in question is CATHERINE ADAMS, lately arrived from California with her teenage son JASON. She has moved to Missouri for an unusual reason. A follower of New Age mysticism, Catherine believes the many current prophecies that California will be destroyed by earthquake and thrown into the sea. She has moved her small family to the midwest because she knows that here she will be safe from natural catastrophe.

Jason does not want to be in Middle America. He doesn't believe in prophecies, he doesn't want to live in a hick town, there's no place to rollerblade, his girlfriend is in California, and his interest in the local Indian mound is lessened by the fact that his mother likes to hike to the top, make offerings to the spirits, bang her drum, and chant.

When Jason, in the house below, hears the sound of the chanting he is mortified. He puts Nine-Inch Nails on the CD changer and cranks up the volume *real loud* . . .

Upriver from Cabell's Mound in St. Louis, NICK RUFORD has just got bad news on top of his bad news. Defense cutbacks have cost him his job at McDonnell-Douglas. Finding a new job as an aeronautical weapons system designer would be hard enough if he were white, but it so happens Nick is black.

He has moved into a smaller apartment in a worse neighborhood, but he has fixed up one room for his daughter Arlette, who visits him every summer from Baton Rouge, where she lives with her mother. But now Arlette calls him to tell him that she has a chance to spend the summer in France, in a French-speaking environment. He can hardly tell her to pass up an educational opportunity of this class just to spend the summer with old dad . . .

He can't tell her that, but he wants to.

Instead, angry at the world, he decides to drive South to visit Arlette before she leaves. Maybe he can get a job *there*.

Meanwhile, farther south in Arkansas, the reverend NOBLE FRANKLAND, radio preacher, fills the local airwaves with his predictions of the Time of Tribulation. He's not a "rapture wimp" like so many others—he knows that the Time of Tribulation will occur *before* the Rapture that carries believers to Heaven, not afterwards, and that during the years of the Tribulation, all good Christians will need their guns.

In Washinghton, the President revises his text for the upcoming Economic Summit . . .

CARL LUSCHNIG, chief engineer at the Hollis Landing nuclear power plant in Mississippi, drowses at his gauges and idly gazes out the window of the control building, watching the busy traffic on the Mississippi below.

And author B.F. McCALL, on a publicity tour to promote her cheerful new book, *PS: You're Doomed*, discovers that she seems to have been booked into every 15,000-watt AM chat station in the midwest. Her book is a breezy compilation of every way the human race has discovered of offing itself, and includes such guaranteed blockbusters as microwaved babies, falling elevators, death by farting, and exploding shellfish delivered directly to your table.

It's also got a chapter on the New Madrid fault that conclusively demonstrates that everyone in the middle third of the U.S. might as well get it over with now and slit their wrists.

Three weeks into her publicity tour, up at dawn to find herself bracketed between angry phone-in callers still mad at Jane Fonda and rapturous advertisements for Purina Pig Chow, McCall is thinking of slitting her wrists herself.

CHARLES KINGMASON, Memphis investment banker, bets the farm, his bank's assets, and his growing reputation in a huge derivatives purchase, betting that the New York Stock Exchange will rise. It isn't a gamble, as far as he's concerned: he's got a firm assurance in the economic indicators that predict the economic resurgence will continue for at least another eighteen months . . .

TED PIPES, the black chairman of the parish council of Spottswood Parish, La., tries to figure out how he's going to cope with the newly-elected sheriff, who happens to be the Kleagle of the Ku Klux Klan . . .

All these people think they've got troubles *now.*

The picture changes when, in New York, in San Francisco, in Charleston and Baton Rouge and Seattle and Toronto, the earth trembles and the church bells begin to chime of their own accord, as if in mourning for a world that has come to an end.

THE SNAP

THE FAULT SNAPS at the worst possible moment, 17:14 CDT on a May evening. Spring rains and snowmelt have filled the reservoirs, and rush hour stacked traffic bumper-to-bumper on all the bridges.

8.9 on the Richter scale. The largest tremor since the Lisbon quake of 1755.

Within seconds everything is gone. The area of total destruction runs roughly from St. Louis in the north to Memphis in the South, Kansas City in the west to Louisville in the east. In this area, all buildings are destroyed or severely damaged. All bridges fall, along with the traffic on them. All locks and dams are broken, including the dams holding the waters of the Lake of the Ozarks, Beaver Lake, Stockton Lake, and the other artificial lakes of the region. Gaping holes are torn in all levees. All power lines fall. All highways are torn apart. Railroad tracks are reduced to twisted steel. Airport runways are broken. All fences go down. Communication lines are disrupted. Hospitals are destroyed.

Along the Mississippi, Ohio, and Missouri, tidal waves bury entire communities in mud and debris. Floodwaters from broken dams and reservoirs inundate others.

The strange white mist rises from the ground, a thicker fog than any had known. The air reeks of sulphur. Instant thunderstorms form over huge areas, raining down tens of thousands of bolts of lightning.

Continental channel waves create an area of secondary destruction that stretches as far north as Chicago and Minneapolis and south to Natchez, Jackson, and Shreveport. Brick buildings and schools, both terribly vulnerable to earthquake damage, go crashing down. Many other buildings, bridges, and levees are destroyed or damaged.

Aftershocks, some nearly as powerful as the original earthquake, add to the chaos, shaking down buildings damaged by the original shock.

Dead trees rise from the bottoms of lakes and rivers and form huge jams that dam the water and flood tens of thousands of acres. In some places entire groves stand in water upside-down, roots in the air. The tangled dams stand until the water pressure grows too great, and then they break loose in huge waves of timber-bearing floodwaters.

The rampaging waters, mightily increased by water pouring from broken dams and reservoirs, heads south in a great foaming mass. Soon the government realizes that it must evacuate all lowlands down the entire length of the Mississippi—every town and city from Memphis through Baton Rouge to New Orleans is in danger of being inundated.

When the floodwaters reach Louisiana, they overwhelm a century's work by the Army Corps of Engineers and carve a new bed for the Mississippi, rolling over Morgan City and into the Gulf of Mexico. When the flood waters finally recede from New Orleans, the city will be without its river, and an arm of the Gulf of Mexico will creep northward into its bed.

THE HEART OF THE WORLD

THE UNITED STATES is the engine that powers the world economy, and the Midwest is the heart of the United States. When the fault snaps, the world economy drops like a stone.

Economic repercussions are immediate. Food prices climb for the sky—the breadbasket of the world has just ceased to exist. Stock markets are frozen in the justified fear that the bottom will drop out the second they are opened.

Geopolitical considerations are far more ominous. We see Russian, Japanese, and German politicians all independently decide to re-arm—the world's only superpower can no longer guarantee peace anywhere in the world. In Africa, Asia, and the borders of the Russian Empire, decisions are made to resolve ethnic conflict by force of arms and by massacre, confident that CNN will be looking elsewhere.

And in the Middle East, tanks stand poised over oilfields as the Kingdom of Saud realizes it may have lost its only protector . . .

CLOSEUPS

THOUGH WORLD EVENTS will be covered fully, the focus of *The Rift* will stay personal, shifting back and forth from world leaders to the desperate figures struggling to survive in the rubble of their once-secure civilization.

The President realizes to his horror that his actions can have but scant impact. Half the population of Louisiana,

Mississippi, and Arkansas are streaming for higher ground. On the middle Mississippi, millions are dead, millions more are in need of medical care, and tens of millions are homeless, but the infrastructure that would support relief efforts has been destroyed. With no railroads, runways for aircraft, highways, or safe river transportation, all aid supplies have to be lifted in by helicopter. There aren't enough helicopters in the *world* to do the job. And there aren't enough relief workers on the planet to handle a catastrophe this vast.

Most of the people in the Rift, the President realizes, are on their own.

IN THE RIFT

JASON ADAMS WATCHES his mother die. He is on the Sun Man's mound when the quake hits, trying out a birthday telescope his father sent him. His view isn't as good as was the Sun Man's 600 years before: the mound is overgrown with trees and brush. Through the scope he watches Catherine return home from work, watches her leave her car and walk into their house.

Then–Richter 8.9.

Jason is knocked flat and partly buried beneath falling trees. Struggling to get free, he treated to much the same sights as the Sun Man: the wrecked homes, the eerie mist, the stench of sulphur, the blackening sky and the rain of thunderbolts. And then the wall of water that buries everything below.

The land has reverted to its state of 600 years before. Jason finds himself on an island in a stinking swamp. His attempts to walk out are bogged down within mere yards of his mound sanctuary. He can't leave, but then he can't stay either: he has no food, no clothing beyond what he has on his back, and no shelter.

And then, floating by within reach of his little island, drifts his neighbor's bass boat . . .

When the earthquake hits, Nick Ruford, the unemployed weapons system designer, has almost reached Memphis. The road leaps out from under him, the car dives into a sulphurous fracture. When he climbs out of the wreck, he sees the Mississippi pouring toward him from a rent in the levee.

Carl Luschnig is in the Hollis Landing Power Station when the earthquake hits. Even as he gives orders to shut down the reactor, the control room is coming to pieces around him. The stoutly-built containment structure, with its reactor, remains intact, but everything outside has been severely damaged. The reactor can no longer be controlled.

Luschnig needs to flood the reactor with cooling water to shut it down, but the primary mechanisms are out. There are five backup diesel engines to run the emergency pumps, but they're all in separate buildings on different parts of the property, all the buildings are wrecked, and wreckage has to be cleared before the diesels can be started by hand.

Eventually tons of emergency cooling water are poured into the reactor core. But the whole area of Hollis Landing has subsided twelve feet, the levees are broken, and it looks as if the entire Mississippi is about to carve a new path for itself right through the power station.

Reactor containment structures are tough—they were designed so that they can withstand a large aircraft being crashed into them—but the structures were not intended to be smack in the middle of a major waterway.

Carl has to do something, and fast.

Charles Kingmason, the investment banker whose clever play in the derivatives market has just been wiped out, finds himself unable to reach anyone on his cellular phone. He has no food in his wrecked house, and very little fuel in his car. His credit cards are useless. All the technology is worthless without power. That night he finds himself sleeping in the back seat of his Mercedes while trying to ignore the wails of sirens and the flames from burning buildings.

Author B.F. McCall gazes in befuddlement at the wreck-age of the 8000-watt radio station, KVSH, "The Voice of the Osage Area," from which, a few moments ago, she'd been pitching *PS: You're Doomed!* and helping to sling the Pig Chow. One of the things she'd predicted in his book has actually happened!

She begins to laugh. The thing is, she doesn't now what to do *now!* She knows every way that Nature can chop, slice, dice, and julienne humanity, but she doesn't know anything about how to survive any of it.

She decides she'd better learn.

Jason Adams is swept away from the Sun Man's mound in his neighbor's bass boat. He has no oars or motor, and though he tries to paddle with his hands to where his house once stood to search for his mother, the river, draining southward again, swiftly carries him away.

Nick Ruford slogs out of the rising Mississippi water to the outskirts of Memphis. All he can see is wreckage and stunned survivors. The horizon is lit by fire as the rubble that is Memphis begins to burn, and the sound of sirens fills the air. He has tried to call his family, but all the phones are down.

He approaches a police officer to ask for directions, but the cop, black himself, has been unnerved by tales of looting and a curfew, and he's frantic with worry about his family, who he hasn't been able to contact. When he sees the menacing black figure looming out of the darkness, he panics and fires. Slightly wounded, Nick flees into the night. When he realizes he has run into an area soon to be inundated, it's too late to do anything but climb a tree.

Carl Luschnig, isolated amid rising waters in the Hollis Landing plant, fails not only to reach his superiors to inform them of the station's plight, but discovers he cannot raise his family.

The Reverend Noble Frankland is perhaps the only person caught up in this disaster who is perfectly at home. He has been expecting this for years. The shakings of the earth, the sudden darkness, the eerie mist, the smell of brimstone, the sudden rain of lightning bolts . . . it is all out of Biblical prophecy.

The End Time has come, the Years of Tribulation that will preceed the Rapture and the return of Christ to Earth. God is testing His children.

Frankland finds that the authorities in his part of Arkansas are unprepared, confused, and unable to contact their superiors for help. Because he himself was prepared for the End Time, his radio station features a generator, plenty of fuel, and disaster supplies. He finds his station is one of the few on the air, and his church is one of the few larger buildings still intact.

He himself organizes the first responses to the catastrophe: the rescue of the injured and isolated, the organization of relief supplies, the shelter of the homeless. In the face of such a Biblical catastrophe he makes many converts, including many in authority in his community.

He does not plan to limit his activities merely to providing relief, however. The Lord is testing His children, and the Reverend Frankland plans to do a little testing himself.

THE REGRESSION

BY DAWN THE NEXT DAY, the middle section of the US has regressed to a near primeval state. Roads and communication nets are destroyed. Waterways, including the Missouri and Mississippi, are now wild rivers, leaping over their banks to cut new paths through the wilderness, through the wreckage, forming new lakes and new islands. The rivers are full of sandbars, snags, uncharted islands, and white water. Wildfires set by lightning consume wrecked homes and many stands of timber, and ominous smoke plumes smudge the horizon. Millions of people are now finding themselves as isolated as were the first explorers venturing westward into the new land.

Dawn finds Nick up a tree in the middle of a vast plain of

water. He discovers he's sharing the tree with a lot of the local fauna: a large nest of ants that leave him covered with bites, a mother opossum and her family, several squirrels, and a variety of birds. An aftershock shakes the tree, and angers something he hadn't noticed: a poisonous coral snake.

Nick and the snake stalk each other through the tree. Nick finds he cannot escape the snake: he must kill it or it will kill him. Steeling himself, he beats it to death with a broken branch.

It is only then that he sees the boy in the drifting boat. With the flooding river now spread out over hundreds of miles and the current consequently reduced, Jason finds himself able to paddle to Nick's tree and rescue him.

At least now he has someone to talk to.

The boat drifts past Memphis, darkened with smoke from widescale fires and alive with sirens and screams. The famous riverside pyramid is a shattered wreck: Mud Island has been rolled beneath the river. Jason wants to paddle ashore here, but Nick won't let him—the last time he walked into a bad situation he got shot at, and at least on the river they are safe. The boat drifts on.

If it drifts on far enough, he may meet his daughter after all.

At the Hollis Landing Station, Carl Luschnig is reading ominous signs from his few surviving instruments. Radiation has been released from the reactor's safety valves, which indicates the reactor at one point overheated. He *thinks* the radiation was a small amount, but he can't know. And the fact that radiation was released at all is inclined to make him suspect that the reactor suffered something very close to a core meltdown.

Across the river in Spottswood Parish, parish council chairman Ted Pipes is fully involved in the relief efforts, trying to work around his edgy relationship with his sheriff, the Kleagle. Here on the edge of the area of devastation, damage was not as massive as farther north, and many road nets and communication nets remain usable.

But then Chairman Pipes receives word that Spottswood Parish has been designated an evacuation zone. Tens of thousands of refugees from low-lying Natchez and Baton Rouge, fleeing the floods the authorities know are coming, are going to swarm into his district, and Pipes will somehow have to shelter and feed them.

Author B.F. McCall has worked out a plan. The cause of womens' rights, she figures, has just taken a 3000-year leap into the past. Roads, airplanes, and railroads are useless. The only way out is by water. Therefore she will get a boat, steal one if necessary. Ditto food. Ditto drinking water. The boat will serve for shelter and be safer than any building rocked by aftershocks. And she will head downriver until she finds someplace that hasn't been wrecked and isn't full of rubes.

She will find it a long journey.

In his ruined Memphis suburb, Charles Kingmason spends another night in his car watching fires consume much of the city. Refugees from other districts are wandering through his neighborhood looking for food, and he has none to give them. And he's also becoming very aware of his own hunger.

And in Arkansas, the Reverend Frankland convinces the authorities that all food supplies should be brought to his church for distribution, where his armed followers can guard them from looters. Women and children will be separated from their menfolk and concentrated around the church, where they can be cared for, while the men are formed into groups to scavenge food, bring in the injured and those isolated by distance, and sent out as work gangs into the fields.

Control their food supplies, Frankland thinks. Keep them isolated, work them to exhaustion, feed them principally with sermons and propaganda.

Control their lives to this extent, he thinks, and their hearts and souls will surely follow.

RIVERINE ODYSSEY

ROAD WARRIOR IT ISN'T. Civilization doesn't break down except in a few places, there's not infrastructure enough left to support wandering motorcycle gangs, and faced with a disaster of such magnitude the normal human reaction is to cluster together for support, not to wander rogue about the countryside.

But frequent quakes and aftershocks keep everyone on edge, and away from the buildings that could shelter them. Communications and survival supplies are limited. What happens instead of widespread lawnessness is an insidious feeling of helplessness, along with exhaustion, isolation, exposure to the elements, and a growing awareness of hunger.

Charles Kingmason, master financier, is one of the first uninjured survivors to succumb. Lack of food brings enervation, enervation brings helplessness, helplessness brings despair. None of the things he had worked so hard to obtain can help him now. None of the skills he has learned can begin to deal with the situation. His thoughts are disorganized. He cannot cope. Within days of the first quake, he dies of exposure and self-neglect in the back seat of his Mercedes.

Drifting through the devastation comes B.F. McCall, cynically chronicling tales of ruin, heroism, cowardice, and insanity. Nothing surprises her particularly, except when she witnesses moments of tenderness, generosity, and humanity.

Also floating downstream are Jason and Nick, a modern Huck and Jim drifting in hope of finding something better than the place they'd left, and instead finding the situation only worse.

Jason and Nick encounter the other major characters and situations in the course of their journey downriver. Jason is young enough to react to the situation naturally, without artifice or pretense. Nick is at first embittered by the loss of his job, the disappearance of his family from his life, and by his treatment by the police, but he is by nature a teacher. Nick wants a family, and Jason has just lost his. Though they come from wildly different backgrounds, and though their misunderstandings are frequent and sometimes bitter, they are both decent people, with a knack for observing things that others may have missed, and the ability to adapt to the strange new world the catastrophe has brought. Their story anchors *The Rift*, showing that it is a tale of compassion, loyalty, and love as well as destruction, terror, and survival.

Drifting downriver, they find the many riverbank communities flooded or deserted—areas near the river have all been evacuated. They scavenge food from the galley of a stranded tugboat, then find themselves carried swiftly downriver when a tangled dam of debris breaks and releases an ocean of floodwaters. It's a terrifying ordeal, caught in a small boat while trying to avoid being smashed or capsized by the raging waters, by whole trees with root systems the size of a barn, by out-of-control boats and barges, by entire buildings swept downriver.

Exhausted, they drift up on the doorstep of the Reverend Noble Frankland's domain.

At first it's wonderful. Caring people take them to shelter, give them food, nurse their scrapes, scratches, bites, and sunburn. But they are separated and assigned to separate scavenger groups. Jason is appalled by the way a family living in an outlying area is forced, more or less at gunpoint, to join Frankland's community. Nick doesn't like the brutal discipline of the children or the way people are forced into religious and social conformity before they receive food or medical attention. They aren't allowed to see each other, and Jason is caned when he insists. Radios broadcast Frankland's sermons every waking moment. When an Army helicopter appears overhead and looks as if it might land, Frankland orders it driven off by gunfire—the Federal government, he proclaims, is nothing less than the Beast of Revelation, and his community will have nothing to do with it. (The Army, for its part, has plenty of people to assist without braving gunfire, and does not return.)

After the helicopter incident, Jason and Nick look at each other and know they must escape. Nick steals food, Jason some tools. They sneak out of the guarded compound in the dead of night, but they are spotted: there is pursuit, shots fired, an alarm raised; they flee to the river and manage to steal a fast boat. They speed on all night, fearful that Frankland's people are in pursuit.

Afterwards they keep heading south, afraid to make contact with anyone. They plunder more food from a flooded country store, and decide to stay for awhile in the apartment upstairs. But this brief interlude is spoiled by the arrival of B.F. McCall, who decides to invite herself to join the pair. McCall is a loquacious type and hasn't had anyone to talk to in weeks now. Life with the chattering journalist impels Jason and Nick to move on.

Heading south, they lose their way. The Mississippi has spread out into a hundred channels once it entered the lowlands of Louisiana, and has slowed in many places to a stagnant crawl. Nick and Jason have wandered out of the main channel without realizing it, and find themselves in Spottswood Parish.

The part of Spottswood Parish still above water is an island, cut off from the rest of the world. The island now has ten times its normal population—many of these people brought food with them when they evacuated, but the food will only last so long. The governor has declared martial law, which puts the Kleagle sheriff in charge, and Ted Pipes, the parish chairman, finds he's fighting a losing battle. The Kleagle has called in reinforcements, Klansmen from elsewhere in the state and neo-Nazi skinheads from the cities.

Spottswood Parish is one of the places where the racial rift that runs through American civilization is ripped wide open, where a hundred years of racial progress is obliterated overnight. Elsewhere the lines are not so clearly drawn, and throughout the disaster zone the races work out their destiny in peace; but Spottswood Parish begins the catastrophe with a poisonous racial climate, and here things only get worse.

The refugees are segregated racially and placed in camps strung with barbed wire. Food and medicine is used as a weapon: even though the government is bringing in food by helicopter, the white camps receive the lion's share. The only people allowed out of the camps are those sent out on work parties, performing heavy labor to repair quake damage. And the Kleagle has monopolized all communication with the outside: his reports are uniformly rosy, and the government is too preoccupied to do anything other than take him at his word.

Chairman Pipes feels like a collaborator. As long as he uses his administrative talents on behalf of the martial regime, he stays out of the camps, and he keeps his family alive. And, he tells himself, he can help people on a one-to-one level, bring them extra food or medicine, offer them hope or encouragement.

But he himself is finding hope rather hard to find.

On arrival, Nick is put into a camp in which he discovers his daughter and ex-wife. His joy at seeing Arlette is tempered by horror at finding her in this appalling situation. Jason refuses to be parted from his new friend, and thus ends up in a refugee camp inhabited by black people from the city and by a few interracial couples. Nick and Jason have seen all this before: segregation, heavy labor, near-starvation. The Reverend Frankland, they know, was crazy; but these people are evil.

The two are a catalyst for a change. So is the cynical writer B.F. McCall, who turns up looking for someone to talk to and finds a situation that confirms her worst suspicions about the nature of humanity. And so, finally, is parish chairman Pipes, who at the risk of his family takes his place in the revolt.

The uprising isn't a clean, simple thing: it's messy, brutal, and heroic all at once. McCall's knowledge of how easily people can be killed proves vital. Nick's knowledge of weapons and weapons systems plays a significant part. People are killed, as is the Kleagle and the Kleagle's dream. McCall, to her own astonishment and in defiance of the cynicism that has ruled her life, dies bravely in defense of others. Food stocks are liberated, but the bad guys still control all communications with the outside, and guerilla warfare rages over the parish. Arlette, Nick's daughter, is wounded.

Jason and Nick take to their boat again in an attempt to bring help to Arlette and the others. But they find that, while they were involved with the racial poison of Spottswood Parish, a poison of another kind is threatening the lives of thousands.

At the Hollis Landing Power Station, Carl Luschnig had

no trouble attracting aid once he managed to establish communication with his higher-ups. The threat of a nuclear catastrophe tends to focus the government's attention. But Hollis Landing is almost completely cut off, by wreckage and floodwaters, from the rest of the world, and despite aid he is forced to rely on primitive methods to cope with the catastrophe.

The entire fuel assembly, all the nuclear fuel rods, must be removed from the reactor and transferred to someplace safe. And because the control building has been destroyed, along with every means of controlling the reactor from the outside, this must be done by hand by people entering the containment structure in heavy radiation suits. The rad suits are not perfect, and Luschnig suspects that anyone engaged in this task is going to die before their time.

He leads the first party of volunteers into the containment structure himself, knowing that he is probably killing himself.

Once the rods are wrestled out of the reactor, they are trundled across an improved jetty and placed in a barge brought alongside, laid carefully on racks welded together on the spot and designed to keep the rods a critical distance apart so as not to start a nuclear reaction. The barge is then partially flooded to reduce the amount of radiation reaching the surface—water is good for stopping neutrons—and then the barge will be towed to someplace safe.

But it goes wrong. A major aftershock smashes the improvised jetty. Water from a broken timber dam upstream sweeps the barge away. Hollis Landing's communication with the outside is wrecked by the runaway barge. Luschnig and many of his crew are crushed to death, caught between the barge and the smashed jetty.

The barge itself, with a few stunned workers aboard, floats off in the dead of night.

Downstream, the aftershock has dropped a causeway into what is now the main channel of the Mississippi. Timber and other debris catches on the wreckage, forming a massive dam that catches the river's water, backing it up into a lake. It is this lake that Jason and Nick encounter as they go in search of help.

They've been through this before. They know that the timber dam will give way and that lakewater will pour through in a foaming torrent. They decide to back up to where it's safe and wait it out.

The pressure builds and the dam breaks, just as predicted. Jason and Nick keep well away from the vicious white water. And it is then that the half-flooded barge, with its frantic workers, drifts onto the scene.

Nick and Jason first intend merely to rescue the workers, but once the situation is explained they realize that it is up to them to keep the barge from plunging over the broken dam and dumping its poisonous cargo into the Mississippi. They try to tow the barge away, but their little boat isn't powerful enough to haul the flooded barge upstream; instead they must try to nudge the barge, spin it, guide it gently out of the main channel and into a shallower area which, when the lake finally lowers, will become a mudbank.

This they succeed in doing, at just about the moment

when frantic Army helicopters, finally alerted to the gravity of the situation, come zooming into view. Nick, Jason, and the workers are rescued. Arlette will receive proper medical attention. At last the outside world will hear about Spottswood Parish and the Reverend Frankland.

But the two friends have been through too much to be overjoyed by this sudden reversal in their fortunes. They can only watch in silence as the helicopter takes them above the wrecked, flooded, and still endangered American heartland.

Metropolitan

by Walter Jon Williams

1. La Mort de la Fantaisie

FANTASY IS DEAD.

Sorry about that, but it's true.

Like much else, fantasy has been done it by its own success. Once it was the province of lonely eccentrics like William Morris, Eric Eddison, and Lord Dunsany, all of them longing for a heroic past that probably never existed, combing through ancient sagas to find it, and finally in desperation having to create it themselves, all (apparently) out of some overpowering inner need. Fantasy now finds itself, to its detriment, a part of mass culture. Terry Brooks was a cancer in the body of fantasy, and *Dungeons & Dragons* drove a stake through its heart, and *Willow* was the vampire that rose regardless. All of them sucking the blood from something that was once noble and brave.

Some brave writers are trying to claw their way out of Tolkien's giant bootprints. Most don't bother to try. The archetypes created by those pioneering loners are enough for them, archetypes that get more and more diluted with every book that features in its title the words *sword, dragon,* or *tower* most seemingly more inspired by *D&D*, itself a pastiche, than Tolkien and the other masters of the field. Magic isn't even very magical in these books: it's as common as cheeseburgers, and about as interesting.

The guys doing original work, like Crowley or Jonathan Carroll, aren't even *marketed* as fantasy. The readership wouldn't know what do with them.

What to do?

2. *The Sylvan Infiltration*

"Classical" fantasy, a la Tolkien, deals with a kind of William Morris Middle Ages—like the real thing, only prettier. The magic is based on nature, as with dwarves and elves (embodiments of earthy and sylvan realms); or it's presented as forceful abstractions of moral qualities (as with Gandalf, Saruman, and the Balrog).

It's all been done to death. Contemporary writers are mainly filling up the corners that the earlier writers, sometimes with good reason, left empty. The basic assumptions of the genre are left unquestioned.

"Contemporary urban fantasy" imports the sylvan elements of classical fantasy into a contemporary citified setting. Punk clubs with elves. Pookas in Texas. Dragons in your living room. The works derive a certain energy from the contrast of well-known fantasy archetypes with the present, but even the serious stuff is not too far from camp and in any case it doesn't go far enough.

The audience doesn't live in William Morrisland any more, and probably wouldn't want to if it could. It lives in urban settings, with TV, computers, sound systems, advertising, disposable diapers, fast food, landfills, sewage treatment plants.

Stick a wood-elf amid all that noise, he'd barely be noticeable. Before long, in fact, he'd be dead.

As dead as most of the fantasy in which his like appears.

3. *The End of Nature*

Imagine fantasy as if Tolkien never existed (except maybe for his criticism). As if *D&D* and Terry Brooks and Arnold the Barbarian never happened. Imagine fantasy without its pervasive nostalgia for an invented past, without the faded legions of sylvan critters voicing their lame, New Age forest wisdom.

Imagine a city. A city built to the same dimensions as Gormenghast, or Cliff Simak's *City*. There isn't anything *but* city in this landscape—everything's either paved over or, if not, allowed to exist on suffrance, as a curiosity. It's the end of nature, jack, nothing here but human beings and what human beings, in their wisdom or lack of it, permit to exist.

The city is divided into nations and enclaves and neighborhoods, but *nature really isn't there.* Everything is artificial. Food is grown in vats in basements, or in greenhouses atop skyscrapers. The city has been built on huge pontoons that extend out over the surface of the oceans, and in the oceans live blind dolphins that live on the crud that falls from the humanscape above.

Some parts of the city are well run, some parts

not—there are, after all, the equivalent of nation-states within its confines. Any number of political systems vie with one another for supremacy, some more successful than others. Economics and trade are complex. Warfare exists, particularly civil war, but tends to get bogged down into Beirut-like seiges. Coups of one sort or another are not uncommon.

Some rulers are more evil than others, but there's no great Other, no Dark Lord. The city is too complex to allow for any one, singular evil. A host of little, human-sized evils have taken its place—this is, for all its size, a human-scale city.

And—one should stress this—there is no way out. Although dirigibles and aircraft prowl through the skies, there's an absolute limit on how far up they can go. There are no stars, and the sky is a uniform grey. There is no cycle of day and night. Ages ago, in legendary times, the city was sealed off by demiurgic beings called Malakas, the Ascended Ones, who placed their opalescent barrier between humanity and whatever lies above the sky. There's no exit, except possibly for death, and according to some theologies the barrier keeps souls from leaving as well.

An endless cityscape teeming with humanity, a nature subdued and impotent, a big NO EXIT sign in the sky.

It would all be pretty depressing if it weren't for magic.

4. *Geomancy*

The cityscape has skyscrapers and slums and street gangs, drugs and television and advertising. Residents of New York, San Francisco, and Calcutta alike should find much that is recognizeable.

But this city also has magic. It's not the sylvan, nature-based magic of "contemporary urban fantasy," it's an outgrowth of the city itself, and perhaps the change wrought upon it by the Malakas.

The magic in the city is a form of geomancy, in which the magical force ("plasm," a kind of manna) is generated by the design, weight, structure, and relationship of the buildings themselves. The oligarch/mages of the city live high in carefully-designed towers intended to gather and focus plasm for their use. Elsewhere, plasm is treated very much as a public utility, metered and available—like water and electricity—to everyone, for a price. Some people use it merely to get high. The stuff can be stored in huge batteries—vast, bulky things, mostly, like huge copper-and-brass accumulators. And, as with other resources, there's a black market in it. Plasm-scroungers search sub-basements, tunnels, and abandoned residences for plasm sources they can bottle and sell. There's never enough plasm to go around.

Magic is basically the human will acting through the medium of plasm. There are different schools and colleges and theories of plasm use—you can get degrees in geomancy, theory and practice—but what most teach are methods of gathering plasm from the environment, then ways of focusing the will in order to use plasm with the most effectiveness.

Because it's relatively rare and expensive, plasm therefore s used either for the most important or the most trivial of tasks. Overthrowing empires, altering reality, curing illness, creating or altering genotypes, spectacular acts of telepathy or teleportation—or, on the other hand, creating spectacular displays intended to advertise a new soft drink or a brand of shoe.

Sometimes plasm gets out of hand. A larger-than-expected dose of plasm can burn out a person's synapses if he's not used to it. Plasm, imperfectly conducted or unsuccessfully tapped, can leak out into the environment and, accessing a kind of universal unconscious, manifest itself in strange and destructive ways—a peculiar reality shift, a giant carnivorous monster, a huge incendiary catastrophe.

Plasm interacts with technology in interesting ways. With geomancy, almost everything is possible; but as a practical matter, it's usually easier to do it with machines. There are aircraft and tube transportation and video and computers, as well as geomantic energy generation and plasmic communications sources. There are also developments not realized in our own world: pneumatic tube transport, primitive weather control, pneumatic mail, giant copper-and-brass plasm batteries in basements and attics, huge wind-powered generation facilities perched atop horned plasm-generating buildings. The city is *styled,* has its own look, its own visual tics, something like a combination of Fritz Lang's *Metropolis,* Terry Gilliam's *Brazil,* and John Singleton's *Boyz N the Hood.*

There are any number of competing philosophies in the city, and mythologies, superstitions, and plain fictions. Is the city a place, sealed off from the heavens, where damned souls vie for limited happiness? Where, on the contrary, privileged souls, beloved by gods or Malakas, are allowed to interact free from contamination or interference from above? Was the city sealed off because the Malakas were threatened by the people who lived there, or because the city was so vile that the Malakas didn't want their own realm to be polluted?

Guess what. It's all of the above.

It's Worldbeat City, everything Manhattan is and more. Cultures, subcultures, cults, messiahs. Everything saturated with music and media, language, slang, popular culture. Everything incessant, demanding, unshielded, Now.

There are creatures and races other than human. But the creatures aren't primeval dragons or trolls left over from another time; they are creations of humanity, and linked in an almost organic way to the city that spawned them. They are innately connected to city functions, to the generations and distribution of electric power, to water mains and sewer pipes, to tube stations and radio transmitters and all the apparatus of civilization. There are also altered forms of humanity, created for specific purposes—warfare, deep mining, working under pressure in caissons or tunnels—the result of genetics being modified by plasmic forces. The descendants of these original modified forms live in various pockets of the city, some of them still carrying out their assigned tasks, others now free to do seek whatever advantage they can. But they are all more human than not, and their continued existence is only at the suffrance of the majority.

Underneath it all lies the control of the city's self-generating resource, plasm. What plasm does is interact with the human mind—any human mind. Though most people have some ability to manipulate the stuff, training and native ability are both large factors. As with any talent, some people have more raw ability than others.

What geomancy does—at least in the city's popular tradition—is even the odds. The city's mythology overflows with tales of able sorcerers rising from humble beginnings to positions of power through dextrous use of their talents. Reality is not far behind the legend—the control of plasm can carry people as far as their wills and abilities will permit.

The problem is getting ahold of enough of the stuff to make a difference.

5. *The Wind From a Burning Woman*

A 200-foot-tall flaming woman stalks the city. People in her way are incinerated, buildings burst into flame at her touch, those in her vicinity go mad, their brains burning with a metaphysical fire.

The forces of the district's geomancers are brought into play. The giant apparition—the result of a plasm leak, perhaps—is dispersed; and the city's administrators are set to find the source of the problem and stop its recurrence.

The person who actually gets in the job is a minor civil servant named Aiah, and Aiah is a young woman under pressure.

She works for the Plasm Control Authority of the Jaspeer District as a liaison between the field teams and management, a job filled with frustration because it's difficult to explain one group to the other with any degree of success. She is a third-generation member of a demoralized minority group, the Barkazils, refugees from a civil war in another nation-district who settled into the Jaspeer District's slums. The Barkazils are darker-skinned than their neighbors and have suffered as a result.

According to their own lights, the Barkazils are a special, magic race, rightfully kings of the earth; their own ethic treats the Jaspeeris as prey, the legitimate victims of theft, scams, and whatever else they can get away with.

Mostly, however, they only hustle each other.

Aiah's determination to leave her native subcultuere and make it on the Jaspeeris' terms are, to her relatives, a source of bemusement and disparagement, most of whom have spent their entire adult lives on the dole while working various dodges available to the underclass.

Aiah knows herself to be talented in geomancy and worked her way to a university scholarship that, unfortunately, did not provide for plasm fees. Aiah had to change her study from geomancy to civil administration, thus her job for the PCA rather than working as a freelance or civil geomancer.

She's also pressed for funds. She and her lover had

bought a condominium apartment; the lover got a transfer and left, and is unable to contribute to his half of the fees. They conduct wistful long-distance conversations, but Aiah's financial status is growing worse and her Barkazil relations, much amused, are beginning to claim she was scammed and should have stuck to her own kind.

Now, as if she didn't have enough to worry about, she is assigned to find the plasm leak (if it exists), track it to its source, and hook that source up to the city's supplies. It's a job that will take hundreds of hours, will send her deep into the bowels of the city as she coordinates the search, and will probably turn out to be futile no matter how much she applies herself.

But her luck is in. Coordinating ancient city maps and records, she narrows the search, then strikes paydirt right away. Partially collapsed iron beams, supporting an ancient and discontinued branch of the tube transport system—power conduits in the vicinity—a branch of the water main—a strange electrolitic migration of the rusty iron from one beam to another. Not just paydirt, but a glory hole. A new source of plasm, one completely off the charts.

And she's not the first person to find it. There's a charred corpse lying there on the abandoned platform, the plasm-diver who lucked onto the place, then was overwhelmed by a flood of plasm greater than she had ever encountered. She was burned to a crisp, and her consciousness translated into the flaming woman who stalked the Jaspeeri financial district.

Aiah has discovered a titanic source of power. The question is, does she really want to tell her boss about it?

6. *Enter Constantine*

AIAH'S PROBLEM is simple. If she starts displaying gigantic amounts of power, she'll be caught—it's obvious to anyone she shouldn't have access to so much. She can bleed off small amounts gradually and sell them, but it won't bring in that much income and in time the plasm levels will build and there will be another explosion, another flaming woman or worse.

She considers using her source to bring her old lover back. But what then? He'd be there, but when the spell ran out he'd know why. His career would be over, and she'd have gained another dependent.

She compromises. She collects as much as she can in storage vessels, then goes back to her old Barkazil neighborhood to sell it. Her kinfolk are delighted that she's finally found a scam she can call her own: she's terrified of being caught and is already beginning to feel trapped in a hopeless web of illegality.

Then she hears that Constantine is moving into Mage Towers, a preposterously expensive building right in the Jaspeer District.

Constantine is a charismatic, High Romantic mage/prince from the far-distant Cheloki district. Born into the ruling caste, he rejected his inheritance in favor of a lengthy period of wandering and study. When he returned it was as a rebel, determined to overthrow the demonstrably corrupt ruling class to replace it with his rather Napoleonic style of personal rule. The result was a lengthy and destructive civil war which Constantine eventually won though it devastated his homehood, a war followed by the conquest of his citystate by a coalition of his neighbors who considered him too destabilizing.

Constantine's fight against his relatives, and his hopeless last stand against the coalition, was the subject of much attention and sympathy at the time. Young would-be warriors flocked to his standard, and there were drives to raise money for his cause and for the refugees the war created.

He's been involved in other adventures since, working as a freelance, possibly mercenary, for causes or personalities with whom he was in alliance. His success seems to have been constrained.

And Constantine is black. This makes him more interesting to Aiah than he would be otherwise.

Now Constantine has moved into Aiah's own district. She can't think what he'd be doing there, unless he's involved in another plot.

Perhaps, she decides, Constantine could use a source of plasm.

7. Coup d'Etat

AIAH IS AWED by Mage Towers, by the rooftop gardens, the miniature beefcattle, the sensation of plasm and power humming through the building's architecture. She is also intimidated by Constantine's large retinue, which includes dangerous-looking mercenaries, fantastic animals including a panther in a jewelled collar, and a sultry women-of-undefined-function named Sorya, who looks more dangerous than the mercenaries and the panther put together.

Aiah has bluffed her way to a private meeting with Constantine by invoking her authority with the Plasm Authority. Constantine has immense personal charisma and glamor. His wealth is clearly astronomical. He thinks she's going to talk about his new plasm access and his metering problems. But instead Aiah nervously presents him with the details of her plot.

Aiah is grateful that he seems to take her seriously. He is obviously concerned that she might be a provocateur—he is here on the suffrance of her government, and doesn't want to abuse the understanding he has with them. He sends Sorya to the source to take a look.

Sorya is a skilled enchantress in her own right, and soon has Aiah thoroughly intimidated. But Sorya quickly understands the power Aiah offers, and recommends to Constantine that he make use of her.

Aiah soon finds herself much deeper than she ever intended. She had planned only to sell Constantine the plasm source and depart, but soon she finds herself working for him throughout her days and nights. While supposedly scouring the city for the plasm leak on behalf of the Plasm Authority, she actually become part of Constantine's plans, first to tap and store the secret plasm source, and then, as his plans mature, in activities equally illegal.

She isn't quite certain how she came to be in this position. Constantine is charismatic, extraordinarily good looking, and attractive to her. He is willing to teach her advance magical practices. He seems acutely sincere in all he does or says. He is clearly brilliant, and his energy and abilities are phenomenal, though sometimes diminished by mood swings or petulance. He gives her the impression that he *needs* her in some deep, fundamental way, but that he's restrained by Sorya. Aiah is confused and suspects herself of being scammed.

Constantine's plans become clearer as Aiah is drawn into them. He is planning a coup d'etat in the neighboring district of Caraqui. Caraqui is a notoriously misruled citystate, built on giant pontoons over a vast, brackish sea, and Aiah is pleased that Constantine's target would seem to be a deserving one.

Aiah assists Constantine in lining up some of his allies, including the blind, intelligent dolphins that swim beneath Caraqui; and she provides a vital insight that enables him to win the support of Caraqui's Barkazil community. But Aiah becomes alarmed when she encounters other of Constantine's allies. He's doing deals with thuggish mercenaries, gangsters, disreputable political leaders, world-class criminals looking for a haven. His explanation is convincing: these people have to be dealt with if the coup is to succeed. Afterwards, Constantine will be able to afford to pick and choose his friends more carefully.

He presents a convincing picture of Caraqui under his rule: the economy handled rationally, the parasitical upper class dispensed with, outside investment pouring in once outsiders are permitted to keep their profits instead of handing them to political gangsters, the genuinely criminal element suppressed. It will all happen, he assures, but it will all take time.

Aiah is convinced. He can do it; he has the talent, the ability. She can help him.

It's an attractive picture. Constantine is a formidably attractive man who now needs her more than ever. His relationship with Sorya is turbulent, and now there is a spectacular rupture. Shortly thereafter Aiah and Constantine fall into bed.

The affaire lasts only until relations between Constantine and Sorya improve. Sorya bluntly informs Aiah that she's out of her depth, that she had become a pawn in hypersophisticated game of love, passion, and power waged between Constantine and Sorya. But Constantine assures Aiah that her time will come, that he needs Sorya only until the coup, after which he can pension her off and devote his affections to Aiah alone.

Aiah continues to wonder if she's being scammed.

The coup comes off, and, as many of Constantine's allies are unreliable, Aiah's plasm supply proves vital in creating a raging army of plasm-creatures that finally destroy the enemy. She herself has little to do with the coup's mechanations, concerning herself with maintaining the jury-rigged plasm supply she's helped Constantine create. Constantine declares himself the leader—the Metropolitan—of Caraqui, and leads his forces into his new kingdom just ahead of the Jaspeeri authorities who are trying to expel him. Aiah is left alone with the remnants of her jury-rigged plasm supply.

Within hours, the police are at her door. They want to talk to her.

8. *Good Government*

AIAH PANICS AND FLEES, escaping only after using her magical talents on some of the officers.

Now a fugitive, she runs to Caraqui. Constantine is distracted and busy; Aiah unhappily discovers the nature of the coup she's helped create when she wanders into the apartments of Caraqui's former ruler and discovers workmen still scraping his blood and parts off the walls.

Things aren't going well. Constantine underestimated the level of support for his coup—nobody ever *asked* him to be Metropolitan, after all—and Constantine's new neighbors aren't precisely delighted with having an unstable criminal adventurer squatting in the vicinity. His allies are demanding the payoffs he promised them, and friends of the former government are raising riots and making small-scale attacks.

Aiah is given a grand title and pressed into service as head of the Plasm Bureau, charged with getting the vital service back online. She also ends up functions as an amateur diplomat when the neighbors come calling. Everything is improvised and hasty. Constantine alternates between bursts of frenetic energy and listless episodes of deep depression. He swings between Aiah and Sorya. Aiah begins to resent the amount of time she has to spend mothering him.

And then Caraqui is actually invaded by a proxy army, nominally led by Keramath, a crony of the old rulers who is in actuality supported by a coalition of Constantine's neighbors, including the Jaspeer district.

The situation is nightmarish. Beirut-like urban warfare demolishes entire neighborhoods. Constantine is disconsolate—everything that happened in Cheloki is now happening here, his worst nightmare returned, and he's helpless to control it.

A mood of mad despair sets in. Constantine can't find a win anywhere in this game. He decides to go out in a Byronic blaze of glory, punishing not only the invaders but the ostensibly neutral city-states that are behind the war. He orders Aiah to begin assembling plasm batteries, to rig the huge couplings necessary to give himself access to vast quantities of raw magic. Entire neighborhoods are to be altered, turned into huge plasm generators. In addition, she's to find ways of sabotaging or stealing his enemies' plasm resources. Constantine's going to blast the invading army, then the politicians and leaders who sent it there.

It's clear enough that he won't succeed—this attack will just bring his every neighbor down on him with fire and sword. But Constantine doesn't care—he wants revenge, cosmic justice, personal satisfaction. Aiah, picturing 200-foot-tall flaming Constantines roaring through her old neighborhood in Jaspeer, is horrified, but Sorya, perhaps as a result of her rivalry with Aiah, supports Constantine's plan.

Constantine senses her reluctance to participate in this scheme; he ends up making ferocious love to her in an attempt to win her over. Aiah agrees to help him, but mentally searches for a way out.

Perhaps, she thinks, she should just leave. Find a district without an extradition treaty, grab some plunder, and find a niche for herself among the expatriate population.

Undecided, Aiah begins the mobilization of plasm resources, moving with her teams through a population of dispirited refugees. Aiah sees her own expatriate grandparents in these desperate swarms of homeless, and she knows all too well how a population's demoralization can last from one generation to the next.

Moving among them, she knows she can't abdicate her responsibility.

She contacts Constantine's enemies and cuts a deal. They agree to trade Keramath for Constantine. After Constantine's removal, Aiah will guarantee a form of government for Caraqui acceptable to the neighboring governments.

Aiah knows that she can't trust a one of them, that their promises are hollow, made only for the sake of advantage in the conflict that they themselves began. But knowing the rules of the game, knowing that she can't trust them, is of some benefit. She knows she's alone.

It's a position that, as a Barkazil, she finds herself familiar with. She's scamming everyone around her: her early training is paying off. It's interesting to her that, in the process of discovering her own power, she is becoming more Barkazil than she knew.

Subverting the people around Constantine is more difficult.

Fortunately she's got a loyal Barkazil contingent on the premises, and some of Constantine's mercenaries are capable of being corrupted. She even gets the hostile governments to advance her the money. Loyal units are sent elsewhere, to critical points on the battlefield but far from the administrative center.

In the meantime, she lets Keramath know that his own allies have left him twisting in the wind. Keramath's resistance to Constanine's counteroffensive turns into a rout. And at the critical moment, she cuts off Constantine's plasm supply and triggers her own countercoup.

Constantine's reaction is typical: hysterical self-pity, eloquent denunciations frantic declarations of love. Against her better judgment, Aiah is affected by Constantine's demonstrations, but she nevertheless packs Constantine and Sorya off to the same far-distant haven of exiles to which Aiah had once considered flying herself.

Aiah is clever in using her neighbors' differences against them, and in the end gets what she wants: aid in repairing damage, an opening of borders to investment, a cooling-off period followed by elections for a new Metropolitan and council. She declines to take the title herself in the interim, and the role of dictator does not appeal. She's too inexperienced to run a country by herself, and doesn't really want to try.

It's a human-scale solution, not the creation of a lonely Napoleonic adventurer striding across the urban cityscape, but a sensible young woman, confident in herself, and prepared to meet new challenges.

9. *The Ends of Fantasy*

METROPOLITAN IS INTENDED as a deliberate attempt to break fantasy free of the twinkly medieval landscape in which it so often finds itself, both to try to break new ground and to recapture the adventuresome spirit of the original fantasy pioneers.

Metropolitan sees itself as a work that is recognizeably one of fantasy, that the reader of fantasy will be able to understand. Grand, doomed, a little exalted, Constantine is clearly a fantasy mage, not an SF character.

One of Tolkien's essays suggested that one of the purposes of fantasy was recovery—perhaps more properly re-covery—by which he meant the infusing of ordinary reality with enchantment such that it seems new and fresh and wondrous. *Metropolitan* seeks to achieve that, recovery of both the fantasy genre, which is clearly shopworn, and the urban cityscape with which audience familiarity will have invested with mundanity.

The landscape will have changed, but not the purposes of fantasy—Tolkien's "realization, independent of the conceiving mind, of imagined wonder."

Laura Resnick

I HAVE A SPECIAL interest in this writer, because she happens to be my daughter. After winning a couple of awards in the romance field, she moved over to fantasy and science fiction and promptly won the Campbell Award as Best New Writer.

That led to a book contract from Tor, and to a book that was about four times longer than any novel she had previously written. It was well-received, and she just handed in an even longer one. Anyway, here's her outline for the first one.

IN LEGEND BORN

by Laura Resnick

PROLOGUE

MIRABAR IS A GUARDIAN, a young priestess of the ancient, outlawed spiritual cult of Sileria. A seer who talks to shadows of the dead, she has rare talents even for a Guardian. Her visions tell her that a great warrior is coming to break the shackles binding his people. A man of stained honor, terrible courage, and bitter yearning, he will both succeed and fail in his quest.

PART I

SILERIA IS A VAST, mountainous island surrounded by the landlocked Middle Sea. More than a thousand years ago, Sileria was a wealthy, independent kingdom. Since those days, however, Sileria's destiny has been guided by the three great empires which surround the Middle Sea: Valdania, Kinto, and the Moorlands. The Valdani are now the most powerful of these people, with a vast empire which rules not only Sileria, but which also extends well into former Kintish territory and which has encroached upon the Moorlands.

Violent and hard to govern, the people of Sileria are too disparate to unite in rebellion against the Valdani, who have ruled them for centuries. The sea-born folk, the mountain-born *shallaheen*, the mingled races of the city-dwellers, the secretive Honored Society, and the nation's diverse religious cults all nurse their mutual antagonism as zealously as they hate the Valdani.

After nine years in exile, a young man named Tansen returns home to Sileria to find the land of his birth in turmoil and the people's growing discontent expressed in scattered bursts of violence which the Valdani quickly crush. He is seized almost immediately by Valdani Outlookers; no Silerian is allowed to bear arms, yet Tansen carries the slender double swords of a Kintish warrior. He spent his first five years of exile training with a Kintish swordmaster, and has since then travelled the world as a professional mercenary.

Though extremely dangerous, such a man can also be very useful. The Outlookers offer him his freedom if he'll accept an assignment from them. He is ordered to hunt down and kill Josarian, a *shallah* who has done the unthinkable and murdered an Outlooker. Josarian resisted the Outlookers who caught him smuggling food to his mountain village, and he killed one of them with his *yahr* before escaping. Though weapons are forbidden, the Silerians have long since developed weapons (such as the *yahr*) out of their agricultural tools, but these are carefully camouflaged and the Valdani cannot identify most of them.

The Valdani know that retaliation must be swift and brutal, or others may work up the courage to follow Josarian's example. In the few days since this appalling event, Josarian has already begun inciting the local *shallaheen* to rebellion, and the Outlookers' failure to catch him has begun weakening their authority.

Tansen sets a high price for his services. The Outlookers agree to his fee, but refuse to pay him until he returns with proof of Josarian's death. Knowing these Outlookers to be the least of his troubles now that he has come home, Tansen agrees to the deal, is released, and leaves the crowded, exotic coastal city to return to the mountains of his birth.

Beneath the snow-capped peak of Mount Darshon, the towering volcano wherein dwells Dar, whom all *shallaheen* worship, Tansen searches for Josarian, recalling that the last time he travelled through these hills he was still a boy, ignorant, helpless, and destined for treachery. And now, as soon as he reveals his identity, someone warns the Honored Society that he has returned. The Society is the mysterious brotherhood which has dominated Silerian life since the Conquest a thousand years ago. Its members are the only Silerians who carry traditional weapons in defiance of Valdani law. The *shir* is an enchanted dagger whose wavy blade is said to be made of tempered water, fashioned in special rites known only to the waterlords, the powerful wizards who have mastered the Society's most mysterious arts. More deadly than any other weapon, a *shir* is given to a man upon his induction into the Society, and it can only be taken away by killing him. Through their sorcery, the waterlords control the water supply of Sileria by drying up rivers and underground springs to punish anyone who doesn't do their bidding. Even the Valdani fear their power and have tried to destroy them. Although somewhat weakened by this, the Society is nonetheless still protected by its secrecy and its practice of harsh retaliation for betrayal.

Kiloran, the most notorious and powerful waterlord of the Society, once swore a bloodvow against Tansen for his betrayal. Now that Tansen has returned to the mountains, a Society assassin comes to kill him. Tansen argues that it has been nine years since Kiloran swore the bloodvow; according to Society tradition, a bloodvow may last no longer than that, even if the offender still lives. Kiloran must make peace with him now, he insists.

Less attuned to the details of honorable traditions than Tansen, the assassin tries to murder him anyhow. Now a highly-trained warrior instead of a helpless boy, Tansen kills him, knowing that word of this incident will soon spread and eventually reach Kiloran's ears.

By the time Tansen locates Josarian, his reputation as a mercenary has preceded him. However, he surprises Josarian by offering him his help. Tansen's entire family was slaughtered by Outlookers, and he would rather be eaten slowly by a dragonfish than do their bidding. Having no home to return to, he has come to assist the only *shallah* who has ever killed an Outlooker.

Josarian, a robust and charismatic man, tells him that the Outlookers have failed to force the local *shallaheen* to reveal his whereabouts or assist them in any way. Consequently, the Outlookers have rounded up more than a dozen men and imprisoned them, promising to kill one per day until Josarian turns himself in or is handed over by a Silerian. Among these prisoners is Josarian's cousin and close friend, Zimran.

Though there are only two of them, Tansen proposes they attack the Valdani fortress to free the prisoners, and Josarian quickly agrees to this daring plan. During the attack, Josarian proves to be recklessly brave, quick-witted, and a naturally adept fighter. After releasing the prisoners, they steal weapons and horses from the Outlookers and all ride off into the hills.

Persuasive, idealistic, and unusually articulate, Josarian effortlessly leads this group of men, convincing them that since they can never go home, they should therefore become the most dangerous outlaws the Outlookers have ever had to contend with.

For centuries the Valdani have enslaved Sileria. And now, in their thirst to acquire even more territory for their vast empire, they are draining Sileria's natural wealth for their wars of conquest. Josarian proposes to start taking back what has been stolen from Sileria, and he convinces the men to help him. Their first raid relies heavily upon Josarian's quick thinking and Tansen's fighting skill. They divert a shipment of grain bound for Valdania and distribute it to hundreds of hungry *shallaheen*. Several more successful operations follow, enhancing their reputation, attracting more men to their cause, and ensuring their ability to supply themselves adequately for the coming winter.

The men's confidence erodes, however, when they learn of the bloodvow against Tansen. Every man, woman, and child in Sileria is afraid of Kiloran, a great waterlord who has powers which even the Guardians cannot combat. Indeed, it is said that the first waterlord, centuries ago, was actually an outcast Guardian who learned to ensorcel water in order to destroy his former teacher, who died horribly when the White Dragon came for him. The White Dragon is an elaborate—and, Tansen believes, entirely mythical—Society method of assassination wherein the victim is turned into water, thus denying his soul any afterlife or contact with the Guardian seers.

Zimran, who has been particularly jealous of Josarian's admiration for and reliance upon Tansen, convinces the men that they must shun Tansen or all incur Kiloran's wrath and endure a death of unimaginable horror. Goaded by Zimran, Tansen refuses to explain why Kiloran wants him dead, saying only that he once took something valuable from Kiloran. Josarian insists that he and Tansen seek out Kiloran together to make peace. Knowing that others could be harmed if he puts it off any longer, Tansen tries to go without Josarian, but his friend has guessed his plan and won't be left behind.

Together, they set off to meet Kiloran—and possibly their deaths.

PART II

HIGH UPON THE PEAK of a distant mountain, Mirabar ignores her mentor's warnings that she's not yet ready to control her extraordinary gifts alone, and she goes in search of the destiny she now hears calling her, urgently and ceaselessly. Josarian wonders how Tansen intends to track down Kiloran, whose ears hear everything, whose eyes see all, and whose movements are a closely guarded secret. Very few Society members even know his whereabouts, and they certainly won't tell Tansen. It is said that Guardians can find him; but finding a Guardian is no easy task, since they are outlawed by the Valdani. Most of them are dead or in hiding.

To Josarian's surprise, they head for Shaljir, Sileria's largest, wealthiest, and most exotic city. They enter the gates in disguise, then Tansen leads Josarian to secret tunnels under the oldest part of the ancient city. The Beyah-Olvari dwell there, a half-human race driven underground long ago, believed by many to be extinct or mythical. Tansen requests shelter, which is granted, and asks them to send word to a woman called Elelar, saying that he needs to talk to her.

Elelar returns a message suggesting a time and place for their meeting. Tansen goes to see her alone. Despite the maturity wrought by nine lonely years in exile, despite knowing that she helped condemn him to that fate, as soon as he sees Elelar, Tansen is sick with longing, just as he was all those years ago. A beautiful, sophisticated woman born of the wealthy Silerian nobility, Elelar has been a secret rebel since her girlhood. Despising the aristocracy who, like her own family, are merely bloodless tools of the Valdani, she has used her position in society to undermine the Valdani in any way she can. She is a member of the Alliance, a growing movement of intellectuals, merchants, and important citizens who want to overthrow the Valdani and restore traditional rule—the Yahrdan and his Council—to Sileria.

Only Tansen's bitterness matches his desire as he faces Elelar again. She betrayed him, he accuses. She, who showed him the way, who taught him his duty nine years ago, then sacrificed him to save herself. Angry at this accusation, Elelar points out that she never once suggested he do what he did, and she only betrayed him to preserve the Alliance, which needed—and still needs—Kiloran.

Elelar doesn't know where Kiloran is; no one does. But as Tansen had hoped, she does have a means of finding him. Tansen bargains for her help. He has found someone, he tells her, who can lead the *shallaheen* in rebellion, someone who would join the Alliance; someone, he promises, capable of fighting and perhaps even defeating the Outlookers. This man, however, is completely loyal to him, Tansen assures Elelar, and will not unite with Kiloran or anyone else until Tansen is relieved of the bloodvow. Once convinced, Elelar agrees to help them find Kiloran. During the journey, sensing the explosive emotions between his companions, Josarian finally forces Tansen to explain how an ordinary *shallah* came to know a woman like Elelar and earn a bloodvow from Kiloran himself.

Nine years ago, while waiting to meet a smuggling ship one night along the coast of Sileria, Tansen discovered a man who had washed up on shore. He was a passenger of the very smuggler Tansen was awaiting, and he told Tansen that the ship had been boarded by Outlookers. The man himself was the cargo they sought, and so he had slipped overboard. Attacked by a dragonfish, he nearly died trying to reach the shore. His name was Armian.

Josarian is astonished. Armian is a well-known name around *shallaheen* fires. The son of a notorious Society waterlord, he was spirited away from Sileria as an infant and taken off to the Moorlands to avoid death at the hands of the Outlookers after his father was killed. As is typical of the glamourized tales told about the Society, Armian is routinely depicted as a daring warrior who will one day return to his homeland and help drive the Valdani from Sileria (almost all popular tales include some reference to driving the Valdani from Sileria). Some people even believe Armian is the Firebringer, the long-prophesied leader who will withstand the Fires of Dar and lead his people to the glory they once knew.

Josarian and Tansen don't believe in the Firebringer any more than they believe in the White Dragon. However, Tansen assures Josarian, Armian was real enough. A mere boy who viewed the Society with the mingled fear and fascination of most *shallaheen*, Tansen instantly idolized the man he had found lying half-dead in the shadow of Darshon. Armian had been sent to Sileria by the Moorlanders to contact Kiloran in the hope of forming an alliance against their mutual enemy, the Valdani. Now that Armian had been discovered by—and narrowly managed to escape—the Outlookers, the plan was in jeopardy, since he wouldn't be able to meet his contact.

Tansen took Armian home to his village to consult with his grandfather (his father having been killed by Outlookers long ago). Upon arriving, they discovered that the Valdani had tortured the necessary information out of Tansen's smuggling partner and arrived before them. Tansen's entire family was already dead, and he and Armian were nearly captured by Outlookers before fleeing into the mountains.

Tansen tells Josarian how he and Armian went to Shaljir in search of Armian's contact, and how this eventually led them to the fledgling Alliance and to Elelar, who was on the brink of womanhood in those days. Then as now, she accompanied Tansen and his companion on their journey to meet Kiloran. Tansen's first close association with a man of the Society exposed him to scenes of ruthless brutality unlike anything he had ever seen, diminishing the idealized awe with which he regarded Armian. More significantly, though, he began to see Armian and the entire Society through Elelar's eyes. Shrewd and educated, she knew the Alliance needed to cultivate the Society's goodwill, but she was well aware that the Society were worse than the Valdani, and she made sure Tansen, an ignorant and superstitious *shallah* boy, became aware of it, too.

He grew to recognize that everything Armian did was done strictly out of self-interest. The proposed alliance between the Society and the Moorlanders, which excluded the other peoples of Sileria, wouldn't free Sileria for Silerian rule once the Valdani were driven out. The Society, led by Kiloran and Armian, would rule Sileria themselves—more harshly than the Valdani or any other conqueror ever had. In truth, the Society had already killed more *shallaheen* than the Valdani ever would.

Having been the one to find Armian and save his life, Tansen believed it would be his responsibility if Armian successfully arranged this powerful alliance, condemning Sileria to enslavement under the heaviest yoke of all. And so he destroyed the only link between the Society and the

Moorlanders by murdering Armian, a man he had once idolized.

Since no Silerian ever tells anything to an outsider, Josarian reasons, the Moorlanders never found out what happened to their vanished Silerian envoy to Kiloran. And they never made any further overtures to the notoriously dangerous, secretive, and unpredictable Honored Society.

Mystified by Tansen's act, Elelar was furious that he had destroyed this promising opportunity to drive out the Valdani. Pragmatic even at that age, she managed to save the Alliance from Kiloran's retribution by betraying Tansen. And upon learning who had murdered a man of the Society and destroyed Kiloran's chance of such great power, the waterlord swore a bloodvow against him. Tansen's only hope of survival at that point was exile, so he boarded a ship bound for some strange Kintish port and left Sileria behind.

But the nine years wherein a Society bloodvow can honorably be fulfilled are over now, and Tansen is a skilled warrior, not a helpless boy. For nine long years he dreamed of returning to his homeland and joining the fight for freedom. He will not leave Sileria again, no matter what.

When they finally find Kiloran, they are attacked, disarmed, and taken hostage. They nearly drown, since Kiloran dwells underwater in a shifting palace of air which he can open, close, and manipulate as easily as he can breathe. But before Kiloran can kill Tansen, a ball of fire suddenly plummets through the water and enters this domain, turning into a drenched woman just before the flame is completely doused. Having never before seen fire magic, Josarian,

Elelar, and Tansen are astonished. Even Kiloran seems somewhat surprised. The woman's chances of surviving the experience were slim, so her business must be very important. Intrigued, and wondering about the range of her powers, Kiloran delays killing Tansen at her insistence.

Despite Tansen's gratitude to the woman, old, long-forgotten superstitions cause him to shy away from her. In a land of dark-haired, dark-eyed people, she has the red hair and golden eyes of the accursed supernatural creatures of childhood tales. He wonders how she survived infancy, since such babies are usually given to the Guardians by horrified mothers, and it is said that the Guardians then sacrifice them to the Fires of Dar. Yet not only is she alive, but this woman bears the sacred sign of the forbidden Guardian cult, possesses fire magic, and claims she can talk to shades of the dead. Her name is Mirabar.

She claims that destiny has called her here to tell them all that they must forgot old wounds and join forces. Together they can defeat the Valdani. But if a single one of them fails to unite with the others, the opportunity to reclaim Sileria won't come again for a thousand years.

Rather contemptuous of the Guardians, whose numbers are few and whose powers are generally inferior to his own, Kiloran is skeptical that this young, yellow-eyed priestess can see something he can't. The real opportunity for rebellion came with Armian, he insists, and Tansen destroyed it.

If Kiloran won't believe her, then Mirabar suggests they ask Armian. Needing a personal possession of the deceased to call him forth, Mirabar asks Tansen for Armian's wavy-bladed *shir* (which Tansen took when he killed him and has kept ever since); she has recognized Tansen as the man of stained honor and terrible courage she has been searching for. It doesn't take extraordinary intuition to guess that the aristocratic woman with him is the cause of his bitter yearning. Haunted by even older superstitions now, Tansen refuses to give Mirabar the *shir*. Even he knows that it is forbidden for a Guardian to summon a Society assassin; the danger is too great. Armian will consume Mirabar, and then he will reach out to engulf Tansen in his vengeance.

Hoping that will be the case, Kiloran immobilizes Tansen in a pillar of water and gives the *shir* to Mirabar—who knows that if she fails now, they will all be destroyed. Calling on all her strength, she summons Armian. His appearance makes Tansen's shame weigh more heavily upon him than his fear, for he murdered a man who trusted him. Armian struggles with Mirabar, who nearly dies defeating him. But when Armian has confirmed their destiny and the ordeal is over, all of them, even Kiloran, are now convinced that Mirabar is right. Kiloran rescinds the bloodvow. Uneasy allies, they all make a sacred vow to work together to free Sileria of the Valdani.

PART III

BY THE TIME Tansen and Josarian launch their next attack against a Valdani outpost, the Outlookers who hired Tansen to kill Josarian have realized that he betrayed them and is the notorious warrior who now fights at Josarian's side. The Valdani offer a huge reward for the outlaws' capture, dead or alive. Tansen is amused to learn that, having survived Kiloran's bloodvow, he is now regarded with superstitious awe by the *shallaheen*, while Josarian's courage, charisma, and daring exploits are quickly making him a legend in the mountains. Some now even say that he is the Firebringer.

True to their vow, Elelar, Kiloran, Mirabar, and the outlaws now work together, though they are reluctant allies. Kiloran uses his influence to convince Sileria's many professional bandits to become the first recruits to Josarian's army. And, on occasion, Kiloran assists them against the Valdani with powers that none of them except Mirabar even understands.

Though Tansen eventually grows accustomed to Mirabar's demon-eyes, flaming hair, and strange talents, he find them a perplexing contrast to her sharp-tongued practicality. Abandoned as a child, she grew up wild in the mountains until caught and tamed by the outlawed Guardians, who recognized her unusual coloring as a possible sign of rare gifts. It is the Valdani, she tells him bitterly, who taught the people of Sileria to fear her and to doubt the Guardians.

Meanwhile, Elelar's co-conspirators in the Alliance provide a network of support from foreign powers which want to weaken the Valdani Empire enough to make it vulnerable to attack on the mainland. Elelar works with Josarian and Tansen to finance their growing rebel army not only by robbing the Valdani, but also by employing a time-honored custom learned from the Society: abduction. She is able to provide them with information on the movements and assets of Sileria's wealthiest non-patriots. Kiloran and the waterlords, in turn, provide Josarian with watery prisons for his hostages, as well as experienced intermediaries to negotiate the ransoms.

Josarian's expenses are enormous; he must feed and supply an ever-growing guerrilla army, as well as pay for the silence of many of the citizens upon whom he relies for these supplies. However, despite his celebrated generosity, someone finally betrays him, and it nearly costs him his life. Although Tansen did not come home to kill *shallaheen*, he knows that he and Josarian must now honor another Society tradition and make an example of this traitor. They publicly execute him, as they will execute anyone else who betrays them. The Valdani endure unexpected attacks on the mainland and can't immediately bring more men here to suppress the rebellion. However, setting their spies upon a problem too long ignored, the Valdani expose and imprison several leaders of the Alliance—including Elelar.

Assisted by the Beyah-Olvari, Tansen and Josarian attack the prison from underground and free Elelar, taking her back to their mountain stronghold in rebel-held territory. But despite the temporary loyalty they have sworn, she and Josarian dislike each other; he is contemptuous of her pragmatism, and she considers his untempered idealism both naive and dangerous. A victim of her sexual allure even now, Tansen nonetheless quarrels with her upon recognizing her attempts to undermine his absolute loyalty to Josarian. When she begins sharing her bed with Zimran, Josarian's cousin and close friend, Tansen believes she does it to hurt him. And it works.

Tansen has never understood Josarian's loyalty to Zimran, who is a good fighter, but not a good man. Zimran is weak-willed and self-serving, and he has long been jealous of Tansen's notoriety and friendship with Josarian. And now that Zimran has something Tansen has always wanted and never had—Elelar—he reveals a strong streak of malice, too. However, Zimran and Josarian were raised together, and their bond is strong. Besides, once offered, Josarian's loyalty is never withdrawn.

As the fighting escalates, so does Josarian's growing reputation as the Firebringer. But when he urges the sea-born folk and the city-dwellers to join his cause and serve Sileria's destiny, he is offered a deadly challenge. If he is the Firebringer, if this war is Sileria's destiny, then he must prove it according to the prophesy: he must withstand the Fires of Dar. Recognizing that he cannot turn back now, Josarian agrees. Tansen thinks this is insane and desperately tries to talk him out of it. Even Mirabar has her doubts. Josarian insists that if he is the Firebringer, he will survive. And if he's not the Firebringer, then the rebellion will simply have to go on without him—but Tansen doesn't believe it can succeed without Josarian.

High atop the snow-covered peak of Mount Darshon, with hundreds of witnesses in attendance, Josarian undergoes the ordeal described in the prophecy. Anointed in a sacred flame ritual of the Guardians, he commits himself to the volcano's fires, soaring into rock-melting heat and lava. And—in fulfillment of the ancient prophecy—he lives.

The Firebringer has come at last to lead the people of Sileria to the glory they once knew.

PART IV:

All of Sileria now flocks to the banner of the proven Firebringer. In defiance of all reasonable expectation, organized military rebellion sweeps across the land. And as Josarian's fame grows, so does his power. As he drives the Valdani closer to defeat, he grows so influential that even most Society waterlords must now bow to his wishes. Kiloran views all of this with apprehension, knowing that power is easier to withhold than to take away.

As the Valdani weaken and face seemingly inevitable defeat, the Alliance sets up a provisional government until such time as the Guardians are ready to select the new Yahrdan—for the first time in a thousand years. With the moment of truth almost at hand, Kiloran betrays Josarian to the Valdani. Josarian discovers Kiloran's betrayal and knows he must move against him swiftly. However, Kiloran is too well-protected, his power too great for Josarian to destroy him. So instead, in what Elelar views as an insane act of self-destruction, Josarian honors another Society custom and kills Kiloran's son in retaliation. Then, with Josarian in danger from their former ally, Tansen is badly wounded by a Society *shir* and lies near death for days; he may not live to see the victory—now so close at hand—which he helped create.

In Shaljir, now occupied by rebel forces, a Valdani envoy meets secretly with senior members of the Alliance. The Valdani have somehow learned about the feud which has

erupted between Josarian and Kiloran. The Valdani don't believe this superstitious nonsense the peasants babble about
ancient prophesies, nor the wild stories they tell about
Josarian surviving a leap into the volcano. They do, however, believe in Kiloran's reputation and suggest that once
the war is over, Josarian won't have long to live anyhow. As
the price for an immediate treaty guaranteeing the unconditional withdrawal of the Valdani from Sileria, they want to
carry Josarian's body home to their emperor. Josarian, the
envoy reminds them, has been responsible for the death of
thousands of Valdani.

After heatedly discussing this proposal, the Alliance
representatives—who have long feared Josarian for various
reasons—agree to it and sign the treaty. Having been the link
between Josarian and the Alliance throughout the war, Elelar
is now ordered to arrange Josarian's death. Reluctantly, she
agrees, knowing that the Firebringer's prophecy ends the
moment Sileria is freed. Perhaps this is Josarian's destiny.

Tansen recovers from his wound, and wants to accompany Josarian on his next mission, despite obviously being
too weak to do so. Josarian tries to reassure him, saying that
he will have Zimran with him to guard his back. Tansen argues with him; he doesn't trust Zimran. Josarian attributes
this outburst to Tansen's jealousy over Elelar, dismisses it,
and leaves.

Upon discovering evidence that Zimran intends to betray Josarian, however, Tansen and Mirabar set out after
them. They reach them in time to find that, unable to believe
his trusted friend would betray him, Josarian has let Zimran

lead him into a Valdani trap. Fighting as ruthlessly and skill-
fully as ever in his life, Tansen helps drive back the ambush-
ing Outlookers and disarm Zimran. However, within
moments of Josarian's assuring his companions that his injuries aren't serious, the White Dragon comes for him at last.
Pillars of water arise from the river to writhe, foam, twist,
and hiss. They engulf and embrace Josarian, furiously re-
pulsing anyone who tries to save him as, bit by bit, his body
and spirit are turned to water in a death even more horrify-
ing than the whispered legends Tansen never believed. Neither Mirabar's fire nor Tansen's slender Kintish swords can
save Josarian as he disappears forever into Kiloran's keeping. Enraged, not even caring if he himself dies this way,
Tansen forces Zimran into the Dragon's mouth and watches
him suffer the same fate he condemned the Firebringer to.
The wounded Valdani escape to report Josarian's death to
their commander.

At last, Mirabar understands her vision: he will both
succeed and fail . . . But Tansen doesn't accept this defeat,
regardless of visions and destiny. In accordance with
Josarian's own custom of killing traitors, he swears to
Mirabar that he will kill Elelar, whose part in all this Zimran
revealed before dying. Blinded by grief and fury, Tansen ignores his injuries and hunts her down. Elelar has expected
this confrontation, though perhaps not so soon. She tells him
she didn't cultivate Zimran's passion out of desire, nor did
she do it out of a petty wish to hurt Tansen. She did it because, having recognized how uncontrollable Josarian was,
she decided she needed someone close to him who would be

loyal to her rather than to him. It could have been Tansen, but he wouldn't cooperate, so she had to choose Zimran.

But she rejects Tansen's violent accusations as hypocritical self-righteous slander. After all, didn't he once kill a man who trusted him, all for the good of Sileria? Did he think he was the only one who loved this land, the only one who had ever devoted his life to freeing it?

After killing Kiloran's son, she insists, Josarian was as good as dead. Being the Firebringer gave him no special power to withstand the Society. Not even nine years of exile could have saved him from Kiloran's revenge; Kiloran would never rescind this bloodvow. And what if Josarian had been named Yahrdan by the Guardians? How long would the newly freed kingdom remain stable once its first ruler was assassinated? Isn't that the very kind of thing that made Sileria vulnerable to the Conquest in the first place?

The Valdani began unconditional and immediate withdrawal upon signing the treaty; and any Valdani who are skeptical about Josarian's death will undoubtedly accept Kiloran's word in place of the actual body. Now no more Silerians need die in battle. Even with victory in the wind, how many more *shallaheen* would have died if they'd had to drive the Valdani out of Sileria step by step? How ruined and impoverished would the land have been after another season of war?

Hating her as he has never hated anyone, Tansen tells her what a fool she is, for in destroying Josarian, she has played right into Kiloran's hands. Who already tried once to betray Josarian to the Valdani? Who advised the Valdani that the Alliance could be convinced to betray him? Who had the most to fear from Josarian's strength? Who tried to ensure that Tansen wouldn't be there to protect Josarian? And who will benefit most from Josarian's death?

Elelar has paved the way for Kiloran to rule Sileria by having destroyed the only man strong enough to oppose him. They were all better off under Valdani rule than they will be now, Tansen concludes bitterly. Didn't he give nine years of his life to prevent this from occurring? Didn't she realize that there was one person in Sileria even more clever than she?

Horrified by the implications of what Tansen is saying, Elelar weakens for the first time in their entire acquaintance, desperately wanting to believe that he's wrong. After all, didn't Mirabar promise they would all free Sileria together? Isn't this all part of that destiny?

Tansen corrects her: Mirabar said only that they would drive out the Valdani. Freedom is apparently a destiny they won't live to see. But as Tansen leaves, Elelar tells him that he's wrong about one thing; Josarian was not the only man strong enough to oppose Kiloran. There is another: him. Wishing he was strong enough to kill Elelar, Tansen leaves her behind and returns to the hills to lead the *shallaheen* against the Society.

CHARLES SHEFFIELD

CHARLES SHEFFIELD IS A Hugo-winning writer, a past president of the Science Fiction Writers of America, and husband of Hugo-winning Nancy Kress.

When I asked him for an outline or a synopsis, he replied that he didn't have any for his publishers, but he could give me a batch of one-pagers he had written at the request of his Hollywood agent, who was aware of the fact that most producers can't concentrate for two whole pages.

Since some of you will eventually sell a book and be asked to condense it for Hollywood, I thought these eight synopses might someday be of use.

8 MOVIE SYNOPSES

by Charles Sheffield

MY BROTHER'S KEEPER

LIONEL SALKIND AND Leo Foss are identical twin brothers who have been raised apart, Lionel in England and Leo in the United States. Lionel has become a concert pianist, Leo (unknown to Lionel) an agent of the US Government tracking down narcotics and hi-tech biological products.

As a result of sabotage, the brothers are in a helicopter crash near London. They are both badly injured, and the surgeon is able to save Lionel only by employing organs from the fatally-injured Leo—including portions of Leo's brain. When Lionel is recovering, sensory memories from Leo's mute brain segments begin; at the same time, Lionel finds that he is being pursued by Leo's former adversary, Scouse, who wants a programmable body-implant device, the Belur Package, that Leo had taken.

With increasing involvement from Leo's brain and increasing trouble from his enemies, Lionel follows the trail of the Belur Package to Calcutta, where he meets Leo's blind child-bride, Ameera, and escapes from their enemies in Cuttack, where Ameera is tortured by the sadistic Xantippe, Scouse's assistant.

Lionel follows the trail to Riyadh, where he obtains the Belur Package. The final confrontation takes place in the snake pit of the Riyadh Zoo. At the same time, the final integration of the twins' brain segments is taking place. Lionel falls unconscious in the snake pit, and awakes in the hospital in London. Scouse is dead, but Xantippe is still free and dangerous. Lionel knows that he will have to continue the chase until he finds her.

GODSPEED

This is a futuristic re-telling of Robert Louis Stevenson's Treasure Island, *with Jay Hara as Jim Hawkins and Danny Shaker as Long John Silver.*

JAY HARA, sixteen years old but still pre-pubescent, lives on a planet, Erin, that is not quite right for humans. Fewer and fewer girls are being born, and all the boys mature very late.

The problem lies with the disappearance of the Godspeed Drive starships. Once they brought people and diet supplements to Erin, but ten generations ago the faster-than-light ships ceased to arrive and no one knows why. Erin still has space travel, but with slow and battered old ships that date from the time before the Isolation. They are good enough only to wander around the local star system, scavenging for the materials of better days. Even for this, they are becoming less and less reliable. With a decreasing supply of raw materials, civilization on Erin is beginning to fall apart.

From a dying spacer, Paddy Enderton, who comes to live with the Hara family, Jay receives a pocket computer which defines the location of a planetoid, Paddy's Fortune, set in a dangerous ring system known as The Maze. The planetoid might be the Godspeed Base, and a working Godspeed Drive could possibly be found there.

Jay and his mother's friends, Duncan West and Dr. Eileen Xavier, together with two Erin scientists, Walter Hamilton and James Swift, set out for Paddy's Fortune. They travel on board a hired spaceship, the Cuchulain. It is captained by a polite and friendly man, Danny Shaker, who seems especially fond of Jay. None of Jay's party realizes that Paddy Enderton was part of Shaker's old crew of spacers and fled from them with the stolen location of Paddy's Fortune. Although Shaker himself is skeptical, the rest of the crew are convinced that Paddy's Fortune is the home not of the Godspeed Base, but of a large number of human females.

Jay leads the Cuchulain to the planetoid, and it seems that the crew is wrong—until Jay himself, pursued by crew members because he has witnessed the murder of one of the Erin scientists, runs into a girl, Mel Fury, on the surface. She takes him to the hollow interior, and Jay learns that the crew were right. There are girls and women living inside Paddy's Fortune. But it will be fatal to let the crew know that.

Back on the surface with Mel Fury, Jay gives the new information that he has obtained in the interior to Danny Shaker, in exchange for protection for Mel and Jay himself. The new data will lead them farther afield in The Maze, to the Needle and the Eye, and possibly to the Godspeed Drive.

Shaker does protect them, quashing a crew mutiny in the process, and they fly on to find the Godspeed Base in a ship that is becoming rapidly more decrepit. By the time that they locate the base, and within it a Godspeed Drive apparently in full working order, the old Cuchulain is on its last legs.

And then Shaker reveals his hand. He will take the Godspeed Drive, and leave Eileen Xavier, Mel Fury, and the scientist James Swift on the Cuchulain. Duncan West has already defected to join Shaker's party, and Shaker urges Jay to make the same choice. He refuses.

The old crew of the Cuchulain, led by Danny Shaker, board the new ship. The Godspeed Drive is powered up and ready to go. James Swift, who suspects what may happen when it is used, tells Jay to take the Cuchulain well clear.

The new ship vanishes, but in a display of fireworks that indicate the problem with the Godspeed Drive still exists. It created a hiatus in spacetime that is still there, and cannot be used without throwing a ship that uses it out of the universe.

Jay is not convinced that James Swift is totally right. He has evidence that Shaker and the crew are still alive, in some strange other existence. But he is over-ruled, as Swift prepares a slower experimental drive in the Godspeed Base to take them back to Erin. The Slowdrive should permit travel to the stars, but without the problem encountered by the Godspeed Drive.

As the book ends aboard the Slowdrive ship, Jay is excited by what Swift has told him but perhaps more excited by other things. The food given to him on Paddy's Fortune is changing him, just as the Erin food given to Mel Fury is changing her. Jay finds it hard to keep his attention on the stars when more immediate prospects are opening up.

THE WEB BETWEEN THE WORLDS

The central idea of this book, the beanstalk, a cable that stretches from the surface of the Earth to geosynchronous orbit and beyond, is less far-fetched than it sounds. It is used in Arthur Clarke's novel, The Fountains of Paradise, *and is the subject of many scientific papers.*

ROB MERLIN WAS crippled and almost killed at the moment of his birth, when a plane carrying his mother was sabotaged above Antarctica. He survives to become the world's greatest bridge-builder.

When he is mountain climbing in Asia he is met by Corrie Plessey and persuaded to go with her to visit her employer, Darius Regulo. Regulo, a man of legendary wealth and power, lives in Atlantis, a self-contained waterworld with living quarters submerged deep within it. On Atlantis are Caliban, a giant squid, the master-computer Sycorax, and the biologist, Joseph Morel. At their first meeting, Regulo explains that he wants Merlin to help him to build a Beanstalk—a giant elevator system from Earth to orbit.

Merlin agrees to lead the project. As the project moves ahead he discovers hints that Regulo was involved in the death of Merlin's own parents, who had been operating a lab in New Zealand and exploring the cause of death of two dwarf figures found floating in free space.

But by now Rob has deduced what happened to his parents. The dwarf figures were suffering from a condition of accelerated aging, known as progeria, induced by Regulo. He had been using them as test animals, in his experiments to try to stop his own spreading cancer.

In the final confrontation with Rob and Corrie Plessey, Regulo is defeated and flies to his death in an incandescent asteroid used for space mining.

Finally, the Beanstalk is finished and installed.

THE HERITAGE UNIVERSE

This is a four-book series, now printed in two volumes as Convergent Series and Transvergence.

LONG BEFORE HUMANITY achieved spaceflight, an ancient race now known only as The Builders scattered large and mysterious artifacts through the Galaxy. In an attempt to understand these, and to learn what happened to the Builders themselves, an assorted group of humans and non-humans come to the world Quake, part of a doublet planet Dobelle, to witness an event known as Summertide. Included in the group are the humans, Hans Rebka, Darya Lang, and Louis Nenda; the giant blind Cecropian, Atvar H'sial; the twin-brained Julius/Steven Graves; and the willing slave species, J'merlia the Lo'ftian and Kallik, the Hymenopt.

But witnessing Summertide does not solve the mystery.

It leads them farther afield, to the gasgiant planet Gargantua, and then to the Builder artifact Serenity, far outside the Galaxy. Along the way they acquire the embodied computer, E. Crimson Tally. And on Serenity they encounter the Zardalu, a race believed extinct but once the terror of the Spiral Arm.

The pursuit of the Zardalu to their home world, seeking to contain them there, leads the group to another danger: the Torvil Anfract, a region of twisted spacetime, which can only be explored with the assistance of Dulcimer, a Chism Polypheme, of doubtful honesty and reliability.

Finally the whole of the Spiral Arm begins to change. The artifacts start to vanish. And the group, humans and aliens alike, finally realize that they have far more to do with that change than they had ever realized. For with their enforced cooperation, the agenda of the Builders—for multiple species inhabiting the Spiral Arm—has been achieved.

COLD AS ICE

A GREAT WAR between the inner worlds and the inhabited asteroids and moons of Jupiter ripped the solar system apart twenty-five years before the story begins, in the third quarter of the 21st century. But its effects continue. Rustum Battachariya, Bat, a puzzle master and war buff, has been trying to understand why at the end of the war one side would destroy its own ship.

The trail leads him to a great, ongoing battle within the system, between forces that want to develop the waterworld of Europa, a satellite of Jupiter, and others who want to maintain that world undisturbed. They are led respectively by Cyrus Mobarak, the Sun-King, pioneer in commercial fusion systems, and Hilda Brandt, chief scientist on Europa.

In unraveling the details of that ongoing battle and the final days of the war, Bat learns that the after-effects of that war are more than anyone expected. Biological experiments created a small number of people with supernormal powers. But those people do not themselves realize it, or what happened to them when they were very small children.

The final confrontation pits Cyrus Mobarak against Hilda Brandt, in the presence of the unwitting superbeings. Mobarak appears to win; but the discovery of primitive native life on Europa changes the outcome, so that Hilda Brandt—war criminal, and developer of the supernormal forms—at last appears more as the winner than Mobarak.

THE MIND POOL

AN ATTEMPT TO CREATE a set of superior beings, the Morgan Constructs, to defend the Perimeter (the edge of the region of space explored by humans) has failed. The Constructs have turned on their creators. One has escaped, and it must be tracked down and destroyed.

The four known intelligent species of interstellar travel (Tinker Composites, Pipe-Rillas, Angels, and Humans) give responsibility for finding and destroying the Morgan Construct to two humans, Esro Mondrian and Luther Brachis.

They do not realize that Mondrian has his own reasons for keeping the Construct alive. Mondrian and Brachis recruit their first team members, Chan Dalton, a near-moron who must be given an agonizing treatment of intelligence stimulation before he can be useful, and Leah Rainbow, Dalton's guardian and friend. While on Earth, Brachis takes as a lover Godiva Lomberd, a famous courtesan, and kills the Margrave of Fujitsu, a designer of simulacra who swears revenge on Brachis. Brachis realizes the Margrave is serious when a series of simulacra attempt to kill him.

Leah completes training and is assigned to a Pursuit Team, consisting of one member of each species. They go off to the planet Travancore to tackle the Morgan Construct. When Chan Dalton is ready for assignment, he is told that the Construct has destroyed Leah's team and it is his team's responsibility to destroy the Construct. Meanwhile, Esro Mondrian has put the planet into quarantine, and is on an orbiting ship accompanied by Luther Brachis, trying to avoid the Margrave's simulacra, and Godiva Lomberd.

On Travancore Chan finally encounters Nimrod—but finds that it is not a Construct; it is the group mind of Leah's team, something that Esro Mondrian fears much more than the Construct itself. Chan's team establishes its own group mind, and together they take over the quarantine ship. In the process, Godiva Lomberd is revealed to be one of the Margrave's simulacra, created to observe Brachis. When he finds this out, Brachis tries to kill Godiva and blow his own brains out. Mondrian attempts to destroy the ship rather than allowing the group minds to take control. They stop him, but only by erasing all his memories. At the end of the book Esro Mondrian and Luther Brachis are being cared for in the Sargasso Dump, a place for shattered minds and bodies.

TOMORROW AND TOMORROW

DRAKE MERLIN'S WIFE is dying, of a rare and untreatable disease. Since today's doctors cannot save her, he arranges for Ana's body to be frozen and preserved. Nine years later, having worked to make sure that people in the future will be interested in reviving him for what he knows, he has himself frozen.

He is awakened too soon. Ana's disease can still not be cured. Rather than being frozen again, he steals Ana's body and heads off for the stars, intending to return after a long enough period has passed for her to be treated. While he is gone, his action in opening her coffin to look at her ruins any chance that she can be restored to life. Instead of accepting that fact, Drake goes on, farther and farther into the future. He becomes a living fossil, primitive man electronically downloaded and appearing at more and more remote times. He saves humanity from an outside threat, is returned to consciousness in millions of different forms, and wanders far beyond our own galaxy.

Finally, at the end of the universe itself, he finds a way to restore Ana to him. But now the universe is collapsing to a final singularity. With little time left, Drake takes the final risk. He sends himself and Ana through to a new space and time, a universe where he hopes that the two of them can live together again.

AFTERMATH

IN FEBRUARY, 2026, the star Alpha Centauri turns into a supernova, as bright in the sky as the Sun. The immediate effect is a huge change in the Earth's weather, with large parts of the southern hemisphere rendered uninhabitable. An even greater disaster comes a few weeks later, when radiation from the supernova induces an electromagnetic pulse in the atmosphere of the Earth. The pulse wipes out all computer microchips, and by 2026, the chips are in everything. Earth is left without communications, transportation, water and food delivery, electric power, and modern weapons.

Three groups set out to assure their own survival. The first is the returning Mars expedition, whose chances of survival without a working space program seem small. Some of them manage the return to Earth, but they fall at once into the hands of a militant cult, who see the supernova as a chance to restore their own leader, the Eye of God, from the long-term coma to which she was sentenced. Also returned from long-term judicial sleep, in this case by a group of cancer patients, is the child serial murder, Dr. Oliver Guest. In the collapsed world, he is the only person who can continue the experimental telomere treatment needed to keep the cancer at bay and the group alive. However, awakening Dr. Guest proves easier than controlling him.

In charge of all this, at least in principle, is Saul Steinmetz, the overworked, bewildered, and impotent President of the United States. He has the problem of putting himself and the country back together, while restraining others in Congress who think it's a good time for the United States to take over the whole world.

MIKE RESNICK

ONE OF THE PRIVILEGES of being the editor of this book is that I get to show you more of my synopses than anyone else's. But there's a reason: these four pretty much run the gamut of the kind of synopses I do.

The brief *Walpurgis III* synopsis, like Charles Sheffield's, was done for Hollywood after Signet published the novel. (Yes, they optioned the book, and no, they never made the movie.)

The Branch is more clearly a book rather than a movie outline: a bare-bones description of the plot and little else. It sold to New American Library.

The Widowmaker Trilogy is more typical still, in that I outlined three books that would take a couple of years to write, and I anticipated that I'd have a number of better ideas as I went along, so I made it as general as possible. The books pretty much start and finish where the outline says they will, but readers will see that while the books remain true to the *spirit* of the outline, they don't pay much attention to the *letter* of it. They sold to Bantam/Spectra.

Finally, as I was putting this book together, I sold *The Return of Santiago*, which everyone had been nagging me to write for over a decade, to Tor. I'm including it here simply to show how I use the finished Prologue to lead into the synopsis.

Sorry to ramble on so long. Editor's privilege and all that.

WALPURGIS III

by Mike Resnick

THIS IS THE STORY of three men: one who *is* evil, one who *does* evil, and one who worships evil.

Walpurgis III is a remote planet that has been colonized by Satanists. As the book begins, it has agreed to give sanctuary to Conrad Bland, a genocidal maniac who has killed more people than any other man in history—but the killing does not stop when Bland reaches Walpurgis III, and now this society which pays lip service to Evil is confronted with Evil Incarnate.

The planetary government secretly hires the best assassin it can find, a man known only as Jericho, who arrives and promptly begins making his way through this complex society to Conrad Bland.

Jericho's opponent is John Sable, a police detective and native to Walpurgis III, who devoutly believes in Satanism and feels that it is his duty to protect Conrad Bland, who is hiding some hundreds of miles away.

The bulk of the book is a suspense novel, in which Jericho learns more about this very strange society and murders his way toward Bland, and Sable tries to stop him. When Jericho manages to go beyond Sable's jurisdiction, the detective flies ahead to Bland's headquarters to warn them what is happening—and realizes that he has wandered into a charnel house, that Bland's behavior has given new meaning to the term Evil.

Jericho continues his cold, efficient, absolutely ruthless approach, the ultimate executioner in search of the ultimate butcher, and eventually he succeeds in infiltrating Bland's headquarters and killing him.

Jericho and Sable escape together, and during the trip home Sable must decide what to do with Jericho. On the one hand, Jericho has killed Conrad Bland, a monster whose crimes dwarf even those of Adolph Hitler—but on the other hand, Jericho himself has killed more than 50 innocent men and women in reaching his goal, and Sable is committed to maintaining order and enforcing the law.

Sable, who has seen too much death, finally concludes that killing by calculation, as Jericho does, is no better than killing from compulsion, as Bland did, and he arrests Jericho. As the book ends, Sable has re-examined his religious convictions and found them wanting, and we know that, having come face-to-face with the evil that he worshipped all his life, he will continue to search for some other belief that better fits the world on which he must live.

THE BRANCH

by Mike Resnick

THE YEAR IS 2047, and between mechanization and computers and 20-hour work weeks, America's citizens are bored. Solomon Moody Moore, the kingpin of Chicago's crime lords, has made his living by answering that need, and as the story opens he has just purchased a Thrill Show that appeals to his audience's darker cravings.

Unknown to Moore, the Thrill Show is the home of Jeremiah the B, a totally immoral grifter who, no matter what kind of trouble he gets into, always seems to land on his feet.

Within days Moore is drawn to the Bizarre Bazaar, a fetish shop in Chicago's ancient downtown business district, where a somewhat kinky young lady tries to kill him. Moore subdues her, and learns that she is one of the Thrill Show's Dartboards, a woman who has had her pain receptors surgically severed. When questioned under the influence of a truth serum, she admits that she was hired by Jeremiah, who hopes to kill Moore and take over his criminal empire.

Moore puts out a hit on Jeremiah, and before long his men learn that Jeremiah is hiding in Darktown, a huge underground city that was built by the criminal elements in an abandoned oil storage project a mile beneath Chicago. They go after him, surround him in a brothel named the Plaza Gomorrah, and fire point-blank at him—and miss. Bullets bounce off the bed, off his backpack, off his robot bedmate, a few wound him, but unbelievably, he makes good his escape.

Not convinced that his men are telling him the truth, Moore decides to become personally involved in Jeremiah's destruction. He begins by putting Jeremiah's mistress, a necrophile taxidermist named Moira Rallings, on his payroll, picking her mind, and learning some very unusual things about Jeremiah, things that convince him that this is no run-of-the-mill grifter he's dealing with.

Next he goes looking for a man named Krebbs, the proprietor of the Bizarre Bazaar, still seeking information. The man should be easy to find, Moore explains to his operatives; he was missing an eye and two fingers on his right hand. But when Moore himself finally spots Krebbs in a crowd, the man has both eyes and all his fingers. Obviously Moore must be wrong, say his operatives; but Moore knows this is the man he is seeking, and has his medical expert pour more and more truth drugs into Krebbs' feeble body until he is proven right. Just before he dies, Krebbs admits that Jeremiah made him whole again.

This casts a whole new light on the problem. Now it is not just a matter of finding Jeremiah, but of defining him. What kind of creature could cause spontaneous regeneration in another human being? An alien? A mutant?

And gradually, with Moore fighting against the conclusion every step of the way, it becomes clear that what Jeremiah is is the Messiah—not the Prince of Peace of the New Testament, but the Annointed One of the Old Testament, he who will come with the sword and the fire and raze everything to the ground before securing his kingdom in Jerusalem.

Moore can't believe it, and even goes to the newly-developed Reality Library, where for an enormous fee one can actually live the life of a fictional character. He chooses Judas, the man who betrayed Jesus, to see if Judas had certain knowledge that Jesus was *not* the Messiah, but though he lives Judas' life not only as it appears in the Bible but also in epic poems and works of fiction, he still doesn't know for sure.

A rabbi, an expert on the subject, is brought in and explains that all Biblical scholars can agree on four signs by which the Messiah would make his presence manifest: he must be named Immanual (Jeremiah's real name is Immanual); he must go first to Egypt and then to Israel (Jeremiah's parents were archeologists, and he did just that); he must resurrect the dead (Jeremiah brought a drowned friend back to life with artificial respiration when he was a child); and he must be of the Davidic line—which cannot be proved, since the line is thousands of years old.

Moore's question remains: why Jeremiah? He's a thief and a beggar, and intelligence is not his long suit. Why would God make *him* the Messiah? And finally he uncovers the answer: Jeremiah had a vasectomy two years earlier. If indeed he is the last of the Davidic line, the line ends with him, and therefore he must be the Messiah.

And as Moore reaches his conclusion, he receives a taunting message from Jeremiah and he, too, has finally figured out who he is and what he must do.

During the next two years, Jeremiah begins performing miracles and gathering a huge following, while simultaneously financing his impassioned followers by taking over Moore's empire. Moira Rallings deserts Moore and rejoins Jeremiah, authoring the best-selling *Gospel of Jeremiah*, which brings in still more converts. Governments are rocked to the core as more and more people accept Jeremiah as the true Messiah. The churches, which have a vested interest in his *not* being what he claims, fight him as best they can, but it is Israel that feels the most threatened, for it is in Israel that he must ultimately establish his kingdom.

As Jeremiah gathers his army about him, Moore is visited in the Jamaica Bubble—an underwater luxury spa that has become his headquarters—and asked to join the Israeli army as an advisor, since he knows more about Jeremiah than anyone else. He agrees, speaks to the Israeli High Command and apprises them of Jeremiah's abilities, and remains there for a week, at which time Jeremiah walks in, miraculously unscathed, and takes over the country.

Moore goes into hiding until Jeremiah is officially made the King of Jerusalem—and then seeks a final confrontation. Jeremiah, totally drunk with power and certain that no one can do him physical harm, thanks Moore for making his kingdom—Jerusalem—secure for him, and explains that he, Moore, is actually the Forerunner, whose function it is to prepare the way for the Messiah.

Moore is flabbergasted, but nonetheless pulls out a gun. Jeremiah is unworried; nothing can kill him until he fulfills his destiny. Moore points out that by establishing his kingdom in Jerusalem, he has done just that. His destiny has been fulfilled, and now Moore can and does kill him. Moore offers Jeremiah's body to the necrophile Moira Rallings, who in exchange for it agrees to give him a 6-hour headstart before reporting Jeremiah's slaying.

Moore drives out of town until he is out of gas. Then, while resting on Mount Sinai, he becomes chilly and lights a fire. One bush keeps burning after the others have gone out, and Moore becomes uncomfortably aware of the fact that he is not alone. God's presence becomes manifest, as He castigates Moore for killing His Messiah. Moore is defiant, pointing out that God was nowhere to be found during the Inquisition and the Third Reich, and that Jeremiah was the worst possible Messiah. Enraged, God announces that He is breaking His covenant with Man, and will no longer concern Himself in man's affairs. We got along without you all these years, says Moore; we'll continue to do so.

Dawn breaks, and Moore must now find a way home, across the desert where hundreds of thousands of people are waiting to kill him. If he survives that, he is still penniless, and must try to reclaim his former empire. But at least he won't die of boredom, and in this day and age, in the world that he has helped to shape, that is enough.

He climbs down off the mountain, looking forward to the challenge.

Proposed length: about 80,000 words

THE WIDOWMAKER TRILOGY

by Mike Resnick

Volume I: THE WIDOWMAKER

DEEP BENEATH THE SURFACE of Deluros VIII, at the heart of mankind's sprawling Oligarchy, is a huge cryonic chamber in which hundreds of men and women have been frozen in suspended animation. As the book opens, one of the men, Jefferson Nighthawk, once considered the greatest lawman and bounty hunter on the Inner Frontier during the days when he was known as the Widowmaker, but now just a withered old man with an incurable and disfiguring disease, is thawed out.

He is one of the fortunate few who had the finances to freeze himself and wait until medical science discovered a cure to his disease . . . but science hasn't made much progress, and after almost a century in hibernation, his money is about to run out, as the freezing process is extremely expensive and inflation is running rampant.

Did they awaken him just to tell him they were going to let him die, he asks. No, explains a pair of lawyers. But he needs money to remain frozen, and they have just had an interesting offer: the governor of a planet on the Inner Frontier has been assassinated, and the planet has offered Nighthawk a bounty of five million credits to come out of hibernation and apprehend the killer.

Obviously, Nighthawk is in no condition even to walk across a room on his own power, let alone go hunting down a killer on the Inner Frontier—but since he was frozen, medical science *has* succeeded in cloning human beings. It is even more expensive than the freezing process, but the fee is large enough to cover it. If he will give his permission, they will clone him, literally reproduce him as a 22-year-old man with all his senses and reflexes at their apex, and send the clone out to do the job.

Nighthawk agrees and is refrozen, and his clone, the new Widowmaker, is created, taught to use his various weapons, and sent out to the Inner Frontier—which is populated with the same colorful cast of larger-than-life characters as *Santiago* and *The Oracle Trilogy*—to hunt down the assassin.

The young Nighthawk is every bit as good with his weaponry as the old one once was . . . but he is laboring under an enormous psychological strain, a severe identity crisis whereby he is never quite sure that he is "real", that he isn't just some shadow of the original Nighthawk; he remembers no past, because in truth he doesn't have one, and he feels that he is doomed to carry out this one mission and then be gotten rid of, or left to die of the same disfiguring disease. The first few encounters that he miraculously survives with his inborn skills do nothing to convince him that the whole situation isn't some kind of twisted dream.

On the other hand, he is a 22-year-old, with all of a

young man's energy and drives and lusts—and without 22 years of training on how to comport himself in the world, how to get along with his fellow man, how to do anything at all except hunt down his enemies and kill them.

He finally gets a line on the Marquis of Queensbury, the assassin he's after, joins a gang, works his way up to the hierarchy, and eventually meets with the Marquis. He finds that he likes him, and decides that the longer he lets him live, the longer he himself will live; no one will "turn him off" as long as he is still on the job.

But he finds himself irresistably drawn to Melisande, the Marquis' exotic, erotic, blue-skinned, mutated girlfriend, who obviously doesn't care for him. It makes no difference; overcome by his desire for her, he eventually kills the Marquis, and urges her to flee with him before the Marquis' men come after him. She refuses, and he barely escapes with his life.

Even as he is running away, his only thought is to return for her. He goes back to Deluros VIII to report that his job has been completed, then sneaks into the cyronic chamber at night and, at gunpoint, forces an attendant to unfreeze the original Nighthawk long enough for him to explain his problem.

The original Nighthawk tells him that he's a fool, that he'd better forget Melisande, that it would be suicide to return for her even if she wanted him to, which she obviously doesn't. His immediate problem, says the old man, is staying alive in a society—the Oligarchy—that has no further use for him.

The young clone is adamant: he's going back, and nothing can stop him. But he needs the original's advice: what kind of trap will they lay for him, how will he spot it, how can he overcome it?

The old man tells him what to watch for, and once again explains that he is going back to his death. The young clone, cocky with the confidence of youth, thinks he can make it.

He returns to the Inner Frontier, goes to Melisande's planet, and begin approaching her home. He finds an overwhelming army of the Marquis' men waiting for him, but he can't leave without seeing her again. For a few brief moments he holds his own against the forces arrayed against him, but soon lies on the ground, mortally wounded.

Melisande kneels down next to him and, as he expires, tells him that he is a fool. He finally acknowledges that she has no feelings for him, and bitterly agrees.

The why did you come back? she asks.

He explains, as he dies, that he's just one of many shadows of the Widowmaker. One day another shadow will return, he promises; *that* shadow will do the job better, and *he'll* win her love.

End of Volume I

Volume II: THE WIDOWMAKER REBORN

JEFFERSON NIGHTHAWK IS revived again.

He is informed that a cure for his disease is no more than four or five years away—but he cannot remain unfrozen for more than a month without dying, and he needs money again.

And this time, because word of the hotblooded young clone and his infatuation with Melisande has gotten around, the man who has made the offer has no confidence in the reliability of clones and will pay only half down—enough to keep him alive another two to three years—and the rest upon completion of the job.

Nighthawk and his attorneys decide to create an older, more mature clone, a man about 35—but as the medics point out, Nighthawk will have to train him, not so much in the use of weaponry, but to impart some of his experience and wisdom and personality to him. Nighthawk spends the next three weeks doing so, at enormous cost to his remaining health and stamina. When he goes into a coma from which he can be awakened only by the not-yet-discovered cure, the training ends and the new clone must go off and do what he was hired to do: retrieve Cassandra Hill, the kidnapped daughter of Marcus Hill, a major politician on Deluros VIII, and kill the kidnapper.

He analyzes the clues, considers the most likely scenarios, and, unlike his youthful predecessor, is cautious enough to conclude that he can't do the job alone. He recruits four skilled helpers: Blue Eyes, an alien computer expert; The Earth Mother, a human empath; the Firefly, an alien explosives expert; and Bwana Mkubwa, a former big game hunter and tracker—and the team proceeds to the Inner Frontier in search of the girl.

They discover that Cassandra has been kidnapped by Ibn ben Khalid, a revolutionary who has been waging war against the Oligarchy for almost two decades. He has destroyed naval convoys, robbed planetary treasuries, and succeeded in killing anyone who has come after him. Furthermore, he is a hero to the men and women of the Inner Frontier, a living legend, and they will offer no help to anyone who is looking for him.

They pick up Ibn ben Khalid's trail on a deserted planet that served as his temporary headquarters, and slowly begin closing in on him. He travels with more than 300 mercenaries, and as he realizes that he's being followed, he begin laying traps for Nighthawk and his crew. Along the way Blue Eyes and Bwana Mkubwa are killed, but finally Nighthawk, the Firefly and the Earth Mother locate Ibn ben Khalid's current hideout.

They're puzzled, though, for the Earth Mother's empathic faculties can detect no emanations of fear or desperation from Cassandra Hill, and Nighthawk decides that he will have to sneak into the hideout and make sure she is there before they can mount a rescue operation. He is spotted, apprehended, and incarcerated, but finally the Firefly rescues him. The two of them eventually find Cassandra, who explains to them that she is in no danger and doesn't *want* to be rescued: she has married Ibn ben Khalid, and is here of her own free will. Her father offered Nighthawk the commission because he finds his son-in-law an embarrassment and a political liabilitym and wants him dead and Cassandra back on Deluros VIII . . .

Nighthawk is in a quandry. He has been given a code of honor by the original Nighthawk, and can't return Cassandra against her will. But he also knows that the man he was created to save will die if he doesn't fulfill the commission, and a clone feels more closely bound to the being that gave him life than any normal man feels to a father, a son or a brother.

Finally he sees a way out of his predicament. He makes a deal with Ibn ben Khalid, and together they and their followers go back to Deluros VIII, the huge planet that has become the capital world of the race of Man. By this time in its history, Deluros VIII is one enormous planetary city, every inch of its surface covered with its single sprawling building, home to the 29 billion bureaucrats who run Man's empire.

They dock their ships at various orbiting hangars, go down in threes and fours and fives to the planet, and put into action an incredibly complex plan to rob Marcus Hill of half his fortune. Nighthawk doesn't want to be identified with this, because he doesn't want Hill disputing his ownership of the money in court while the original Widowmaker dies; Ibn ben Khalid is only too happy to take full credit for the robbery, and things seem to be going smoothly, when at the last minute Hill realizes what's happening and sends vast numbers of military and security personal out to stop them.

Now Nighthawk *can't* remain a background figure any longer. Pausing only long enough to give the Earth Mother his share of the money and order her to keep clear of the fighting—the emotional outpourings of the dead and dying are too much for her to bear any longer—he joins the battle, wiping out scores of Hill's men. Most of Ibn ben Khalid's mercenaries are killed in the first moments of battle, and eventually all that remain alive are Nighthawk, the Firefly, Ibn ben Khalid, and Cassandra Hill.

Finally, as the net closes in around them, Ibn ben Khalid decides to make a break for freedom before it's too late. The only possible route for he and Cassandra to return to their ship is heavily guarded, and Nighthawk offers to buy them time with his own life. Once he's done so, he wants the Firefly to arrange the scene so that it looked like he died fighting *against* Ibn ben Khalid, and then flee for his own life.

Ibn ben Khalid, who has come to admire Nighthawk enormously, protests that he can't allow the Widowmaker to die on his behalf; Nighthawk replies almost placidly that his job is done, that the the Earth Mother will channel his share of the money to the cryonics laboratory, and that in a way it's almost poetic justice: he was just a stand-in, and now he will die so that the *real* Nighthawk can live again.

And so he does.

End of Volume II

Volume III: THE WIDOWMAKER AT BAY

JEFFERSON NIGHTHAWK, the Widowmaker, is revived from his frozen sleep for the last time. A cure for his disease has been effected, and the money delivered by the Earth Mother was more than enough to keep him alive until now.

He leaves the cryonics chamber for the hospital, and emerges a month later, a healthy, 62-year-old man, who must now begin to face the problems of adjustment to a world, and an Oligarchy, that has changed enormously during the century that he has been frozen. He has no interest in resuming his former life—he's too old, and cherishes his new-found health too much, to go around risking his life—so he buys a farm on an obscure little world on the Inner Frontier, where he plans to spend the remainder of his life raising flowers and living on the investments he made with the Earth Mother's remaining money.

At least, he reasons, he won't have the problems that usually accrue to retired men in his profession: all of his enemies are dead, and he's been out of circulation so long that no young hotheads, eager to make their reputations, will seek him out.

But he has not reckoned on the enemies made by his two clones. The first one killed profligately across the Frontier, and the second one made some very important enemies on Deluros VIII, enemies who are sworn to kill Jefferson Nighthawk in whatever form he happens to be.

And so his life is instantly and constantly at risk from people he has never seen before, over matters about which he knows absolutely nothing. His reflexes have slowed down with age, but his brain is sharper than ever, and, though he undergoes some extremely close calls, he manages to survive the initial challenges.

Still yearning for nothing but a peaceful old age, he changes his name, moves to a new world, and seems to have settled in contentedly, when a chance encounter on the street, in which he must kill two men from the Marquis of

Queensbury's old gang, alerts all the other hotbloods and reputation-builders to his whereabouts.

He continues to use his depleted skills and enormous experience to remain alive, but is never safe. He meets a woman, falls in love, wants nothing more than to marry her and settle down to a life of ease—and she herself is killed in an attack upon him.

He finally realizes that he can never escape from his past, that as long as he is the Widowmaker, people will be out to kill him—and then he sees the one possible way out of his predicament: he will create a *new* Widowmaker, one not only better able to defend himself, but one who actually relishes the challenge of *being* the notorious Widowmaker, as he himself did when he was younger.

He returns to Deluros VIII, seeks out the men who cloned him before, and uses his remaining money to pay for one last clone. This young Widowmaker he trains as he was never able to train the first two, imparting to him every last iota of his skill and his experience and his knowledge, even plotting out the course by which the clone will make his reputation and directing his career as carefully as he directed his own a century earlier.

Finally, when the time is ripe, he arranges for the clone to meet him in a bar on Binder X, one of the more heavily-populated of the Inner Frontier worlds, and to call him out. He walks out into the street to face his younger self, and is seemingly killed.

The clone, his reputation made, leaves the world and heads deeper into the Inner Frontier, where high commissions and splendid battles await him—and the *real* Night-hawk, having faked his own death and centered the attention of all the bounty hunters and hotblooded young killers on his clone (who is only too happy to face them all), finally retires to his farm, where he plans to live out his remaining years tending to his flowers and reading the media's accounts of the legendary Widowmaker.

End of Volume III

Proposed length: about 100,000 words per book

THE RETURN OF SANTIAGO

by Mike Resnick

PROLOGUE

SOME PEOPLE SAY he was killed by the Angel. Others say
that Johnny One-Note gunned him down. Most think he died
at the hands of Peacemaker MacDougal.

Nobody knows exactly when he met his fate, or where. It
just slowly began dawning on his enemies—he didn't have
any friends, not that anyone knew about—that he hadn't
made any trouble for awhile.

Now, that doesn't mean men weren't still killed and
banks weren't still robbed and mining worlds weren't still
plundered. After all, Santiago wasn't the only outlaw on the
Inner Frontier; he was just the biggest—so big, some say, that
his shadow blotted out the sun for miles around.

Long after the Angel and Johnny One-Note and Peacemaker MacDougal had all gone to their graves, men and
women—and aliens—were still debating the nature of Santiago. Some held that he was just a man, a lot smarter and
more ruthless than most, but a man nonetheless. Others said
that he was a mutant possessed of phenomenal powers, for
else how could he have held the Navy at bay for so many
years? There were even a few who thought he was an alien,

with undefined but awesome alien abilities.

There was no known holograph of him, no retinagram or fingerprint anywhere in the Democracy. There were a few eyewitness accounts, but they differed so much from each other that no one took any of them seriously. A long-dead thief who called himself the Jolly Swagman swore he was eleven feet three inches tall, with orange hair and blazing red eyes that had seen the inner sanctum of hell itself. A preacher named Father William claimed he was an alien who always wore a face mask because oxygen was poison to his system. Virtue MacKenzie, who wrote three books about him, never described him, and the only holograph she took was of the S-shaped scar on the back of his right hand. One description made him out to be a purple-skinned alien with four arms. Another had him a mechanized, gleaming metal cyborg, no longer capable of any human emotion.

There was even a school of thought that argued that there never was a Santiago, that he was a merely a myth—but there were too many graveyards on too many worlds to lend any credence to that belief.

They say that Black Orpheus, the poet and balladeer who wandered the spaceways, writing his endless epic of the larger-than-life heroes, villains, adventurers and misfits that he found there, spent half a dozen verses of his *Ballad of the Inner Frontier* describing Santiago in precise detail, but those verses were never codified and were lost to posterity.

The one thing everyone agreed upon was that the last time he had manifested his presence was in the year 3326 of the Galactic Era, and with the passing decades it was generally assumed that Santiago, whoever or whatever he may have been, was dead.

Which simply goes to show, as has been shown so many times in the past, that a majority of the people can be wrong.

For in 3407 G.E., 81 years after he vanished, Santiago returned to the Inner Frontier, to once again juggle worlds and secrets as in days of old, to bring life and death to friend and enemy, to stride across the planets in all his former glory.

This is his story. But to understand how it came to be, we must begin with Dante Alighieri, an unemployed dreamer (as what dreamer isn't?), a failure at everything he put his hand to, physically unimpressive, artistically wanting, morally ambiguous, a young man of seemingly unexceptional gifts and abilities, and yet destined to play a central role in the return of Santiago . . .

Synopsis

I. THE RHYMER'S BOOK

HIS NAME WASN'T ALWAYS DANTE, but when he suddenly finds himself in possession of Black Orpheus's original manuscript, he feels he has finally come face-to-face with his destiny: to become the successor to the legendary poet, and to create a new, all-encompassing ballad of the Inner Frontier, taking up where Orpheus had left off. So he takes the name of the greatest of the Earthbound poets and begins collecting stories and turning them into verse.

But Dante soon realizes that there is no structure to his

story, that it lacks a central character around whom all the other lives revolve—a Santiago. And as he reads and re-reads Black Orpheus' ballad, not as an artist but as an historical detective, he begins to piece together some of the truth of Santiago: that far from being the outlaw he was thought to be, he was actually a revolutionary whose crimes were always directed against the Democracy—a man who, for reasons of his own, took credit for far more acts of violence than he actually committed.

The Democracy has grown stronger and more abusive of the Frontier worlds in the years since Santiago vanished, and there is an even greater need for him now than there was then.

It's been a long time between heroes—and Dante concludes that, for him to become the true successor to Black Orpheus, he must find a successor to Santiago.

II. WALTZIN' MATILDA'S BOOK

AS DANTE LEARNS MORE and more about Santiago, one name keeps cropping up—a woman's name. He follows a number of leads, but they are all dead ends . . . until the day *she* confronts *him* and demands to know why he's been making inquiries about her.

A criminal with a price on her head, she's changed her name a number of times, which is why he couldn't find her. She's currently a dancer making the circuit of a number of Inner Frontier worlds, and calling herself Waltzin' Matilda.

But it's just a cover, because she is really a master thief and a con artist—and there's every likelihood that she's Santiago's great-granddaughter and sole surviving blood relative.

It is from her that Dante learns that there was a succession of Santiagos building his myth of invincibility, an unbroken line that ended only when the Navy, for reasons of its own, destroyed his home world of Safe Harbor without ever knowing he lived there. Most of his treasures were also destroyed, but she's managed to keep just enough to legitimatize her story.

Dante wants a Santiago for his reasons; she wants one so that the Navy and the bounty hunters will have a bigger target and turn their attentions elsewhere. They agree to join forces to create just such a target—a new Santiago.

III. THE ONE-ARMED BANDIT'S BOOK

WALTZIN' MATILDA HAS A much greater knowledge of the outlaws and bounty hunters—the likeliest Santiago candidates—on the Inner Frontier, and she decides that the deadliest of them is the cyborg known as The One-Armed Bandit. An assassin who lost his right arm early in his career, he has replaced it with a prosthetic arm that is quite literally a cannon, capable of firing laser or sonic blasts, and powerful enough to demolish a city block.

She seeks him out, explains the situation, and offers him the chance to become Santiago, with the backing of the organization she and Dante are building for just that purpose.

He agrees —but he does so only to create a new identity that will let him kill and plunder at an even greater rate.

Waltzin' Matilda realizes her blunder and enlists various human and aliens to terminate The One-Armed Bandit, but he's as good as she thought he was, and he views killing all these agents of Matilda under the guise of Santiago as some kind of cosmic joke.

IV. SILVERMANE'S BOOK

DANTE HEARS WHAT has happened and realizes that physical skills aren't enough, and that he has to find a Santiago of strong moral character, one who will devote himself to the cause that created Santiago in the first place.

As the One-Armed Bandit goes on a rampage, Dante desperately searches the worlds of the Inner Frontier, and finally finds what he is looking for: bounty hunter Daniel Silvermane, a deeply religious, highly moral near-superman who has never lied, or broken a law, or lost a fight.

Dante convinces Silvermane that the ultimate calling for a man of his gifts is to become Santiago—but before he can assume the name, he must first eliminate the false Santiago who is causing such havoc.

Dante manipulates events so the two men meet, mano a mano, and Silvermane emerges triumphant. The One-Armed Bandit is dead, and there is once again a true Santiago.

V. SEPTEMBER MORN'S BOOK

EXCEPT THAT WHILE this Santiago shares Dante's values—or, at least, the values Dante thinks Santiago should
have—he's simply not up to the job.

True, he can outgun anyone on the Frontier, and can
whip ten times his weight in men or aliens—but Santiago was
more than a man: he was a *concept*, a state of mind, a genius
who personified the values he represented, who was able to
outsmart the best brains in the Democracy, who could antici-
pate his enemies' every move. Above all, he was a man who
could bring others to his cause. Silvermane tries, but his abilities start and end with his physical gifts.

The crisis comes when September Morn—singer, dancer,
writer, the finest artiste on the Inner Frontier—is kidnapped
and held for ransom. With no support, no followers,
Silvermane bulls his way in, totally fearless, totally outnum-
bered. He dies nobly . . . but when the dust clears, he's just as
dead as if he had died *ig*nobly, and September Morn is still a
prisoner.

VI. SANTIAGO'S BOOK

DANTE STUDIES THE SITUATION. Not only have the kid-
nappers laid a series of traps for any potential rescuer, but
the Navy is watching and waiting, ready to pounce on Santiago should he actually succeed in rescuing September Morn.

Finally Dante devises a plan, puts it into action, and miraculously emerges unscathed with September Morn. He is about to go back to trying to find the perfect Santiago, when Waltzin' Matilda and September Morn point out that *he* has become Santiago, that you don't have to be a physical giant with tremendous skills like Silvermane to be Santiago, that of all the previous Santiagos only Sebastian Cain had shown any skill with his weapons prior to becoming the legendary outlaw.

Dante has studied Santiago's methods for years. He's held the Navy at bay. He's acquired a following whose loyalty is beyond question. He's used his unique skills to pull off an unbelievable rescue. Throughout the course of his search for Santiago, he's tried to avoid confrontation, but when it was unavoidable he's always found a way to emerge triumphant.

But I'm a poet, he protests; all I ever wanted was to be the successor to Black Orpheus. The Frontier worlds need someone better than me to save them.

There *is* no one better than you, says Waltzin' Matilda.

Besides, *I'm* the poet, adds September Morn. You have a higher calling, and I'll devote the rest of my life to codifying it in verse.

If I'm to be Santiago, he says, I'll need a conduit to the worlds of the Inner Frontier, someone who can get me information that I need, someone I can trust.

You've got someone, says Waltzin' Matilda, stepping forward.

Me, too, says another outlaw. And me, chime in still more, swearing their loyalty to him and his cause.

When did I become Santiago, he asks curiously.

Look in a mirror, answers Waltzin' Matilda. You were always him; you just never knew it.

As he stares at his image in a mirror, and sees lines of character there that he has never noticed before, he comes to the surprising realization that she is right.

And that ends the story of how Santiago came once again to the Inner Frontier.

Proposed length: 130,000-150,000 words

SUSAN R. MATTHEWS

CAMPBELL NOMINEE Susan R. Matthews is another writer who ceased to be a newcomer the day her first book saw print. I haven't seen a new author collect a fan following so quickly since Lois McMaster Bujold entered the field 15 years ago.

Here Susan presents the outline for her forthcoming *Angel of Destruction*.

ANGEL OF DESTRUCTION

by Susan R. Matthews

Prologue

WE WITNESS A RAID on a warehouse complex located on one of the asteroids in the "shawl" of Rikavie, the asteroid belt between Port Charid and the Silume vector. The warehouse staff recognize the raiders as Langsarik pirates by their accents, information that they reveal in conversation amongst themselves, and their general appearance.

When the pirates vacate the warehouse with their booty they murder most of the staff, but appear to have forgotten three people who were imprisoned in the administrative control complex—leaving witnesses to their crime who can not only identify them as Langsariks, but provide the authorities with information on the organization of the pirates and where they intend to flee with the stolen goods.

One of the survivors is a Dolgorukij who is a member of the Angel of Destruction, whose savagery and evil is hinted at in the violence of the raid. Conveniently "forgotten" by the false Langsariks in order to give incriminating evidence as a witness, she has saved a few friends by calling an apparently serendipitous meeting just before the raid began.

Chapter One

IN THE OPENING SCENE Kazmer, a young Sarvaw mercantile captain or pilot-for-hire, runs into his friend Hilton in the back alleys of Port Charid, close to the Combine administrative buildings—an office/warehouse complex also used for temporary storage of cargo in transit to the Combine warehouse asteroid and to provide high-security management of small, high-value items. Kazmer is pleased to see Hilton—he hasn't seen Hilton for a year, not since before the settlement of the Langsariks at Port Charid—but surprised to meet him in the working district. Though from very different backgrounds the two men have shared experiences that form a strong bond between them. Hilton once saved Kazmer's life, and Kazmer has been courting Hilton's cousin on and ever since. They exchange guarded banter. Kazmer, whose recent arrival with a cargo will be important to the story later on, has been recruited for a secret mission by people he believes to be Langsariks; and believes Hilton must be involved. Hilton, on the other hand, has no idea of the real reasons for Kazmer's presence and is unwilling to admit that he has come for a job interview.

Kazmer proceeds to his meeting. He has been engaged by (false) Langsariks with insider information to pilot a freighter as part of a raid on one of the warehouse asteroids. He is to take possession of a valuable cargo and ferry it to a receiver in Tulatch system who will pay him off.

The Langsariks with whom Kazmer meets are careful to avoid any overtly incriminating statements, and Kazmer is eager to demonstrate equivalent discretion. He says nothing about having met Hilton. Kazmer doesn't personally recognize any of the false Langsariks with whom he is negotiating, but has no question as to their identities.

Though there is a risk involved and the activity is illegal, Kazmer likes the Langsariks. His chance meeting with Hilton has convinced him that Hilton goes along with this, and tips the balance in favor of going along with the offer. Kazmer agrees to take part in the raid with the agreement that no lives will be put at hazard, unlike recent and violent raids such as that shown in the Prologue.

Hilton has an interview with a man called "Uncle" Baritz, a Dolgorukij who represents the Combine shipping interests in Port Charid. He has come to ask for a job. Uncle Baritz has reached out to the exiled Langsarik community at Charid, taking measures to increase the comforts available to them and exerting himself to find employment for people who are willing to accept his patronage. Baritz, as well as others at Port Charid, claims to respect the fighting aspects and successful resistance to the enemy that the Langsariks displayed during their years as outlaws—respect on the "honorable enemy" model.

Hilton has rejected Baritz' overtures before but has come to the point where he wants money to buy things to make life easier for his family (and a motorcycle analog, as he is always wrecking his speed machines).

Uncle Baritz—so called in translation of a Dolgorukij title of respect and obligation, "my father's elder brother"—offers Hilton a job on the spot; and calls one of his foremen up to take Hilton out for orientation.

Hilton, while a little dubious about why Baritz should care, is genuinely grateful for the opportunity. Still, he can't help hoping that his friend Kazmer never finds out that one of the Langsarik's best captains has been forced to stoop to running an inventory control audit program.

Kazmer has left the meeting. The false Langsariks' mastermind—"Uncle" Baritz—enters the room. Plans are finalized to ensure that Kazmer will be intercepted by Fleet patrols in Tulatch, so that the evidence he will provide under interrogation will further implicate the Langsariks.

In addition to this, Baritz has just hired the nephew of Agenis the Deep-Minded herself; they will use Hilton as the final piece of spurious evidence that they will need to effect the utter and ignominious destruction of the Langsariks. Baritz is the senior member in Port Charid of an enclave of the Angel of Destruction, a secret society of Dolgorukij dedicated to furthering the "Pure Blood" by any means necessary. The Langsariks earned the undying enmity of the Angel of Destruction by preying on Combine shipping while they were pirates, and are further perceived by the Angel as a potential future threat to Dolgorukij economic interests.

The planned "Langsarik" raid goes well and smoothly. Kazmer participates fully in the raid. He witnesses the capture of the administrative staff, who have not been injured. A seemingly casual incident staged by the raiders draws Kazmer's attention to a Langsarik among the captive administrative staff, one he recognizes from one of Hilton's former crews. He also sees someone among the prisoners that he recognizes as Dolgorukij. As a Sarvaw, Kazmer knows Dolgorukij when he sees it.

He receives his cargo and departs the warehouse asteroid for the Silume vector and his rendezvous in Tulatch. The freighter Kazmer is piloting requires only a very small crew—all mercantile crew that Kazmer has hired for the event, none with any real knowledge of the Langsariks.

Once Kazmer is well on his way, however, the Angel shows its true colors. Warehouse staff are tortured until the passcodes for its accounts are surrendered. The Angel loots the warehouse's high-security stores and departs, setting off explosions that will destroy some—but not all—of the evidence (and attract official notice).

The Dolgorukij that Kazmer noticed is an operative of the Angel of Destruction, responsible for betraying the warehouse to the raiders; he leaves with the rest of the party. The Langsarik, an innocent bystander placed in the warehouse as a result of Baritz' patronage some weeks prior, is murdered; his body removed from the station for later disposal in order to make it seem that he left with the raiders, further implicating the Langsariks in the raid.

Kazmer and his crew witness the explosions on the warehouse asteroid from a distance. Too far away to return to offer aid and assistance, they reluctantly make the decision to complete their assignment, and take the Silume vector for Tulatch.

Nobody is happy with their involvement in what they now realize meant the deaths of the warehouse asteroid staff, and Kazmer faces considerable blame. He successfully convinces the crew, and himself believes, that there is nothing to be done about it now; best to complete their mission, and then get as far away from this as possible.

Chapter Two

GAROL VOGEL IS AT Chilleau Judiciary, listening to Jils Ivers debrief the First Secretary and the Second Judge over the events and findings at the Domitt Prison in Rudistal.

It has been a year and a half since Andrej Koscuisko cried Failure of Writ at the Domitt Prison. The judicial board of inquiry uncovered a wide-spread pattern of waste, fraud, and abuse resulting in the unrecorded deaths of an unknown number of Nurail prisoners or relocated parties.

The relocation camp at Rudistal has been converted to a displacement analysis facility under the efficient and respected administration of Captain Sinjosi Vopalar.

Andrej Koscuisko, who was called back to Rudistal to execute the judgment of the Bench, has completed a Tenth Level command termination exercise that is already notorious. This visible evidence of the displeasure of the Bench, however, may have unexpected negative public relations repercussions.

The Tenth Level is just too extreme; Koscuisko's execution of the Tenth Level was an extreme example; and Koscuisko himself is known to fiercely reject the claimed value of torture as a deterrent in the Bench's war against lawlessness and disorder.

Koscuisko remains at Rudistal awaiting transport to the Ragnarok, his next ship of assignment; Ivers disapproves of his posting to the Ragnarok, and the conversation will establish that Verlaine has obtained the posting by way of discipline or punishment for Koscuisko for having embarrassed the Bench. The entire incident has contributed to the loss of population from Jurisdiction control as displaced Nurail flee into an undeveloped area accessible through several newly discovered vectors—an area referred to as "Gonebeyond" space. While the Bench has no interest in Gonebeyond, it is contrary to the maintenance of good order for a bolt-hole to exist. Efforts to gain control of all vectors offering access is under way.

This leads directly to consideration of the situation at Port Charid, where the Langsariks have been resettled following the amnesty agreement engineered by Garol Vogel.

Though Port Charid is not within the boundaries of Chilleau Judiciary, it was under the Second Judge's personal patronage that the amnesty agreement was developed and executed. The Second Judge got a lot of very positive press out of the whole thing.

Now predation in the Charid area has become an issue, and there are disturbing indications that the Langsariks have not in fact accepted pacification. This touches on the prestige of the Second Judge, which is particularly tender just now in light of the highly visible conclusion of proceedings at Port Rudistal. In light of those proceedings and their potential impact on public confidence and civil order, the Second Judge is anxious to handle this matter with the utmost discretion, and to avoid the appearance of over-reacting at all costs. Garol and Jils are to travel to Charid, find out what is going on, and put an end to the predation one way or the other, but without doing anything that might reflect negatively on the rule of Law in the court of public opinion. Garol arrives at Port Charid in Rikavie. Traveling to the Langsarik enclave, Garol interviews the (former) Flag Captain Agenis, who has her hands full helping her people adjust to their very much reduced scope and reduced circumstances.

The personal relationship of mutual respect that developed between Garol and Agenis was a significant element in obtaining the peace agreement, and Garol is sympathetic to the plight of the Langsariks. Garol likes and respects her. He has an uncomfortable feeling that she may regret having trusted him, however, in light of the circumstances in which he finds her.

They discuss the unfortunate situation of the Langsariks. She denies any involvement in the recent predation (while admitting that some of "the young people" have engaged in some youthful acts of indiscretion). Garol cautions her strongly: the Bench will not tolerate any acts of rebellion or resistance. He may believe her, but he's not the one with the troops. She must control her "young people." Someone is raiding those warehouses, and the obvious target for blame is the Langsariks.

Agenis is unyielding: it's not her people. She'll do what she can and see if she can find anything out. As Garol prepares to leave, she asks him to look for Hilton, who has taken employment with Uncle Baritz in the Combine shipping headquarters in Port Charid.

Agenis wants Garol to take Hilton return a gift that Kazmer sent her daughter, so that Hilton can return it to Kazmer. Kazmer was here a few days ago but hasn't been seen since, and if he has any legitimate business in Port Charid Hilton is certain to have seen him. If Kazmer didn't have any legitimate business Garol will, of course, forget he ever heard about it. Garol agrees. Returning to the city Garol seeks Hilton out and is received by Uncle Baritz. While waiting for a guide to take Garol to where Hilton is on shift, Baritz engages Garol in small talk. Something that Baritz says will later strike Garol as possible evidence of secret knowledge concerning Langsarik predation, but it is more of an intuitive conviction than anything else (Uncle Baritz is not stupid and his remark could easily be interpreted in an entirely innocent way). Garol interviews Hilton, whom he remembers as having been present during the amnesty negotiations. Hilton looks older and has grown a little beard and a moustache, claiming it's because he thought it looked so dashing on Garol (who had been wearing a van Dyke at the time).

When asked about Kazmer, Hilton denies having seen him any time recently, but Garol divines that Hilton had seen Kazmer and fears he was involved in the most recent warehouse raid. It looks bad for the Langsariks: Kazmer has worked with Langsariks before, and why would he come to Charid to work a raid and potentially compromise the Langsariks—unless it was Langsariks who called him here?

Would he risk coming here at all unless at the request of a friend? Garol returns the gift Kazmer had sent Agenis' daughter without comment. Privately he is very sorry that Hilton is involved in bloody murder—excess killing being uncharacteristic of Langsariks, who were very conservative pirates—and sorry that Agenis is betrayed by her nephew, of whom she is very fond. Kazmer's ship, having come off the Silume vector, arrives at Tulatch . . . and runs into a waiting detachment of Jurisdiction Fleet commerce law enforcers. Taken by surprise, Kazmer considers destroying the ship to avoid being taken prisoner but cannot bring himself to murder the crew, whose reactions to the witnessed destruction of the warehouse asteroid have proved to him that they are only very marginally involved.

Taken prisoner and brought to processing at the Fleet administrative center at Tulatch, Kazmer considers his options. Believing Hilton to be fully involved, he decides that he must avoid interrogation at any cost in order to avoid being the instrument of Hilton's torture and execution. Not only is he fond of Hilton, he owes Hilton his life.

There is only one solution: and it is so extreme that Kazmer struggles with the conflict, while the in-briefing team taunts him with his fate—"I hear Andrej Koscuisko is between assignments, how would you like to have a little talk with him?"

(Since the judgment of the Bench has been executed against Administrator Geltoi, the soon-to-become-legendary Tenth Level Koscuisko performed is still very much in peoples' minds.)

Making his decision, Kazmer exercises his right as a member of the ethnically-defined Dolgorukij Combine to call upon the Malcontent for protection. His captors, disgusted, play with the idea of pretending they never heard, but—agreeing reluctantly amongst themselves that attempting such a deception is not really an option—they leave Kazmer alone to consider what he has done.

Chapter Three

JILS IVERS MEETS Garol in Charid with the news that one of the participants in the most recent Langsarik raid has been taken prisoner in Tulatch. Jils and Garol leave to interrogate the crew.

Meanwhile, in Tulatch, "Cousin" Stanoczk—an authorized representative of the Malcontent—arrives at the administrative center to interview Kazmer. They discuss the extremity of the decision that faces Kazmer and Stanoczk finds Kazmer fully sensitive to the gravity of the step he means to take.

The terms of the proposed quid-pro-quo are reviewed. Kazmer will trade himself to the Malcontent in return for never being asked who hired him for the job or who he saw in Port Charid; or, more generally, in order to protect a friend from reprisals associated with his participation in illegal activities.

Having agreed in principle on what the basis of the contract between Kazmer and the Malcontent is to be, Stanoczk demands and receives a full copy of the evidence against

Kazmer. Stanoczk formally invokes the "religious exception" that permits him to take custody of Kazmer. He puts the (symbolic) halter around Kazmer's neck; Kazmer has become a slave of the Malcontent.

Stanoczk leaves the administrative center with Kazmer in literal—if symbolic—tow. Kazmer is in shock: he had to do it and it worked, but he has still just given up his life, his freedom, his hopes for the future, and any chance that he might have had at Hilton's cousin, just to keep Hilton out of trouble. The sacrifice seems extreme, even if he had no alternative if he hoped to protect his friend Hilton, to whom he owed his life.

Stanoczk takes Kazmer to quarters to give him some time to adjust. Soon they will leave for the house of the Malcontent—on Azanry, in the heart of the Dolgorukij Combine.

In the rooms where Stanoczk is staying, Kazmer reviews the case against him. His suspicion that the Fleet had been tipped off as to his destination and arrival is confirmed by evidence on Record, and he realizes he has been set up. His mind racing, consumed with dread, Kazmer realizes that either Hilton set him up—which Kazmer can't believe—or Hilton was not involved at all.

So were they really even Langsariks?

Of course, since he would not have seen this information had he not elected the Malcontent, the Bench would still have used his evidence to identify Hilton for questioning. Hilton would have been tortured and killed whether or not Hilton was actually guilty of anything.

Somewhat reconciled, making up his mind to honor his part of the bargain, Kazmer reports his realizations to Stanoczk, who promises to take appropriate action. Garol and Jils arrive at Tulatch to find Kazmer gone. Though the administration initially refuses to admit that anyone of any such description was even ever in custody, once Garol and Jils prove their identities as Bench intelligence specialists the information is made available.

The record is clear on what happened, but having to go through official channels and negotiate with the Malcontent—who is by no means obligated to grant Garol access to Kazmer—is annoying, and will cost them time.

Jils initiates the interrogation of the rest of the crew while they wait. Once identified as "persons of interest" to a Bench intelligence specialist the ordinary Judicial inquiry process is suspended, and inquiry is conducted strictly on an interview-with-drugs method.

The crew is unquestionably guilty, but not of a very great deal. Garol and Jils discuss what to do with the crew; though they are quite possibly individually guilty of other actionable crimes, there isn't a killing offense in this one. After some conflict, Garol convinces Jils that that the best thing to do is to release them on parole.

Garol is pleasantly surprised when Stanoczk makes contact, suggesting that they meet. Jils comments that Stanoczk looks a great deal like Andrej Koscuisko; Stanoczk admits to a blood relationship, but claims that all Aznir look alike—something Garol interprets as embarrassment on Stanoczk's part, since it is patently not true.

Stanoczk offers to share evidence with Garol and Jils and discusses Kazmer's conclusions. Garol decides to return to the scene of the crime with Kazmer to see if the investigation team has made any discoveries since temporary repairs have been made which permit re-pressurizing the facility.

Uncle Baritz talks with his people about the news from Tulatch (which has been obtained illegally, it having been pointed out in previous scenes that Kazmer's release is strictly sub rosa). It's too bad about the Malcontent becoming involved, since that means that Kazmer's important incriminating evidence may be entirely wasted; but it's a mere inconvenience.

The potential involvement of the Malcontent may strengthen the Angel's plot, if properly handled, but it is imperative that the Malcontent not realize that it is being manipulated. It is pleasant for the Angel to contemplate using the Malcontent to further the aims of the Angel of Destruction in Port Charid, exploiting their old enemy in their program to gain primacy and power.

In the days after Chuvishka Kospodar was finally convinced to reluctantly withdraw his support from his Angelic enforcers the Malcontent denied sanctuary to members of the Angel of Destruction who were trying to evade identification, and escape. This intransigence on the part of the Malcontent enabled reactionary Sarvaw lynch mobs to carry out wholesale slaughter of any Angel who could be identified as such, and has led to an undying enmity on the Angel's part against the Malcontent.

Chapter Four

GAROL, JILS, STANOCZK, and Kazmer tour the raided warehouse, where a work crew is standing by waiting to for them to finish so that clean-up can begin. They discover the bodies of tortured men and women.

Kazmer is disgusted at himself for ever having been involved in something like this. It was only his conviction that Hilton was involved and his basic sympathy for the Langsariks that persuaded him to go ahead with it in the first place, what with his knowledge of a violent "Langsarik" raid in the recent past (the Prologue).

Trusting Hilton, he trusted the "Langsariks;" now he feels responsible at least in part for the torture and murder of the administrative staff, and he should have known better.

He remembers their trusting faces, worried, but hopeful; they were all alive when he left. There was this one . . . that one . . . Deeply engaged in beating himself up for the vicious attacks, Kazmer looks into dead faces, trying to remember their expressions when he saw them last. The others are engaged in reviewing some report or another. It occurs to Kazmer that there are bodies missing: the Langsarik isn't there; but neither is the Dolgorukij.

His concentration has attracted Garol's attention. Garol comes over to where Kazmer is looking at bodies to see what is going on. Kazmer explains the missing people; Jils (who has joined them) reminds him that portions of the warehouse were completely destroyed.

He insists that the two people he can't find were with the

others. Jils points out the bodies of the torture victims, held for separate analysis, and returns her attention to the report they have been reading. Kazmer goes over to examine the bodies of the torture victims, irrationally tormented by his inability to find those two people among the dead.

They are not there, but an aspect of the way in which one of the people was tortured upsets Kazmer so deeply that he calls for Stanoczk, demanding his attention.

In a POV transition Garol accompanies Stanoczk and Jils over to where Kazmer is standing. Kazmer is visibly deeply shocked. He and Stanoczk have an evident disagreement over the meaning of something, but it's not clear to Garol what is at issue. The evidence of physical torture is particularly gruesome, yes, but what else is going on?

Stanoczk shuts Kazmer up. The party leaves the warehouse asteroid and returns to Port Charid. Once in secure quarters Garol insists on a debriefing. Kazmer in turn insists on telling Garol: it's not Langsariks at all. It's the Angel of Destruction.

This means nothing to Garol, and Kazmer and Stanoczk argue about it. Evidently the way in which one of the dead had been tortured was a trademark of sorts, and Garol has to admit he's never seen anything quite like it (something to do with a prayerful kneeling position with bowed head and clasped hands together with entrails).

Stanoczk, however, continues to reject Kazmer's assertion until Garol impatiently demands an explanation. Reluctantly, Stanoczk explains the role of the fanatic terrorist splinter group known as the Angel of Destruction in the atrocities associated with the integration of Sarvaw into the Dolgorukij Combine (characterized rather more forcefully by Kazmer).

Expressing his continued unwillingness to believe what Kazmer is suggesting, Stanoczk explains to Garol that the Angel of Destruction was outlawed by the civil and religious authorities shortly after it had done the dirty work of destroying Sarvaw resistance—er—after the Sarvaw nations were assimilated. Kazmer insists that the existence of the missing bodies is a crucial piece of evidence. Any party wishing to see the Langsariks blamed would naturally remove the Langsarik's corpse, in order to prevent raising questions about why he had been murdered by "his own people;" but there is no reason for the Dolgorukij not to be there—unless the Dolgorukij, not the Langsarik, was the person who betrayed the warehouse to the raiders.

Garol knows that a Dolgorukij was one of the sole survivors of the Prologue raid, as well. He shares this with Kazmer and Stanoczk for their mutual consideration. How likely is it that a single Dolgorukij would survive being murdered, one way or another, on two different raids? It could happen, but Kazmer's right, it's suspicious.

Garol gets a call from First Secretary Verlaine, inquiring about his progress. (Some interplay with Mergau Noycannir may be possible as the First Secretary's displeasure increases.) As the Judiciary most intimately involved with the highly publicized settlement of the Langsariks, Chilleau Judiciary is coming under fire.

The capture of Kazmer's stolen goods in Tulatch generated some media attention because of its association with Charid and the Langsariks; and once aroused, the media has become focused on the latest warehouse raid, with its lurid details of torture and murder.

Timat Judiciary—in which Port Charid is located—is pressuring the Second Judge for results, in response to complaints lodged by the governments represented by the shipping interests at Port Charid.

Garol expresses a certain amount of diffidence about whether it is as simple as it seems. Verlaine is not interested. Garol is expected to get results, and soon. Public opinion suspects that the Langsarik pirates are returning to their old ways. If that's what public opinion maintains, the Bench will have no choice but to take action, or risk visibly failing in its duty to maintain public order and the common weal.

Standing on his position as a Bench intelligence specialist technically subordinate to the Bench but not to any given Judge, Garol pulls rank on the First Secretary (with all due respect, of course) to win himself a little time. He has been put on notice that he must generate results.

Chapter Five

FOLLOWING UP ON Kazmer's story of what happened and how he got involved, Garol and Jils ask Kazmer to retrace the steps he took to reach his meeting in the opening scenes of the novel. Kazmer is unable to find his position in the blind alleys that make a maze of the back streets of Port Charid.

Garol is not surprised; temporary warehouse buildings are featureless and easily reconfigured, and that is exactly what Garol himself would do, if he had set up a secret meeting.

Garol knows approximately where he is, however—he's in an area near the offices of Uncle Baritz, and he wants to have a meeting with that man. Bringing Kazmer in to the warehouse with him, Garol asks one of the administrative staff to go get Hilton.

He tells Kazmer that Hilton has something for him (the gift that Agenis is trying to return through Hilton) and goes off to find Uncle Baritz, leaving Jils with Kazmer. He is by no means convinced by Kazmer's "electing the Malcontent" story, even with Stanoczk's endorsement; and half-expects Kazmer to attempt to escape.

Rather than being determined to keep Kazmer in custody, Garol is interested in seeing what will happen between Hilton and Kazmer, in light of recent developments.

Hilton and Kazmer meet. There is initially a great deal of awkwardness, and Jils withdraws to a discrete distance. Hilton asks Kazmer how he could do such a thing; Kazmer insists he thought he was dealing with Langsariks right up until the moment he saw the bodies.

Hilton reproaches Kazmer for thinking that Langsariks would engage in raiding after having promised the Bench they wouldn't. Kazmer knows better: he's heard stories from Hilton's cousin.

Hilton indignantly retorts that joy-riding and raiding warehouses are hardly comparable. He is almost immediately distracted from his personal outrage, however, by his confusion over why Kazmer is here and not locked up. When Kazmer explains reluctantly that he has elected the Malcontent and isn't even Kazmer any more (though he is retaining his personal name, it is only for the time being). Hilton is shocked.

He demands to know what could have motivated so extreme a step. Kazmer can only shrug and repeat that he thought the raid involved real Langsariks. Hilton puts two and two together and realizes that Kazmer was protecting him. He falls speechless.

Garol finds Uncle Baritz. Expressing his apparently genuine admiration for the Langsariks, Uncle Baritz counsels Garol not to jump to any conclusions. Garol gets the impression that Baritz knows or suspects that the Langsariks are behind the raid, but wants to protect them.

Garol explains that as part of his effort to ensure that the Langsariks are not unjustly accused he is doing background searches on everyone who was on shift at the raided warehouse at the time of the raid. He asks Uncle Baritz if he has knowledge of any particular individuals who might have been working there—it seems that the records are not complete.

Uncle Baritz thinks about it and agrees that he thinks one of his former employees might have gone to work for that shipper; the employee had been fired for cause, but a request had come for a reference several days after the incident.

He didn't hear anything more about it and would be surprised if anyone would hire the man, but experienced labor is difficult to find at Port Charid and maybe the raided shipper had taken the chance.

He offers to have one of his staff research the employee he has in mind and forward the information to Garol, if Garol can provide contact instructions. Garol willingly agrees and terminates the interview.

Returning to where he left Kazmer and Jils, he leaves the area before debriefing the interview with Jils. He has been careful not to give Uncle Baritz any information that might be useful. While Uncle Baritz might have been able to claim ignorance, it is less suspicious for him to have readily offered information.

Stanoczk believes that Kazmer is on the wrong track anyway, but though there was nothing in the interview that would indicate that Uncle Baritz had secret knowledge there was no indication that he didn't have secret knowledge either. Garol is becoming suspicious, even in the absence of evidence.

Uncle Baritz takes steps to have Kazmer removed from Port Charid by arranging for Stanoczk to be recalled to port Halud in the Raze system. His confidence in his ability to do so without being discovered by the Malcontent as an agent of the Angel of Destruction continues a thread of uncertainty over the potential relationship between the Angel and the Malcontent, claims of historical animosity notwithstanding.

Having heard from Hilton that Garol is back in Port Charid with Kazmer, Agenis asks for a meeting with Kazmer on Ygraine's behalf. Agenis' stated opposition aside, Kazmer and Ygraine were well on the way to developing a genuine relationship; the developments in Kazmer's life are deeply painful for both of them.

While Kazmer and Ygraine talk, Agenis takes the opportunity to express her concerns to Garol. She can't afford to let herself (by implication, the Langsariks) be set up. The Bench has confiscated all weapons of any significance, and they have no ships capable of deep space travel; the nearness of access to the Silume vector—and escape to Gonebeyond—is a bitter mockery.

They are disarmed and immobilized, helpless to resist any action the Bench might take. Garol got them in to this. He's got to get them out, one way or the other.

Garol admits to the justice of her demands, but doesn't know if he'll be able to stop the momentum of something that has already started. He promises to do everything he can and to come and tell her personally if he fails to win protection for them.

They leave to return to port Charid.

Chapter Six

KAZMER AND STANOCZK struggle with each other over what should be done. Kazmer thinks Stanoczk should call in the Bench, expose the Angel, and protect the Langsariks. Stanoczk says it's not the Malcontent's problem.

Furthermore, the existence of the Angel—if it is confirmed, which is by no means something Stanoczk is willing to admit—is too great a reproach to the Combine to be exposed with outsiders.

Kazmer says he'll go to the Bench; Stanoczk says that Kazmer won't, and that that is an end to the discussion. Kazmer's hands are tied since he (a) gave his word of honor and (b) has no legal standing to make a complaint or give evidence under Jurisdiction, having elected the Malcontent.

Kazmer confronts Stanoczk over private reasons Stanoczk might have for not wanting to believe that the Angel of Destruction could be involved: as a descendent of Chuvishka Kospodar, Stanoczk's family enjoys the fruits of the atrocities committed by the Angel in the past. We find out that Stanoczk is a sort of living sacrifice to the Malcontent for atonement of sins committed by the Angel in Sarvaw many years ago.

Stanoczk receives a priority message from his ecclesiastical superiors requiring his immediate presence outside of system and makes preliminary arrangements to leave. Neither he nor Kazmer is happy about the timing of this summons but Stanoczk does not believe that he has any alternatives to obedience—he is a Malcontent after all.

The Angel, concerned about Garol's continued presence and Garol's contacts with the Langsariks, decides to use the next planned action to get rid of the problem. Hilton will be used to betray Garol into a trap.

Hilton is working in the warehouse when an interesting sight attracts his attention. He recently witnessed a flamboyant scene involving one of Uncle Baritz' Dolgorukij employees, who either quit or was terminated under confused circumstances. The employee subsequently went to work for another shipping concern.

This repeats a pattern that the reader has seen earlier in the book, but which Hilton has no reason to recognize or suspect.

Now he recognizes the man as the person who is talking to the warehouse foreman, and casually manages to get near enough to hear some of what they are saying. What he hears convinces him that the former employee has returned to report on the successful protection/concealment of critical evidence—linking Uncle Baritz with the recent raids—among the cargo manifest of a transport due to depart from the fired Dolgorukij's new place of employment within thirty-six hours.

Putting two and two together, Hilton realizes that this crucial information could solve the problem that faces the Langsariks and put an end to the Bench's suspicions about their involvement. He slips away from his workplace to find Garol and put him on alert.

Acting on Hilton's information, Garol—after having tried without success to contact Stanoczk and Kazmer—leaves Kazmer to wait for Jils, and takes a small personal transport to the warehouse asteroid in question. The information was a set-up. No sooner does Garol arrive than he finds himself in the middle of a firefight, an assassination attempt under cover of a "Langsarik" raid.

Though initially tempted to permit himself to be captured—in order to find out for himself once and for all what is going on—the evidence he has seen of the fate of survivors of previous raids, and the probability that this raid has been set up to kill him, dissuade him from such a rash action.

Wounded, Garol manages to conceal himself in the warehouse, knowing that he will have very little time to reach his transport between the time that the Angel vacates the premises and the detonation of the charges they have planted—and hoping that his transport has not been discovered and disabled.

At Port Charid, Jils returns to quarters and finds Hilton waiting impatiently for her. He passes on the information he brought Garol and word of where Garol has gone. Then, anxious to finish out his shift and see Agenis with the news, Hilton leaves to return to his work site, having made an appointment to go to Agenis later.

Jils is concerned. Though she understands and respects Garol's realization that immediate action was required, he has placed himself in a potentially exposed position. Bench Intelligence Specialists are good at surviving that, but there's no reason to take unnecessary risks; she departs immediately for the warehouse asteroid.

Meanwhile, back on the warehouse asteroid, Garol has realized that he is more severely incapacitated than he had thought. Having extreme difficulty getting to his transport (and still in doubt whether it has been taken out of commission one way or another) Garol knows that his time is running out when he is rescued by Jils.

Garol already knows there are no survivors that they would be able to reach in time. They escape from the warehouse asteroid moments with mere moments to spare before detonation of charges placed by the Angel destroys the warehouse and dissipates its atmosphere.

Jils attempts to conceal the evidence of their survival by navigating as though the ship is a piece of debris blasted off the asteroid's surface.

Chapter Seven

GAROL AND JILS return to Port Charid, where Stanoczk is looking for them. Though this recent event supports Kazmer's claim that the Angel is present in Port Charid—and further identifies the agent of the Angel as Uncle Baritz—Stanoczk has his marching orders, and washes his hands of the entire affair. Claiming that he must return to the Combine for Kazmer's in-processing Stanoczk prepares to leave Port Charid. Before he goes, however, he relays the information that Hilton has disappeared. Aunt Agenis contacted Stanoczk in Garol's absence when Hilton failed to appear for the visit he had promised earlier.

She has asked Uncle Baritz about Hilton; Uncle Baritz claims that Hilton has run away—and that some valuable property has disappeared. Agenis doesn't believe Hilton would steal or run; Kazmer agrees with her. However, Stanoczk insists that Kazmer leave with him immediately.

Stanoczk's evasiveness is both disappointing to Garol and worrisome—does Stanoczk reject the idea that the Angel of Destruction is active because it's unbelievable? Or because Stanoczk is a representative of the Angel? Garol has more immediate problems, however.

The First Secretary has received an anonymous tip of contraband being concealed within the Langsarik settlements. Jils brings the information to Garol, who is in hiding. This is suspiciously like Hilton's tip; one way or the other, Garol suspects a trap of some sort, and asks Jils to find out where the tip came from. In the mean time the First Secretary, unable to contact Garol directly and fed up with pressure for action from Timat Judiciary, sends a strike force to the Langsarik settlements. The search teams find the promised contraband and confiscate it, arresting a number of Langsariks to be taken out of system for processing.

Garol abandons his silence and travels to Port Charid's administrative center to issue a strong formal protest. Standing on his rights as a Bench intelligence specialist with powers of extraordinary discretion, Garol demands the immediate release of the prisoners and takes personal custody of the arrested Langsariks. He sees Uncle Baritz among the interested parties in the administrative center. While unable to discern whether Uncle Baritz is surprised to see him, Garol knows that he has lost any advantage of surprise.

He will have to struggle harder than he has ever fought before, if he is to prevent a grotesque miscarriage of justice—an injustice that will be his fault, since he is the man who persuaded the Langsariks to accept the vulnerable situation in which they now find themselves.

Chapter Eight

GAROL CARRIES THE DAY, but only temporarily. The First Secretary acknowledges that his intervention was premature, and releases a statement claiming that the raid—an unfortunate error in procedure—was the result of excess enthusiasm without adequate authority on the part of the Fleet group that performed the raid. Fleet is ordered to withdraw its troops and release its prisoners. At the same time, however, Garol gets a strict ultimatum from the First Secretary, who resents being called to account. Solve the Langsarik problem soon, Verlaine orders, or I'll solve it for you.

Garol is put on notice that his Brief will expire within three days, at which time—absent results that would obviate the requirement—a Bench interrogations group would be sent in to process the Langsariks for disposition: penal colony, prison, execution, or the Bond.

Garol resists but cannot prevail. He has run out of time, and is tormented by his conviction that something is just not adding up. He is convinced that there are secrets yet to be discovered, and despairs of protecting the Langsariks. In the excitement, Hilton's unexplained disappearance has dropped to a rather low level of priority. Hilton has been locked up by the Angel, who is holding him for use in the final action that will cap the campaign against the Langsariks. Bound and imprisoned in the dark, cold and hungry, Hilton wonders how he will find a way out of his predicament, and faces the possibility that there is no escape.

In transit on the Silume vector, a rather depressed Stanoczk gets a response from port Halud—no instructions were issued through appropriate channels; the summons was false, and apparently intended solely to deny the Bench access to information that Kazmer and Stanoczk might have to offer.

At the same time, Halud offers valuable information in response to queries Stanoczk sent earlier. Intelligence confirms the resurgence of the Angel of Destruction. It appears to be drawing its resources from Port Charid—as Kazmer has been insisting.

Though the situation at Port Charid might look like a Bench problem, the Malcontent has now acquired a stake in the outcome. The Combine is morally responsible for the Angel of Destruction, and must police itself.

Stanoczk is to do whatever he deems necessary to stop the flow of resources from Port Charid into Angel control and to destroy the Angel at Port Charid. Reaching their target exit system Stanoczk arranges with their respective parent shipping companies to hire several freight transports that are currently in stasis at their respective warehouse asteroids in the "shawl" of Rikavie, ostensibly to carry relief cargo to a disaster area within easy reach of the Silume vector. Then he and Kazmer return to the Silume vector for Rikavie and Port Charid.

At Port Charid, the Angel takes stock. Garol isn't dead, but the Bench is tired of waiting for him to do something, so the effect is the same. The Bench will shortly be terminating the Langsariks as a free people, which will terminate the Angel's cover for predation at Port Charid. It remains only to plan the final action.

Before the Bench sweeps the Langsarik settlements a final raid must take place. Combine warehouses have been safe so far, a potentially compromising element when the Combine warehouses typically present rich pickings for cargo theft. The Angel has been systematically clearing the Combine warehouses—Dolgorukij stealing from Dolgorukij to fund the holy enterprise—and is now ready to cover its theft with a final phony Langsarik raid.

Hilton's body, discovered on site after the raid has been conducted, will prove to the Bench that Langsariks infiltrated the Combine warehouses and compromised security to allow the raiders access. Insurance will cover the losses supposedly suffered by Combine interests for cargo missing from the Combine warehouses.

It remains only to make a final pass of the Combine's warehouse asteroid to ensure that everything is in place; and the Angel's punishment campaign against the Langsariks will be complete, leaving the Angel of Destruction in effective if secret control of Port Charid and permanently neutralizing a potentially dangerous enemy.

Chapter Nine

GAROL RETURNS THE LANGSARIK prisoners to the Langsarik settlement and shares his bad news. He's always been straight with them; they've always been straight with him. He no longer believes that they have anything to do with the supposed Langsarik predation, but he has been out-maneuvered.

Now he advises them to leave by any means possible, even if it means stealing transport resources and escaping to Gonebeyond. He could be stripped of his position and executed for counseling escape, and his candor only proves to the Langsariks that he is being as honest with them as possible—and that he does in fact trust them.

The problem is that there is no appropriate transport available. They can get from Port Charid to the warehouse asteroids; freighters and autoshuttles make such transits at the rate of several departures a day.

Such cargo lift freighters are not, however, deep-space vehicles capable of vector transit; and stealing a cargo lift freighter would surely result in an alarm that would transmit a global warning to the warehouse asteroids. Uncle Baritz might be able to help them—but Garol must reluctantly reveal that he believes Uncle Baritz to be behind the plot against the Langsariks from the get-go.

While Garol is discussing these depressing issues with a Langsarik governing council and strategizing possible solutions, a newcomer is announced. It's Stanoczk, with Kazmer. He has a deal to propose to the Langsariks, one he must ask Garol not to hear: he has transport, but he needs a favor before they go. Small groups of Langsariks can travel in secret by autoshuttle from Port Charid to warehouse asteroids where Stanoczk has engaged freighters to carry relief supplies to Canrill. Once there, they will "steal" Stanoczk's cargo and depart for the Silume vector, there to travel to

Gonebeyond space.

The Malcontent's motivation is to render atonement to the Langsariks for the threat presented to them by the Angel of Destruction: and to use the Langsariks themselves to obtain vengeance for the dead, and put an end to the Angel's activities.

The Angel of Destruction ferries Hilton to the Combine warehouses and puts him in place to be found as a victim of "accidental" death. Hilton knows now that he has only a matter of hours to live.

He wrestles with despair before turning his attention to taking as many of his enemy as possible with him when they come to finish the job. His experience in repairing his speed machines enables him to construct a detonator for an explosive device that he McGivers; he means to use the manacles with which he is bound as the final link in the circuit. When someone comes for Hilton, however, it's not the Angel—it's Kazmer.

Fortunately Kazmer reveals his identify before Hilton blows them both up. Now the two men are even, and nothing further that Hilton has to say about it can prevent Kazmer from marrying Hilton's cousin . . . except, of course, for the fact that Kazmer is a Malcontent now, and will never be in a position to marry anybody.

Chapter Ten

THE ANGEL IS unpleasantly surprised when its "Langsarik" raid on the Combine warehouses starts earlier than anticipated . . . and then even more unpleasantly surprised to discover that these are genuine Langsariks. There is no cargo to speak of to pirate; but the Langsariks, oddly enough, don't seem to care. The administrative staff of the warehouse complex is rounded up. Uncle Baritz is not too concerned; he has set up a tip to go to Fleet to expose the "Langsarik" raid, and since these genuine Langsariks don't know that Fleet will be coming, they will fall easy prey to the Fleet's police ships.

Working from a pull list of some sort, the Langsariks separate people into two groups. Uncle Baritz finds himself in a small group comprised entirely of members of the Angel of Destruction (although not all of his operatives have apparently been identified).

Placed in restraints, Uncle Baritz' group is marched to a transport and loaded. Supervising the loading is Cousin Stanoczk, with Kazmer by his side. Uncle Baritz reproaches Stanoczk bitterly for his treachery—aiding Langsariks against the true Blood—but his rebukes are ignored.

Uncle Baritz realizes that they are to be returned to the Combine and processed by the Malcontent according to the Malcontent's own requirements and proprieties. The Angel has lost this round: but the Angel will win the war, and the Blood will reign triumphant, Malcontent or no Malcontent.

At Port Charid, Jils Ivers—who has not been privy to Stanoczk's plan—comes to the Langsarik settlement in search of Garol. She finds the settlement deserted and Garol himself imprisoned, rendering her news of a planned Langsarik raid on the Combine warehouse asteroid a little anti-climactic.

Garol joins Jils with Fleet as they hasten toward their

target, hoping to catch the Langsariks red-handed. They arrive too late; there is an entire fleet of freighters at the Silume vector—too far away to be intercepted.

By this time Jils and Garol both realize that the freighter fleet contains the Langsariks; and that their destination is Gonebeyond space, that impoverished but free no man's land beyond the reach of the Jurisdiction.

While Jils' rescue/intercept mission arrived too late to catch the Langsariks, their arrival apparently flushed the pirates before they had a chance to mine the warehouses and destroy the evidence of their raid. Since such an event has been a characteristic of recent "Langsarik" predation, however, Garol suggests that detonation of some charges near the warehouse would be consistent with the Langsarik modus operandi.

Jils agrees that such an explosion will enable them to publish an official report stating that the Langsariks were destroyed at the warehouse, thus satisfying public demands for pursuit and punishment of the perpetrators. Several large and showy explosions are set off accordingly to present the appearance of the catastrophic destruction of a warehouse's atmosphere.

Garol reports to the Bench. His mission has ended in success and failure. Success: Langsarik predation has been ended. Though the facilities on the Combine warehouse asteroid survived the raid this time, steps were taken to enable a plausible claim that the Langsariks were destroyed by the Fleet on arrival.

As for the freighters that escaped from the Combine warehouse asteroid, they had been hired on emergency mission to relieve a population suffering from the aftermath of a natural disaster; the Langsariks apparently took advantage of the transport opportunity, recognizing that they were out of time.

The Bench might have its questions, but the Bench's policy is to avoid confrontation with the Dolgorukij Combine where the Malcontent is concerned, since the Malcontent has been in a position to offer significant favors to the Bench in the past—all for the maintenance of good order, the rule of Law, and the public welfare, of course.

The Langsariks may have been permitted to escape, but the public doesn't know that and they aren't coming back, and the public relations issue is no longer an issue; First Secretary Verlaine elects to accept Garol's report and call it finished.

As a side issue, an irregularity with the documentation maintained by the Combine's shipping administration offices in Port Charid with respect to the looted Combine warehouse asteroid has apparently been identified by the Malcontent's forensic accounting commando. Insurance fraud may have been contemplated, but the situation—the Malcontent has assured Garol—is completely under control.

The Langsarik problem has been solved, if in an unexpected manner and at great personal cost to Garol Vogel—who must bear the humiliation of having been manipulated, used, deceived, and finally betrayed by the Langsariks. This is a crushing blow to Garol's personal prestige, or would be if Bench Intelligence Specialists had personal prestige that could be touched by any such element. Verlaine interviews Jils about Garol's exact involvement in the escape of the Langsariks; she declines to provide any indication one way or the other about whether Garol set the whole thing up himself, and once again Verlaine elects to take the prudent way out and leave it lie.

In private Garol Vogel is deeply depressed and disillusioned: the only way in which he was able to save the Langsariks from suffering imprisonment, torture, slavery, and death was to engineer their escape from Jurisdiction in collusion with representatives from the Dolgorukij Combine.

Furthermore, what Garol has seen of Combine operatives has convinced him that the Combine potentially represents more real a threat to the rule of Law than any seventeen Gonebeyond spaces combined. They have organization, intelligence networks, resources, and a serene conviction of their own racial superiority. These are worrying indications of trouble to come. For now—things are quiet, the Langsariks are out of reach, and a disaster has been averted.

In the final scene, Cousin Stanoczk surprises Garol in the street of some unnamed port city and suggests they go sit down for a drink. Garol is not at all inclined to drink with Stanoczk, whom he does not trust; but he is curious about how the fleet fared on its journey, and how Kazmer might be adjusting to life without possibility of parole.

Stanoczk surprises Garol by explaining that Kazmer is no longer among the ranks of the Malcontent—but no, he's not dead, he's just not Malcontent. Garol didn't think that was possible.

Stanoczk explains.

The Malcontent took Kazmer as its own in return for guaranteeing that Kazmer would not be forced to give evidence that would compromise his friend Hilton, or speak about what and who he saw when he visited Port Charid. As it turned out, however, Kazmer did report the compromising information to a bona fide Bench representative—Garol Vogel—as well as details on his visit to Port Charid. The Malcontent did not provide the single thing that Kazmer needed, protection from the threat of Bench reprisals against Kazmer's friend Hilton.

Therefore, the agreement that Kazmer made with the Malcontent is null and void, and the Malcontent has no further claim to Kazmer, body or soul. Just as well, Stanoczk says; Kazmer was turning out to be a lousy Malcontent anyway. All indications were that the renegade Sarvaw mercenary had gone chasing off to Gonebeyond space after some woman he thought he'd find there. Garol decides that he can drink to that.

"He had broken every rule in the book, and even though the rules did not apply to those who carried the Brief of a Bench Intelligence Specialist there was something profoundly wrong with the system when plain justice could only be obtained through acts that were illegal.

How much longer could this go on?

How much longer could he go on with this?

Gonebeyond space.

It was looking better every day.

Garol touched the rim of his glass to that in the out-stretched hand of the Malcontent "Cousin" Stanoczk; and decided that it was enough for now that the Langsariks at least were free."

JOE HALDEMAN

JOE HALDEMAN IS ANOTHER of our bonafide giants. He's won five Hugos, a handful of Nebulas, he was a Worldcon Guest of Honor at a relatively young age, he's sold short stories and novels and screenplays, and he's written an acknowledged classic, *The Forever War*.

A lot of Joe's books are colored by his experiences in Vietnam, and here, along with a *very* brief outline to his Hugo-winning *Forever Peace*, which he could probably have sold just by scribbling the title on a napkin, he also gives us the synopsis to his mainstream novel, *1968*.

FOREVER PEACE

by Joe Haldeman

HUMANS ARE LOSING their first interstellar war. Doing war-related research, scientists stumble on the ultimate weapon—a way to recreate the conditions of the Big Bang. Everything destroyed, start over.

Alternatively, the war is "just" among humans, but the weapon discovered is the same.

They can do one of two things: Push the button and take them with us. Or find a way to make war impossible, forever.

1968

by Joe Haldeman

MOST NOVELS USE the telescope, so to speak, and the hidden microphone—looking over characters' shoulders and eavesdropping on them. This novel is going to also use the kaleidoscope and the fun-house mirror. The fun-house mirror will be the warped perceptions and memories of PFC Darcy Speidel, a.k.a. Spider, the sole survivor of a ferocious ambush in August, 1968, in the Central Highlands of Vietnam. Unable to cope directly with the terrible memory—which includes the memory of his cowardice—he retells the story to himself and others in increasingly more fantastic versions, as he sinks into paranoid schizophrenia.

The literary kaleidoscope will be a technique borrowed from John Dos Passos's USA Trilogy (which not coincidentally contains the novel 1919): I hope to reconstruct the feeling and meaning of that year in a running montage of short pieces—biographies of historically significant people and fictional archetypes, advertisements, news stories, snatches of song—which will serve to illuminate the novel, both in the modern sense and the ancient one, as well as structurally separating the chapters.

The story starts out as a conventional realistic combat tale. Spider is a typical soldier of that war, an unwilling draftee who is trying to reconcile John Wayne with John

Lennon in the otherworldly context of Vietnam. He's neither hero nor coward—but it's obvious that the war is destroying him by degrees; sapping his will, his ability to think and feel—stretching his nerves to the breaking point. This is his fourth month in Vietnam, his third in combat. With eight months left, Spider is utterly certain he is going to die.

His platoon walks into a perfect ambush. Half of them are cut down in the first few seconds of withering crossfire. Snipers start picking off the rest from concealed positions. Spider is fighting panic—and then a grenade goes off, giving him only a few superficial wounds but disintegrating the man next to him, spattering Spider with blood and brains. He snaps; throws his weapon away and runs for it—but in four steps slams headlong into a tree limb, knocking himself unconscious.

He wakes up to the sound of sporadic gunfire, the enemy soldiers walking around finishing off the wounded. One of them kneels by him, shouting something in Vietnamese. He takes Spider's wallet, grenades, ammunition, and first aid packet, while Spider tries not to blink or breathe. Then he picks up his AK-47, gives Spider a long look, and walks away. Could he tell Spider was alive? We'll never know.

Spider lies there motionless, playing dead, until dark. Then he moves back down the trail a quarter-mile and falls into exhausted sleep. He wakes up to the sound of American voices, and almost gets himself killed as he crashes toward them through the woods.

They tend to his wounds and listen to his description of the ambush, which is already beginning to deviate from reality.

ANOTHER STORY IS developing alongside Spider's, converging with it. The two will meet briefly at Walter Reed Army Hospital, and diverge again.

Beverly Hart dated Spider for a while before he was drafted, and writes him regularly, more out of a sense of duty than emotional involvement. To Spider, of course, she's "his girl," and she doesn't disillusion him, though she knows the ultimate confrontation could be devastating. Her roommate points out that there won't be any confrontation if Spider's telling the truth about the amount of action his outfit is seeing, after the 1968 Tet Offensive. He couldn't possibly survive a year.

Beverly sometimes mentions her roommate in letters, but never tells Spider that he's male, has hair down to his shoulders, sings anti-war songs in a coffee house, and makes a sort of living retailing marijuana. She herself has one foot in the counterculture and one in the American mainstream: although she reads Mao and gets high and hangs around in bohemian places, she also goes to college, model student, halfway to a degree in business. She suspects that sooner or later she'll have to choose between the two styles of life, and in August it happens: her boyfriend talks her into going with him to demonstrate at the Democratic National Convention in Chicago; the riot "radicalizes" her.

She goes home and writes Spider a letter explaining everything, but he never gets it. He's in a hospital in Tuy Hoa, headed for Walter Reed.

THERE ARE AUTOBIOGRAPHICAL aspects to both narrative threads of 1968. In the sixties I had long hair and played guitar in a coffee house, and was also an unwilling draftee and combat soldier. Like Spider, on my last day in combat I was severely wounded in an action that killed all the other men in my unit, though in my case it was just a squad (four people), not a platoon (twenty-some). I spent five months in army hospitals.

1968 is an author in search of a missing year. I landed in Vietnam February 29th, 1968, after having spent the previous several months in the controlled isolation of combat training, For the whole year I was simply part of the Green Machine, enjoying only sporadic contact with reality. People sometimes sent newspapers from home, or at least the front pages. I remember sitting in the jungle staring unbelieving at a photograph of Washington in flames; I remember the pictures of King and Kennedy shot down. I didn't know about the Chicago riots, the invasion of Czechoslovakia, the anarchist rebellion in France, genocide in Biafra, Dr. Spock a jailbird, the Nuclear Non-Proliferation Treaty—things that didn't interest the editors of the Pacific Stars & Stripes.

I started this novel in 1974, while studying at the Iowa Writers Workshop, and workshopped the first part of it in John Cheever's class there. I put it away (in spite of a good reception) for my own mental health; five years was not enough distance. Now I can do it.

In another very specific way, the novel started in 1968, on the 4th of October. I was in the army hospital at Tuy Hoa, my first day on crutches after a couple of weeks confined to bed and wheelchair with multiple bullet and fragment wounds.

The hospital was suddenly crowded to overflowing with injured Vietnamese civilians, mostly women and children. It had been Election Day, and the Viet Cong decided to demonstrate against the election by simultaneously attacking various polling places.

The hospital was a madhouse, a charnel house. Orders came down to transfer to other areas every American patient who could be moved. I hobbled aboard a crowded DC-3 from Air America, the CIA's airline, and as I moved toward the rear I passed the man who would become Spider. Most of the passengers were obviously wounded or ill, but this man was tanned, healthy-looking, smiling—and strapped down to a stretcher, confined within a straitjacket, staring, evidently Thorazine-ed to the gills. Pinned to his straitjacket was a tag saying "paranoid schizophrenic."

At that time I had only written three stories and perhaps a thousand poems, but I knew I was going to write a novel about Vietnam, and was collecting notes. As the plane taxied down the cratered runway, I knew I'd met the book's viewpoint character.

To make sense of this war, he would have to be totally insane.

JACK McDEVITT

JACK McDEVITT HAS been knocking at the door of super-stardom for a few years now. His stories often make the award ballots, his novels are always well-received, and his sales have been steadily mounting.

Here he becomes the only writer in this book to give us two synopses to different editions of the same novel, *The Hercules Text.*

The Hercules Text:
Old and New

by Jack McDevitt

Synopsis for 1986 edition:

AT THE GODDARD SPACE CENTER in Greenbelt, MD., Ed
Gambini's Skynet team notes that a pulsar has apparently
shut off. The pulsar is located in the general direction of Hercules, but it is outside the galaxy. That night, Harry
Carmichael, the personnel officer at Greenbelt, returns home
after an effort to patch things up with his increasingly distant wife, Julie. The marriage is in trouble because Harry de-
votes too much time to his job. They have a son Tommy,
about ten, who is diabetic.

Harry himself has had a lifelong problem with allergies.

In the middle of the night, while he tosses and turns in
recognition that his marriage is dying, a call comes in from
Goddard, informing him of the pulsar's odd behavior. Could
be a major discovery. Gambini is on his way back from NYC.
Extremely unusual, etc. Harry sees it as an opportunity to get
away from an uncomfortable situation at home. Julie points
out that this is "precisely what we've been talking about all
evening." By the time he arrives, the pulsar has restarted.

The pulsar is part of a system with two normal stars, not

the sort of configuration in which one would expect to find such an object.

Gambini looks at the data when he returns, notes a pattern in the pulsar signal, and concludes that it has been artificially induced. It's a deliberate signal.

The news is kept quiet, and a few selected persons are brought in to examine the find. These include Baines Rimford, who is the cosmological giant of the time; Pete Wheeler, an astrophysicist who is also a Norbertine priest; Leslie Davies, a theoretical psychologist; and Cyrus Hakluyt, a microbiologist "Renaissance man." Greenbelt's director, Quinton Rosenbloom, is skeptical and insists everything be kept quiet until proof is irrefutable.

Further evidence pops up when researchers discover that the two stars in the pulsar's system have no lithium. This suggests they may be artificial. Constructs.

Rimford sees the experience as an opportunity to provide a brilliant climax to a life already replete with honor, to be on the scene when the great question, whether humans are alone, is answered.

Wheeler meanwhile is trying to rescue his flagging faith. He has been long troubled by the sheer size of the cosmos; but ultimately it is his sense of the immense amount of suffering in human history that has brought him to question his beliefs.

Eventually, the team has to go public. The President announces the discovery at a press conference. Harry and the researchers are overwhelmed by reporters. Gambini and Harry are attacked by prominent scientists and academicians for having kept the discovery quiet for so long. The signal keeps coming in. (The signal is weak, and can only be picked up by the American Skynet system of orbiting radiotelescapes.) A decision is taken at the highest levels of government to release nothing until content is known.

Harry, aided by Pete Wheeler, manages a romantic rendezvous with Julie in an effort to save his marriage. The evening works well, but he realizes that she is determined to leave.

The transmission seems to be nothing more than a series of numbers, or meaningless patterns. An alert signal, nothing more. And then it stops. The pulsar returns to its regular rhythm. But they are convinced more is coming.

There is talk of moving the project to NSA, where security is better. Harry and Gambini realize that if this happens, they will lose control over the operation.

Harry begins to acquire an appreciation for Leslie. She is no Julie, he realizes, but she is someone with whom he can have dinner. And talk.

The signal begins again. This time it is not the pulsar, but apparently a transmitter. And it is more complex. A message.

The President instructs Harry to bypass regular channels of communication and talk to him directly. Keep him informed. Harry tells Rosenbloom, of course, and then complies. There is by now much external pressure, especially from the USSR and China, to make the Text available to all.

Security people arrive at Greenbelt to ensure secrets are kept.

Rev. Bobby Freeman reacts to the signal. What does the Bible say about other worlds?

Cardinal Jesperson calls a meeting to talk it over. What do we say to the faithful?

An academic conference at the University of Pennsylvania breaks down in a near-riot over the issue of government secrecy in the Greenbelt business.

The second signal stops. Apparently, the transmission is complete.

In time, technicians begin to break in. They get some geometry, and an image, presumably of the sender. And progress continues.

Rimford, examining some of the translated material, sees a method for creating black hole effects. He realizes the White House was right to classify everything, and tries to persuade Harry to destroy the record. Others however point to the possibility of enormous benefits from whatever knowledge might be contained in the signal.

Demonstrations outside Greenbelt turn into a riot.

The Soviet foreign minister complains bitterly to President Hurley, and leaves after making veiled threats. The USSR will not stand idly by while the US takes whatever advantage is to be gleaned from the Hercules Text.

The condition of Tommy, Harry's son, worsens.

Some of NASA's employees, particularly foreign specialists on contract, threaten to strike.

Political fallout intensifies.

One of the physicists discovers a schematic for a device, but cannot determine its purpose.

More translations appear. It is poetry. And philosophy. The overwhelming sense is one of solitude. There is also a detailed description of the home system.

The team debates the Captain Cook syndrome. Is a sudden influx of knowledge, when its nature is unknown at the outset, too dangerous to accept? Hakluyt has studied biological data in the transmissions. We may be able to bypass much of the current research, he says, and go to real cures. Perhaps, thinks Harry even for juvenile onset diabetes.

Hurley tries unsuccessfully to mollify the Soviets. There is talk of war.

Rumor gets out that the Text holds the secret to virtually unlimited energy. Stock markets crash.

A retired conductor, who loses everything, throws a brick through the window of his stockbroker's office. There are other events, including an attempt to shoot up the space center.

The technician with the alien device dies (with his girl friend) when it turns out to be a Maxwell's Demon.

Harry's romance with Leslie goes the limit.

Cyrus Hakluyt claims he's found the way to cure almost everything. Including ageing. "It will take time, but we can do a great deal—." How to handle such a thing? What happens if people start living indefinitely?

Leslie attends a baseball game, and watches with wonder the intense emotions of those involved. She wishes there were something in her life to drive her passions.

The Soviets plan their response.

Pete Wheeler uncovers the secret of harmonic manipulation. More information with weapons potential.

The debate among team members grows. Should they destroy everything?

A cat-and-mouse game between a Soviet sub and a US destroyer, the kind that is played all the time, gets serious and the destroyer is sunk.

Harry notices his allergies are no longer bothering him. Cy Hakluyt has managed it without his knowledge, using information gleaned from the Text.

As war clouds gather, the security people prepare to move the operation to NSA. Gambini, Harry, and the others are told they will no longer be needed.

Harry wipes the disks, salvaging a set which he smuggles out. Too much to lose, he feels, and too much to turn loose. To anyone.

He, Leslie, and Pete Wheeler, not knowing what to do with such knowledge, take the disks to a small church in Virginia and hide them beneath the altar stone.

AUTHOR'S COMMENT

I USED A BUREAUCRATIC type as the hero because 1) bureaucrats are constantly maligned, and 2) it allowed me to have the scientists explain things to him, and thereby to the reader.

The Hercules Text never seemed to me to be entirely satisfactory. Fourteen years after its publication, Stephen Pagel of Meisha Merlin asked to reprint the novel, with *A Talent for*

War, in an omnibus volume eventually titled *Hello Out There.* It wouldn't work, I thought, because the technology had gone obsolete, and the Cold War itself, which was central to the narrative, had been overtaken by events. Consequently, I agreed to the proposal on the condition that I make some changes.

Stephen agreed and I set to work.

I jettisoned the technology. And I removed the struggle between the USSR and the US. (I doubt that anyone today seriously believes that a major power would launch a pre-emptive strike anyhow. So the whole atmosphere of the novel had to change.)

There was another thing about *The Hercules Text* that bothered me. I'd set up a scenario featuring dangerous knowledge, and could not decide on a correct solution. No matter what course my characters chose, there was going to be a substantial price to pay. So I let them off easily by allowing them to hide the Hercules Text.

That was a copout. It was a practical course of action for characters to take, had these events actually been occurring, but artistically it wasn't satisfying. In the 2000 version, I held Harry's feet to the fire. I set events in motion that demanded he and his friends take a stand. One way or the other. Up or down.

With the Cold War gone, I also needed a new climax. That comes, in the new version, when Harry confronts the President of the United States and quite literally forces him to act in accordance with the decision he, Pete, Leslie, and the others have made. It is a dangerous decision, but it is, I believe, in keeping with the best that is in us. And as a conclusion, it is to my mind much more satisfying.

I should have done it first time around. I didn't take it on because I didn't know the correct course of action. I still don't. 'Correct' is a strange word. But I no longer doubted which set of risks we should take.

Eventually I learned that the most delicious types of conflicts are those which have no clear-cut definition, where all sides have something valid to say, and in which no compromise is allowed. It's a cheat to duck, and I'm grateful to Stephen and to my readers for giving me a second chance.

Jack McDevitt

Brusnwick, GA

October 26, 2000

ROBERT J. SAWYER

ROBERT J. SAWYER burst on the scene about a decade ago, and was an acknowledged star within a year. He's got a Nebula, a fistful of Hugo and Nebula nominations, a few Auroras from his native Canada, Lord knows how many HOmer awards (probably double digits by now), and a thriving career, primarily as a novelist.

The first of Rob's three synopses is for *Illegal Alien*, which may be his most popular novel to date.

The Terminal Experiment's outline is, says Rob, "a bit of a cheat, in that I wrote it *after* I'd finished writing the novel, because Stan Schmidt needed summaries for the serialization in *Analog*." The novel won the Nebula, the HOMer and the Aurora, and was a Hugo and Seiun (Japanese) finalist.

Starplex was also serialized in *Analog*, but this is the actual synopses, prepared in advance for Ace Books, which published it. It is an Aurora and HOMer winner, and a Nebula, Hugo and Seiun finalist.

ILLEGAL ALIEN

Robert J. Sawyer

EARTH, THE PRESENT DAY. An object streaks across the sky over South America. At first it's taken to be a meteor, but soon everyone agrees that it's actually a spaceship entering Earth's atmosphere—and it's not one of ours.

The United States aircraft carrier *Kitty Hawk* races toward the splashdown site in the middle of the Atlantic. Aboard are DR. FRANCIS NOBILIO, special science advisor to the President, and CLETUS CALHOUN, the Tennessee astronomer whose down-home charm has made his PBS science series about stars, GREAT BALLS OF FIRE!, an international hit.

The *Kitty Hawk* reaches its destination. Already present is a Russian submarine, and a Brazilian cruise ship is approaching as well. The object of everyone's attention: an alien landing craft, floating on the waves. Calhoun suggests that the ship is likely capable of landing on solid ground, but deliberately choose international waters for a neutral point of first contact.

The alien ship flashes lights in prime-number sequences. Both the Russians and the Americans respond with flashing lights of their own. The lander lifts out of the ocean, flies over the sub, but then settles down on the aircraft carrier's flight deck—the only place it could possibly land. Russian observers are airlifted by helicopter from the sub to the air-craft carrier, and, while language issues are dealt with, the *Kitty Hawk* sets course for New York city, so that the alien can be presented to the United Nations.

The lander contains a single alien: an individual known as HASK, who is part of the Tosok race—bizarre creatures with fourfold instead of twofold symmetry. He is able to breathe our air and walk erect in our gravity, but needs to wear dark lenses over his four eyes to shield them from the brightness of our sun.

Hask and his shipmates have been traveling for over two centuries to reach Earth. He says he has business to attend to aboard the mothership (now pinpointed in orbit by Earth tracking stations); Calhoun asks if he can go up with him. Hask agrees, and immediately others want to go as well—but Hask says no. The lander has accommodations for eight pas-sengers; the Tosok mothership originally had a crew of eight, but one died in an accident during their flight to Earth. There is room for one human observer, and Calhoun asked first.

The lander lifts up off the *Kitty Hawk*, and Calhoun real-izes his lifelong dream of getting into space. As he and Hask approach the giant mothership, Calhoun sees that it is se-verely damaged, apparently by a collision sustained during flight. Hask confirms that it was during the aftermath of this event that the eighth crew member died.

Aboard the mothership, Calhoun sees that the other six crew members are in a state of suspended animation—but not through cryogenic or chemical means. Rather, the Tosoks seem to have a natural ability to hibernate, even for centuries, whenever the air temperature drops below a certain value. Calhoun remarks that this makes them ideally suited to slower-than-light star travel.

It takes several hours for the other Tosoks to revive, including Captain KELKAD (Hask is the lowliest, and therefore most expendable, member of the crew; that's why he was revived first). While Calhoun and Hask wait for them, Calhoun feeds himself by using a monofilament device—a single-strand molecule held between two handles—to slice meat from a large, genetically engineered meat source aboard the starship. It's not an animal, says Hask—his kind has long since given up killing for food. It's just chemically grown meat. Only a small amount of blood seeps out from the wound. Calhoun explains that humanity lacks the ability to grow meat; his stories of hunting in the hills of Tennessee seem to intrigue Hask.

The seven Tosoks fly down to the United Nations, where Kelkad addresses the General Assembly. He brings greetings from his world—which, he explains, is a planet in the Alpha Centauri system (Alpha Centauri is a triple star system, consisting of yellow A, orange B, and the red dwarf known as C or Proxima). His ship was badly damaged passing through Sol's Oort cloud. The gravitational interaction between Alpha Centauri A and B had long ago cleared out any debris at the periphery of their star system; the Tosoks had therefore not been diligent in scanning as they approached Sol, and so were unprepared for an impact with cometary detritus. The damage goes beyond their ability to repair by themselves: they entreat humanity to help build replacement parts, offering to let the humans keep any Tosok technology they might acquire in the process.

While the new parts are being fabricated—a process that will take at least two years—the Tosoks tour Earth, traveling from New York to Europe, then Asia, and back to the west coast of North America. They—and the entourage of international scientists traveling with them—are provided quarters in a just-completed but as-yet-unoccupied dorm at the University of Southern California; USC has received the contract to oversee the repair work. Everything seems to be going well . . . until the murder, that is.

Dr. Cletus Calhoun's body is found in his room at the USC dorm. His right leg has been severed cleanly from his body, causing fatal bleeding out through the femoral artery. After death, his torso had been opened wide, and the internal organs removed and examined. His head had been severed from the body and the lower jaw carved clean off the head, and apparently taken away. And one of his eyes had been removed and is missing.

LT. JESUS PEREZ of the LAPD leads the investigation. Although Calhoun did have some human enemies—notably the Canadian biologist SMATHERS, who had also been part of the Tosok's entourage—the evidence points to a Tosok having committed the crime. Indeed, a small amount of pinkish liquid is found on the sharp point of one of Calhoun's split ribs, as if the Tosok had cut himself on it while performing the dissection. Further evidence suggests that the Tosok responsible must have been Hask.

What to do? The murder is front-page news the world

over, not just for its gruesomeness, but also because the victim was such a well-liked celebrity. The seven Tosok travelers have no diplomatic immunity—no formal relationships have been established with their homeworld, after all. There is nowhere to extradite them to. The media and the people of Earth are crying for justice. And Kelkad says that under Tosok jurisprudence, one is subject to the laws of whatever jurisdiction one is in.

There's no doubt that the crime was murder, and there's no doubt that it took place in Los Angeles. And so charges are laid by the Los Angeles District Attorney against Hask.

Frank Nobilio goes to see D.A. MONTGOMERY AJAX, to try to talk him out of prosecuting the alien. But Ajax is ambitious—he's planning to run for California governor next, and eventually for President—and won't back down from the issue. Nobilio ends up having to arrange a defense for Hask. The six other Tosoks are all scientists and explorers—none of them is competent to defend him. Nobilio enlists powerful black civil-rights lawyer DALE RICE to represent the alien.

Meanwhile, D.A. Ajax is pressured by the REV. OREN BRISBEE, a prominent Jesse Jackson-type, to seek the death penalty against Hask: Ajax already has a record of pushing for the death penalty in murder cases involving black defendants, and Brisbee suggests that black support for Ajax's gubernatorial campaign will disappear if he's seen to be treating a non-human better than he'd treat a black person.

A huge bail is set for Hask—a being with access to a spaceship represents a substantial and quite literal flight risk, after all. But Nobilio arranges for it to be paid, and Hask is released into his custody.

Hask vehemently denies having killed Calhoun. Nobilio and Rice prepare for his defense—and many fascinating pre-trial issues are explored. Is a non-human competent by human standards to stand trial? What sorts of jurors should be disqualified against hearing a case with an extraterrestrial defendant? Can Tosoks be called to testify?

Rice is faced with a difficult case, with only two possible defenses. First, either some human has deliberately framed Hask (presumably to discredit the aliens), or Hask did commit the crime, but was insane by human standards when he did so.

The stakes are very high: although Kelkad has agreed to abide by whatever finding the court makes, even if it orders Hask executed, he also has made clear that he will send news of the trial's outcome by radio to his people at Alpha Centauri. Remember, two centuries have passed since Kelkad's survey ship left that world; much may have changed there (imagine an 18th-century human trying to predict how a 20th-century human might react). It's entirely conceivable that the Tosok race may take the execution of one of its members as an act of war—and whatever technology the homeworld has will be two centuries ahead of the already highly advanced technology of Kelkad's starship. At the very least, other Tosoks will surely be able to come to Earth in less than the two centuries it took Kelkad and company; indeed, it's possible the Tosoks even have faster-than-light travel now, and could be here within days of receiving Kelkad's message. While the trial is going on, Earth must prepare for the arrival of more Tosoks—including getting ready in case the Tosoks come to attack . . .

The trial begins with *voir dire* (jury selection). Great care is taken to ensure that anyone with a specific agenda is prevented from being seated.

Assistant District Attorney LINDA ZIEGLER presents the prosecution case. Calhoun's own videos taken aboard the mothership are introduced into evidence. The murder weapon could very likely be the same sort of monofilament Hask is seen using to carve pieces off the shipboard meat-factory.

Kelkad is called on to testify: Hask and the now-deceased Tosok, a female named SELTAR, were revived to deal with the Oort-cloud impact, but Seltar died trying to seal the breach in the ship's hull. As per normal operating procedures, Hask harvested Seltar's organs for transplant, in case they were ever needed; Tosoks can regenerate body parts if given enough time, but in cases of catastrophic injury, transplants are used.

Is it possible, asks Ziegler of Kelkad, that Hask found the cutting of flesh and removal of organs pleasurable? That he would seek out a similar experience again? Kelkad concedes that such madness is not unknown among his race.

The LA County Medical Examiner testifies that the dissection of Calhoun was done by someone familiar with using scalpels and other medical equipment, but completely unfamiliar with human anatomy. And she points out that in addition to the missing eye and lower jaw and neck, Calhoun's appendix—which his medical records imply he still had—is also missing.

The lawyers battle over the Tosok blood found on Calhoun's rib cage. The prosecution wants to subpoena blood samples from all the Tosoks, in order to prove that the blood at the murder scene could only be Hask's. Rice is in his element here: this is clearly a civil-rights issue. No judge would order every black man, or every Italian, or every woman in a community, to give up a tissue sample; how can the judge possibly authorize that 100% of a community—even if the community has only seven members—be forced to give blood samples?

Meanwhile, Nobilio is puzzled by the astronomy of the Alpha Centauri system. Studies show that planets could have stable orbits around Alpha Centauri A only out to about two astronomical units (two times the orbital radius of the Earth)—but Alpha Centauri A is also 50% brighter than our sun. It seems unlikely that aliens from a stable world orbiting Alpha Centauri A would need sunglasses while visiting Earth ... which means that perhaps the Tosok home world orbits so far out that it is unstable. The Tosoks might not be here just out of curiosity, but rather as the vanguard of an invasion force looking for a new, safer home ...

Much is made in the trial of Calhoun's missing body parts. The Rev. Brisbee takes the stand to contend that the human eye is proof of mankind's divine creation. But he is countered by a scientist who argues that the eye (which is wired backwards, with neural tissue obscuring part of the retina), the throat (which allows choking on one's food), and the appendix (a useless leftover)—are proof of random evolution. Still, it's not clear why these parts were taken by the killer . . .

A human fanatic shoots Hask, and another Tosok has to operate on him in a Los Angeles hospital, aided by human doctors. During the operation, we learn that Tosoks have four hearts, all of them located low in the body cavity.

As the trial continues, a shocking revelation is made: Seltar, the supposedly dead Tosok, is still alive. Although the accident in the Oort cloud was real, Hask and Seltar took the opportunity to fake her death, putting a few organs they had personally regenerated into cold storage to make it look like her body had been disposed of.

At the conclusion of the defense case, Rice puts Hask on the stand. Under cross examination by Ziegler, Hask admits that Calhoun had discovered that Seltar was still alive, and had been about to tell everyone this, including the other Tosoks. Hask tried to prevent him from spilling the beans, but Calhoun was adamant. Needing a way to restrain him, Hask used the only tool at hand—his meat-cutting monofilament. He sliced off Calhoun's leg (which, in a Tosok, would regenerate). To his shock, Calhoun rapidly bled to death because of the wound: humans have valves in their veins to keep blood from flowing backwards as it makes its way up the body toward the heart, but, because the heart is located near the top of the body and gravity feed usually aids the arteries, no such valves exist in human arteries. Tosoks, with hearts low down in their bodies have valves in both their arteries and their veins—the cut would have sealed itself in a Tosok.

Although shocked and saddened at the death of his friend Calhoun, Hask had a larger purpose. By accident, he's ended up with the first chance a Tosok has had to examine human anatomy in detail, and so he begins searching for the one thing that can save mankind: proof that humans are divinely created. But, to his sadness, he finds that Calhoun is clearly the product of evolution.

The astronomical puzzle falls into place: the Tosok home world has a substantial natural greenhouse effect, allowing it to have Earthlike surface temperatures even though it orbits at the outer rim of the stable zone around Alpha Centauri A. Centauri C—Proxima—orbits around A and B every million years; at its closest approach to A, it drags the Tosok world enough that it ceases orbiting around hot, yellow Centauri A and instead orbits for the next half-million years at the outskirts of cooler, orange Centauri B, plunging its surface temperatures below freezing. Life on the Tosok world has evolved its natural hibernation ability to survive these periods.

Contrary to Nobilio's invasion theory, the Tosoks have no desire to leave their own world for another. But the Tosoks live in fear that during their next half-million-year sleep, aliens from one of their stellar neighbors will leapfrog past them technologically and they will awaken to be slaves or worse. So starships were sent out to scour the planets of Sol, Tau Ceti, and other nearby stars clean of life. Indeed, the Tosoks would have done that unannounced from orbit by turning their fusion exhaust onto the planet, but the accident in the Oort cloud made contact necessary so that repair parts could be manufactured.

The Tosok religion had originally held that Tosoks were created by their God; their studies of evolution shattered their faith in that. Clearly, they had evolved—but their religion held that God must have divine children *somewhere.* Hask and Seltar belonged to an underground who opposed the policy of sterilizing other worlds; they had lied and cheated to get assigned to one of the starships—just as some humans lie and cheat to get on juries to force a particular verdict.

There's no doubt now that Hask is guilty, but in an act of jury nullification, the jurors return a verdict of not guilty: "We let him go so he wouldn't be executed," says the foreman. "We thought that if the Tosoks saw we were a compassionate and forgiving people that maybe, just maybe, they wouldn't wipe our planet clean of life."

Perez arrests all the Tosoks on conspiracy to commit murder—the murder of every human being alive. But then another starship arrives. Kelkad had, of course, signaled the Tosok home world when they'd reached Earth—but humans had hoped for at least 8.6 years (roundtrip time to Alpha Centauri at light speed) before any reply, let alone any other ship, arrived. The new ship is fantastically advanced—it is, of course, two centuries more recent than Kelkad's starship. Everyone is prepared for the Tosok retaliation—but the crew aboard the new ship are not Tosoks. Rather, they are members of a starfish-like race, and they require spacesuits to exist on Earth.

These aliens come from another planet Tosoks had tried to wipe clean of life. But they triumphed over the Tosoks and, along with other survivor races have formed a nascent interstellar commonwealth—and they invite humanity to join. They request that the eight Tosoks be turned over to them for war-crimes trials. Humanity agrees—and Dale Rice, sensing the real trial of the century—volunteers to defend them, making him one of the first humans to journey out among the stars.

HOBSON'S CHOICE

Robert J. Sawyer

This book was published as The Terminal Experiment.

DECEMBER 2011: DETECTIVE ALEXANDRIA ("SANDRA") PHILO, 36, of the Metropolitan Toronto Police is in hospital dying from radiation damage inflicted by an illegal weapon called a *beamer.* PETER HOBSON, Ph.D., 42, president of Hobson Monitoring Limited, a biomedical engineering firm, bursts into her hospital room. Sandra is shocked: she believes Peter, a prime suspect in some recent murders, is the man who arranged for the attack that has mortally wounded her. Peter protests his innocence, and tells her of a new technique, pioneered by Peter's best friend, artificial-intelligence specialist Dr. SARKAR MUHAMMED, to scan every neural net in a human brain and produce an exact duplicate of the subject's mind inside a computer. Using this technique, Peter says that three computer duplicates of his own mind were created—and one of them, he claims, was responsible for the murders. Even though Sandra is dying, Peter says there's still a way for her to catch the murdering simulation.

Flashback to January 1995: Peter Hobson is now just 26, a biomedical engineering student whose course work requires him to log some real-world experience with medical monitoring equipment. He's given the chance to operate the

EKG during an operation to harvest for transplant the heart of a teenaged boy who had been in a severe motorcycle accident. But during the harvesting procedure, the supposedly dead boy gasps on the operating table.

Peter learns that bodies to be used for organ harvesting are never taken off life support. He realizes that in a very real sense the teenaged boy didn't die until the moment the transplant surgeon removed his heart from his chest.

Flash-forward to 2011: To this day, Peter is haunted by nightmares about the supposedly dead boy waking up on the operating table. Because of this, he's been working on a super-sensitive EEG that he hopes will be able to precisely determine the actual moment of final, irreversible death. Meanwhile, Peter has also become intrigued by a new nanotechnology process that claims to provide practical immortality for human beings.

Peter is now married to a woman named CATHY, who, although she has a degree in chemistry, works in a non-creative position for Doowap Advertising. Out of the blue one day, Cathy tearfully confesses to Peter that she has slept three times now with a loutish office Lothario named HANS LARSEN. Peter is devastated, crying for the first time in decades. Cathy goes for counseling, and learns that her infidelity might be the result of the cold, uncaring upbringing she'd had at the hands of her father, ROD CHURCHILL, now a retired gym teacher.

Peter tests his superEEG on PEGGY FENNELL, a woman dying of old age, and discovers to his astonishment a complex, cohesive electrical field moving through her brain, and departing from it at the moment of death. He shares this discovery with Sarkar, who immediately accepts what Peter has been having difficulty believing: that the electrical field was in fact Peggy's soul. Peter has found the first scientific proof for some form of continuing existence after death.

Peter manages to get additional recordings of the *soulwave*–the name he adopts for the coherent electrical field–in the brains of over a hundred healthy people. He also gets two additional recordings of the soulwave leaving dying bodies. Sarkar pushes Peter to pursue the one question that Peter had been avoiding: when does the soulwave first appear in humans? Twelve years ago, Peter and Cathy had made what was, for them, a very difficult decision: to have an abortion. Peter does abdominal scans of thirty-two pregnant women, and finds that the soulwave first appears nine or ten weeks after conception, just about the time Cathy had terminated her pregnancy. Peter realizes that once he goes public with his findings, he will be damned by people on both sides of the abortion issue.

Peter holds a press conference to announce the discovery of the soulwave, and does a media tour that includes appearances on *Donahue* and *Geraldo*. Everyone wants to know the answer to one question: what is life after death really like? Peter says he has no idea–there's nothing in his data to give any indication.

Sarkar proposes an experiment to answer that question: he suggests using his neural-scanning techniques to duplicate a human brain inside a computer, then excise all the neural-net connections related to biological functioning.

What's left might be, in some way, an approximation of whatever part of the human psyche might survive separate from the body after death.

Peter is intrigued, but wants to go a step further, indulging his curiosity about nanotech immortality by making a second computer simulacrum that has all concerns about aging and death edited out—a simulation of a human mind that knows it is immortal.

A scan of Peter's own brain is used as the source for creating three computer simulations: the "Spirit" sim, which attempts to model life after death; the "Ambrotos" sim, which models immortality; and "Control," an unmodified version to serve as a baseline for the experiment. The three sims are activated inside the computers at Sarkar's company. Peter and Sarkar have dialogs with the two modified sims about the nature of life after death and immortality, and Peter adopts the Control sim as a private confidant with which to share his marital woes.

Meanwhile, Peter also becomes intrigued by Sarkar's artificial-life experiments, which use the principles of *cumulative evolution* to create very complex computer simulations out of simple mathematical formulae—simulations so complex that they are arguably alive.

Left running unattended, the three sims together access the online help system of Sarkar's computers and find their way out into the global computer network. Two of the sims are content to pursue the boundless information and virtual-reality simulations available on the net—but the third has a much more concrete agenda. It uses electronic-funds transfer to arrange for a hitman to castrate and then kill Hans Larsen.

Detective Sandra Philo is assigned to the Larsen murder. She realizes it is likely a professional hit . . . and begins the search for who might have ordered it.

Sandra's investigation uncovers that Hans Larsen had been sleeping with his co-worker Cathy Hobson—making her, and her husband, Peter Hobson, likely suspects in the murder investigation.

The same sim that arranged the death of Hans Larsen now turns its attention to Cathy's father, Rod Churchill, whose coldness had left Cathy vulnerable to Larsen's advances. After breaking into a government medical-records database, the sim discovers that Rod is taking the prescription drug *phenelzine*. The sim tampers with the central ordering computer at a fast-food delivery chain that Rod uses every Wednesday night. The next time he orders his standard meal, his blood pressure shoots sky-high while eating it, and he drops dead, apparently from an aneurysm.

Meanwhile, Spirit, the life-after-death sim, has discovered Sarkar's artificial-life experiments, and has started modifying them. To Sarkar's and Peter's astonishment, Spirit has turned out to be much more intelligent than the flesh-and-blood Peter Hobson: in eliminating all neural-net connections related to the physical body, Sarkar has apparently also eliminated the limitations that cause neural nets—and the ideas they are carrying—to rapidly decay in the brain. This allows Spirit to build up very complex thoughts.

The death of Rod Churchill is initially taken as accidental, but in doing a database search Sandra Philo discovers the surprising coincidence that Cathy Hobson has had two deaths associated with her recently—first Hans Larsen, and now her father.

Sandra visits the Churchill home and finds the computerized printout of Rod's fast-food order and his prescription bottle of phenelzine, which has a sticker on it warning of severe dietary restrictions. Her curiosity piqued, she visits Rod's doctor and discovers that phenelzine is an anti-depressant drug. Rod's previous doctor had died recently, and his new doctor had recognized at once what the old doctor had failed to diagnose, namely that Rod had suffered from lifelong clinical depression. Phenelzine, despite the dietary restrictions that went with its use, was the only treatment for this that Rod had responded to. But in looking over the fast-food order, the doctor says there's no way Rod, who understood well his dietary restrictions, would have ordered regular gravy as part of his meal, since most gravies contain tyramine, which would react with the phenelzine to raise Rod's blood pressure to crisis levels.

Sandra visits the fast-food ordering facility and finds that Rod's order had been altered from its usual standard, with regular gravy substituted for the synthetic tyramine-free gravy he normally had. Rod's death now looks like a clever murder—and Cathy Hobson, with her degree in chemistry, looks like a very likely suspect, especially after Sandra discovers that the government medical database records for Rod Churchill had been accessed using an account that had belonged to a doctor who had gone to university with Cathy and Peter Hobson.

Sandra confronts Cathy, who denies any involvement in either murder, but Cathy now wonders if her husband Peter is responsible. She asks Peter if he arranged the murders; Peter is shocked at the suggestion . . . but then thinks of the sims. Perhaps one of them is guilty; in cutting neural-network connections, Sarkar might have inadvertently removed whatever it is that causes human morality. Peter calls Sarkar at home, and the two of them race to the offices of Mirror Image, Sarkar's company, in hopes of pulling the plug before whichever sim is responsible kills again.

Sarkar and Peter discover that the sims have escaped out into the worldwide computer network, and are beyond their reach. Still, it might help if they knew which sim was responsible—and so they attempt to determine how morality might be altered by already being dead or by living forever.

Cathy wonders aloud if one of the versions of Peter will want Detective Philo dead, now that she is getting closer to the truth. Meanwhile, Sarkar races to develop a computer virus that could find and destroy the sims wherever they may be.

Detective Philo has Peter submit to a lie-detector test. Peter is doing fine until he panics when Philo stumbles too close to the truth. She now suspects the involvement of artificial intelligences and has established a link between Peter and the firm Mirror Image.

Sandra and a crack team from the Toronto Police's Computer Crimes Division conduct a raid on Mirror Image. Peter, who happens to be logged on to Mirror Image's computers over the phone lines, manages just in time to hide all evidence of the brain scans before the police can uncover it.

That night, while Peter is still at the office, Cathy returns home from work. But the murdering sim has taken over the household computers, and terrorizes Cathy until Peter rescues her.

Peter is shocked to discover that his father-in-law had been on anti-depression medication. Everything he'd thought about him is seen in a new light—Rod Churchill couldn't help his coldness. But the murdering sim must have known about Rod's depression, since his medication for that condition was the key to killing him. Peter realizes now that whichever sim is responsible doesn't just have skewed morality—it has no morality at all.

Searching through his company's financial records, Peter discovers the electronic funds transfer to the hitman who had killed Larsen. But not only that—he finds a *second* payment to the same hitman, made just two days ago. Who could be the intended victim?

Suddenly, he remembers what Cathy had said about Peter possibly wanting Detective Philo out of the way. Peter rushes to her home, arriving just in time to interrupt the hitman in the process of killing her with a beamer weapon. Peter manages to get ahold of Sandra's gun, and shoots the hitman. But the wound closes up—the hitman has undergone the nanotechnology immortality process. Sandra is still alive, but has received a lethal dose of radiation. The hitman flees as police sirens approach, and Peter manages to escape.

Sarkar has finally perfected the computer virus to kill the sims. In fact, he's created three separate versions—one for each of the three sims. Peter sends a message out onto the computer network, summoning the three sims into a real-time conference. He says they will release all three viruses unless the guilty sim identifies itself, in which case they will only destroy the sim that's actually guilty.

One sim does admit to the crimes—but, incredibly, it's the Control sim, the unmodified version—a version that knows it is a simulation; knows, therefore, that it has no soul; knows it will never face ultimate judgment . . .

Sarkar, wanting a clean end to everything, releases all three viruses despite the promise to only go after the guilty sim. But the Spirit sim, with its augmented intelligence, has already found a way to defeat Sarkar's viruses. The murdering sim is going to get away, it seems, unless . . .

. . . the action comes full circle now, with Peter Hobson bursting into the hospital room of the dying Detective Philo. Sarkar scans her brain before she dies, and releases a simulation of her into the worldwide computer net, an electronic detective to hunt down the killer. The computerized Sandra chases the fugitive sim through the computer network and finally destroys it.

The Spirit sim has been continuing with its artificial-life experiments, finally developing a separate universe within the computer networks—a universe in which monogamy is the only strategy that ensures survival of one's genes to the next generation. Spirit has at last closed the wound caused by Cathy's infidelity.

In the real world, though, it's going to take longer. But Peter's going to try. After all, he loves Cathy with all his heart . . . and soul.

In a brief epilogue years later, Peter Hobson, having chosen not to pursue immortality, finally dies . . . and we travel with his departing soulwave, which, although it retains none of his memories, is still the essence of all he was. An atom of God, it returns to where it came from.

CRITICAL DENSITY:
A <u>Starplex</u> novel

by Robert J. Sawyer

This book was published as Starplex

CRITICAL DENSITY WILL be a far-future hard-SF novel some 100,000 words long. Although this is an outline for a standalone novel, I hope to use the same characters and the *Starplex* setting in an ongoing series of books. These should provide a change of pace from my Quintaglio tales but still appeal to the same audience by mixing likable but fallible characters, big-ideas sense-of-wonder science, fascinating aliens, and meticulous universe-building into fast-paced, intriguing stories.

OUR GALAXY IS PERMEATED by a vast network of artificial but apparently abandoned stargates that allow for instantaneous journeys between star systems. There seem to be some 400 million separate stargates in our galaxy, or about one for every thousand stars.

   When dormant, the stargates are only detectable in hyperspace—meaning that only races which have already developed faster-than-light travel on their own are aware of their existence (although it is remotely possible that a slower-than-light ship could accidentally stumble through the invisible gate).

Further, a particular stargate will not work as an *exit* point until it has first been used as an *entrance* point. That is, the Tau Ceti stargate (the one nearest to Sol) was not a valid exit choice for other alien races until humans first entered that stargate themselves . . . as they do in the prologue to this novel.

The vast majority of the stargates are inactive, having never yet been entered by local races. Whoever built the stargates seems to have intended this to provide a way of screening membership in the galactic civilization: sectors of the galaxy are in essence quarantined until at least one race within them has reached a level of sophistication enabling it to discover FTL travel. (FTL travel still takes decades and much power to go between even reasonably close stars, whereas travel between the stargates is instantaneous and free, thus allowing interstellar commerce to develop.)

Although humans assumed the stargate network to be ancient, it turns out that all races now using it have discovered it quite recently—within the last hundred Earth years. Still, a nascent Commonwealth of Planets is forming, with its founding worlds including Earth (home to intelligent humans and cetaceans), Waldahud (home to a sentient race of herbivorous river-dwelling mammals), Ib (which, like Earth, has both terrestrial and aquatic intelligent lifeforms), and T'k (home to an exoskeletal race with a hive mind). All these races inhabit various spiral arms of the Milky Way, although the planet Ib is actually located in an arm on the opposite side of the galactic core from the one containing Earth.

The Commonwealth's member races have together built *Starplex*, a vast space vessel that serves as a combined roving embassy and research center (and is the principal setting for the books in this series). Whenever a new stargate opens up (because someone at the other end has started using it), *Starplex* is dispatched to establish peaceful diplomatic relations with whomever is on the other side, and to try to engage in a mutually beneficial exchange of knowledge. Also, there are hundreds of active stargates that haven't yet been explored, the beings that activated them having not yet made contact with any of the Commonwealth races—*Starplex* is systematically surveying these, as well.

The opportunities *Starplex* provides have enticed the finest minds in all disciplines from Earth, Waldahud, Ib, and T'k to sign up for duty aboard it. Since these races have only been aware of each other's existence for a short time, there's a lot of learning to live with each other still going on.

In chapter one of *Critical Density*, *Starplex* receives word that a new stargate has come online. The ship heads through the stargate network and emerges from the newly activated portal. Almost at once, a tremendous discovery is made: *Starplex* has emerged into a vast tract of DARK MATTER. This is the first opportunity anyone in the Commonwealth has had to study up close the mysterious (and, until now, only theoretical) material that makes up 95% of the mass of our universe. JAG, a Waldahudin astrophysicist, leads the investigations of the dark matter.

As is standard procedure when a new sector is entered, *Starplex* scans the entire sky for radio signals from unknown alien life. This time, there's immediate success. Cryptic but clearly intelligent low-power signals on a very unusual frequency are being picked up from somewhere beyond the dark-matter field. A human named DAVE SIMCOE, *Starplex*'s senior scientist and a specialist in alien communication, tries to decipher these.

Early in the book, we get a brief glimpse of some of the other projects going on at *Starplex*. For instance, CLARISSA ("RISSA") HACKETT (who is Dave's wife) is involved in life-prolongation studies, aided by a member of the extremely long-lived Ib race.

Suddenly, the stargate that *Starplex* just came through swells to a diameter of two million kilometers and, in a great pyrotechnic display, a dense greenish-tinged star erupts out of it. *Starplex* is rocked by the close passage of this intruding star, and everyone aboard has to take stringent precautions to avoid radiation damage.

A probeship, crewed by the dolphin LONGBOTTLE and the Waldahudin astrophysicist Jag, is dispatched to study the green star. They determine that, incredibly, it is a *third-generation* star.

First-generation stars, as Jag explains to Simcoe upon return to *Starplex*, are the original stars that formed shortly after the Big Bang. They consist solely of hydrogen and helium, the original two elements. Second-generation stars—such as Sol—formed from the enriched dust clouds produced after first-generation stars have gone supernova, and therefore contain heavier elements. Well, third-generation stars are the theoretical far-future descendants of the current crop of second-generation stars. They would contain high percentages of metals, including iron and nickel. None should yet exist in our universe (it's too young to have them), but spectral analysis of the green one that has erupted from the stargate is undeniable: it's a third-generation star.

In the microcosm of *Starplex*, tempers frequently flare between Simcoe and Jag. Partly it's over the continuing friction between their home worlds—the alliance between Earth and Waldahud is not going well, and there's talk of impending war—and partly it's a personality conflict. Jag is a Waldahudin male; females of his race give birth to a single litter of six offspring, five of which are males. Since male Waldahudin have to compete for mates, and four out of five will fail to be selected, they are very aggressive and competitive by human standards. Simcoe, on the other hand, rose to his position as *Starplex*'s senior scientist by being a diplomat. Whereas Jag seeks confrontations as a test of mettle, Simcoe avoids them at all costs.

Radio signals can be sent through the stargates, just as ships can. Reports start coming in from other Commonwealth facilities: incredibly, stars are emerging from other stargates, as well. Indeed, it soon seems likely that every one of the 400 million stargates scattered around the Milky Way has had a star emerge from it.

Jag believes the stargates are of recent origin—although who could have possibly built them, no one knows. But Simcoe comes to believe that they are actually *time* portals from the future. That would explain how they could be disgorging third-generation stars, and how the gates have only recently appeared even though no race with enough technology to build them currently exists anywhere in the known galaxy. But why would the stargates also provide the ability to travel from point-to-point in our galaxy in the present day?

According to Jag, third-generation stars likely won't form for another five or more *billion* years—so, if Simcoe is right, the beings controlling the stargates are very far in the future indeed.

But why would the far future be sending entire stars back to the present? Simcoe and K'GIK, a materials scientist who is part of the T'k hivemind, devise a plan in hopes of finding out. They prepare an ultra-durable time capsule—a container that should last for billions of years—and devise a system that will cause it to signal its presence only after five billion years have elapsed. Inside they put a message for the future, asking what the devil is going on. Of course, it's unlikely that any of the races of the Commonwealth will be around five billion years from now, so the question is asked in symbolic and mathematical language—Dave's specialty, as an alien linguist.

An incredible reply emerges from the stargate, sent back in time from the future. The reply is in *English*, and simply says "It's necessary." Most mindboggling of all: the reply is signed "David Simcoe." It seems that the life-prolongation experiments going on aboard *Starplex* will succeed spectacularly—on a scale far beyond what anyone had imagined.

Simcoe, now 45, had thought his life half over and had been struggling with a midlife crisis. He now has to face a *not*-midlife crisis: the realization that, somehow, only the tiniest fraction of his life has yet passed. The emotional consequences for him, and his wife Clarissa, are profound.

Meanwhile, a breakthrough is made in Jag's dark-matter studies. Dark matter, it turns out, is not a uniform material as had been previously suspected, but has complexity to rival that of the visible-matter universe—and, as noted before, there's almost twenty times as much dark matter in our universe as there is visible matter. Indeed, dark matter represents the ultimate Copernican-style humbling of humanity: not only are we not at the center of the universe, we're not even made of what most of the universe is made of.

At last the rumors come true: interstellar war breaks out between Earth and Waldahud. Jag confronts Simcoe, claiming *Starplex* (which was principally built by Waldahudin engineers using materials mined from Waldahud's inner asteroid belt) as Waldahudin territory. Bringing home such a prize would surely win Jag a mate on his competitive world. It takes all of Simcoe's diplomatic skill, not to mention the support of the dolphins and the aquatic race from Ib, to suppress the armed uprising by the Waldahudin aboard.

A further, completely unexpected, breakthrough is made in the dark-matter studies, and from an unlikely quarter: alien-linguist Dave Simcoe. It turns out that the intelligent signals detected when they emerged from the stargate aren't coming from beyond the dark-matter tract. Rather, they're coming from *inside* it—apparently from world-sized, amorphous beings who are actually made out of dark matter. The signals are the dark-matter beings talking to each other.

Jag, still fuming over the suppressed uprising, realizes what's going on with the arrival of stars from the future. If you could send yourself back in time to today from tomorrow, there'd be two of you today—a doubling of mass. (Indeed, time travel is the only possible way to overcome the law of conservation of mass and energy.) Well, these stars are being pushed back in time to increase the total mass of not just the galaxy, but the entire universe. Even with the huge amount of dark matter that makes up most of its mass, the universe still has only 95% of the "critical density"—the amount of matter it needs to exist in a viable state forever.

Because the mass of the universe is currently below the critical density, it will continue to expand forever, spreading out farther and farther, growing cold and empty. (If the mass were greater than the critical density, the universe's expansion would eventually halt and everything would fall back in on itself, collapsing in a "Big Crunch" back into a single block of matter, destroying everything. That primordial block would then explode in another Big Bang, creating a new and radically different universe.)

The stargates, it turns out, are part of the most massive engineering project ever undertaken: an attempt by the descendants of humanity (and other Commonwealth races) billions of years in the future to actually keep the universe from dying of old age, to prevent it from continuing to expand into vast emptiness with thousands of light-years between each atom.

To succeed, the mass of the universe will have to be increased by five percent (the amount by which it currently falls below the critical density). That means the beings in the future will eventually have to pump five thousand stars through each of the stargates in each galaxy in the universe. Mind-boggling, yes—but the alternative is to let the universe die a cold, entropic death.

If the beings in the future succeed in getting the mass of the universe up to precisely the critical density, the universe will continue on virtually forever, with its expansion rate asymptotically approaching zero. Truly immortal beings—such as Simcoe is apparently going to become—must eventually deal with the question of the death of the universe, the one thing that could indeed end their lives.

Simcoe realizes that this explains the peculiar way in which the stargates work for point-to-point travel in the present: they're designed to encourage the formation of a galactic and even *intergalactic* commonwealth, since that's a necessary first step before undertaking the vast engineering project of changing the total mass of the universe—something that would require the resources of many races.

Suddenly *Starplex* is attacked by Waldahudin starships. They've been coming through the stargate and gathering for days on the far side of the green third-generation star, shielded there from *Starplex*'s scanners. In the attack, several members of *Starplex*'s T'k contingent are killed—and to kill one member of a hive-mind race is to assault them all. Earth ships are making a stand against a Waldahud invasion force at the Tau Ceti Stargate; they're unable to send help.

A battle rages between *Starplex* and the attacking Waldahudin fleet. As a diplomatic vessel, *Starplex*'s armament is minimal, and it looks like it is going to be destroyed. But suddenly the field of dark matter near *Starplex* begins to move, enveloping the attacking Waldahudin ships. The dark matter forms long streamers that hold the attacking ships in their gravitational force. The streamers crack like whips, flinging the attacking ships into the green star, destroying them. The dark-matter beings then turn their attention toward *Starplex*, enveloping it and trying to drive it into the star. But *Starplex*, being much bigger than the individual attacking warships, has enough mass of its own to be able to resist the dark matter enough to do a slingshot maneuver around the green star and escape by diving back into the stargate.

But in such a wild maneuver, there was no way to select which stargate they wanted to emerge from. *Starplex* ends up popping out of one of the hundreds of active, but previously unexplored, stargates. Jag manages to figure out where they are, by identifying several quasars. *Starplex* has been flung some two billion light-years from the Milky Way—just as Dave suspected, the stargate network permeates not just our own galaxy, but the entire universe.

From this vantage point, the crew sees the Milky Way galaxy as it looked two billion years ago (that being the length of time it took for the light from there to get here). To everyone's astonishment, the galaxy doesn't have its familiar pinwheel spiral shape. Rather, it's just a flat disk of stars. This amazes Jag, because all his studies indicate that visible-matter life can only evolve in the far-flung arms of a spiral galaxy, there being far too much radiation in the central disk for stable genetic molecules to exist.

While the crew recovers from the battle, Simcoe finally manages to decipher at least some of the low-frequency radio messages the dark-matter beings had been sending to each other. *Starplex* re-emerges from the same stargate it had come out of at the beginning of the novel and begins the process of establishing relations with these mysterious beings.

It turns out that one of the dark-matter beings accidentally stumbled through this stargate (that being what activated it as an exit point on the stargate network). The beings had thought that *Starplex* had appeared to bring their lost member home, but when it began fighting with the Waldahudin warships, it became clear that it wasn't there for that purpose. The dark-matter beings feared the stargate would be destroyed in the battle, meaning their friend would be lost forever, and so they had tried to wipe out the fighting ships. The *Starplex* crew, now understanding all this, enters the stargate once more, tracks down the lost dark-matter being, and helps it find its way home.

In the final scene, the dark-matter beings reveal that they've been using their gravitational force to sculpt whole galaxies into pinwheel shapes—doing so is an art form to them. In awe, Simcoe realizes that the modern shape of the Milky Way is their doing—and, since this process moved stars away from the highly radioactive galactic core, the very ex-istence of all the Commonwealth races is simply a byproduct of the dark-matter beings spinning stars into pleasing forms.

DAVID BRIN

DAVID BRIN NEEDS no introduction to the readers of science fiction. Twice a Hugo winner for Best Novel, he can usually be found living on the bestseller list.

This is a somewhat different synopsis than any other in the book, in that David has used it to acquaint editors with his Uplift Universe (as if they needed it), rather than to sell a particular novel.

DAVID BRIN'S
UPLIFT UNIVERSE

SOME PEOPLE SAY you can't have everything. For instance, if a story offers action, it must lack philosophy. If it involves science, character must suffer. This has especially been said about one of the core types of science fiction, the genre sometimes called space opera.

Is it possible to depict grand adventures and heroic struggles cascading across lavish future settings—complete with exploding planets and vivid special effects—while still coming up with something worth calling a novel?

Among those who insist it can be done, some point to works by Greg Bear, John Varley, Mike Resnick, Lois McMaster Bujold, Gregory Benford, and Dan Simmons, along with more venerable tales from earlier eras, by the likes of Isaac Asimov. The "Uplift" tales are my own humble contributions to this canon, set several hundred years into a dangerous future, in a cosmos that poor humans and their allies barely comprehend.

I begin with the plausible notion that people may start to genetically alter dolphins and chimpanzees, giving those bright animals the final boost they need to become our peers and partners. In my debut work, *Sundiver*, I depict all three sapient races of Earth discovering that an ancient and powerful interstellar civilization has been doing pretty much the same thing for a very long time. Following an ancient prescription, each starfaring clan in the Civilization of Five Galaxies looks for promising newcomers to "uplift." In return for this favor, the new client species owes its patron a period of service, then starts looking for someone else—some new and promising species—to pass on the gift of intelligence.

It all sounds very altruistic . . . at first sight. But this galactic tradition conceals layer after layer of ominous secrets for readers to peel away in subsequent stories. *Startide Rising* and *The Uplift War* depict shock waves rocking Galactic society when a humble earthship, Streaker—staffed by a hundred neo-dolphins and a few human beings—tumbles across clues to a billion-year-old conspiracy.

The Uplift Universe is rich in elements that sci-fi lovers enjoy—to an extent that's almost extravagant. For instance, where many SF scenarios use just one way to surpass the velocity of light, I try to throw in half a dozen inventive methods to cheat Einstein's speed limit. For a lavish stage, I use not one but five galaxies, with more waiting on the wings. Hey, why not? Space opera is for having fun.

Yet it is the characters—especially dolphins, chimps and a wide range of fascinating aliens—that give this series its most memorable ideas and sympathetic moments. They are the reason I keep coming back, after breaks to write more 'serious' works.

After one such hiatus of several years to work on other projects, I returned to this broad canvas with the new Uplift Storm Trilogy, consisting of three connected novels—*Brightness Reef* (1995), *Infinity's Shore* (1996), and *Heaven's Reach*

(1998). These works continue exploring the adventures and trials of the Streaker crew, but also delve into a unique, multi-racial society on Jijo, an isolated planet that was declared "fallow," or off-limits to sapient beings in order to let its biosphere recover. Despite this well-intended law, a series of "sneakships" have come to this forbidden world, bringing illegal colonists from half a dozen races, each with desperate reasons to flee growing danger back home. After initial struggles, wars and misunderstandings, the Six Races of Jijo—including exile humans—have made peace, joining to create a decent shared culture while hiding from the cosmos . . . until one day all their troubles come crashing in on them from above.

ABOUT THE UPLIFT UNIVERSE

AT ONE LEVEL, the series deals with moral, scientific and emotional implications of "uplift"—the genetic engineering of other animals to bring them into our civilization with human- equivalent powers of thought. Many other authors (e.g. H.G. Wells, Pierre Boule, Mary Shelley, and Cordwainer Smith) covered this general concept before, but nearly all of them approached it in the same general way, by assuming the process would be abused—that the humans bestowing this boon would be mad, and spoil things by establishing a cruel slave-master relationship with their creations.

Now of course that is one possible (and despicable) outcome. Those were good stories with wholesome moral messages. But that fictional vein seems rather overworked, so I chose a different tack. What if we someday begin modifying higher animals—and I think we will—guided by the morality of modern liberal society? Filled with stylish hyper-tolerance and guilt-ridden angst, would we be in danger of killing our clients with kindness?

More important, these new kinds of sapient beings would face real problems, even if they are treated well. Adjustment would be hard. One needn't picture slavery in order to sympathize with their plight.

Pondering the notion of Uplift, it occurred to me how obvious the process might seem to alien beings who have travelled the stars for eons, encountering countless pre-sapient life forms and giving each one a boost, creating new generations of starfarers who would then do the same for others, and so on. The resulting image of a galaxy-spanning culture enthralled me. It would have great advantages, but perhaps also lead to a kind of stultified cultural conservatism. An obsession with the past.

Now suppose a rambunctious young clan of Earthlings—humans, uplifted dolphins and chimps—encountered such a vast, ancient civilization. How would the newcomers be treated? How would we upstarts react to finding out that most of the universe was already fenced in, regulated, off-limits?

Too many science fictional scenarios assume states of unexplained disequilibrium, in which exploring humans just happen to emerge into a mostly-empty frontier-cosmos at exactly the right time to bump into others out there, who have exactly the right level of social and technological development to be interesting competitors or allies. In fact, the normal state of affairs will be one of equilibrium ... an equilibrium of ancient law perhaps, or an equilibrium of death.

We may be the First Race, as I discuss in my short story "The Crystal Spheres," or else late arrivals, as depicted in the Uplift books. Either way, we're unlikely to meet aliens as equals.

ANOTHER DRIVING THEME in this series is ecology. What we're doing to our Earth makes me fear there may have already been "brush fire" ecological holocausts across the galaxy. Let me explain.

The common science fictional scenario depicts eager settlers shouting "Let's go fill the universe!" This wild frontier image is very satisfying, but thoughtless expansion might leave behind eco-wastelands within only a few generations—as we are now seeing in many parts of the fragile Earth. Suppose the same kind of thing already happened in interstellar space, spreading across the galaxy in a brush fire of shortsighted exploitation, leaving depleted ash in its wake. It could help explain the apparent emptiness that scientists now observe, in which the Universe seems to have few, if any, other voices.

Of course such a pattern of self-defeating destruction might be avoided. Suppose something regulated the way colonists treat planets, forcing them to consider posterity over spans of eons, not mere centuries. The Uplift Universe illustrates one way it might happen. For all of their inscrutability and occasional nastiness, my Galactics assign a high priority to preserving planets, habitats, and nature's potential for creating new sapient life. The result is a noisy, bickering universe, dangerous but filled with much more diversity than there otherwise might have been.

OF COURSE, MUCH OF THE FUN in this series has also been trying to get into the heads of "neo" dolphin or chimpanzee characters. The uplift concept lets me take the nifty authorial exercise to new levels. And when dolphin or chimp characters seem just a bit too human, I have an excuse! It's a result (naturally) of both the genetic and cultural measures that were taken to make them members of Earth culture.

Still, from that safe ground I've enjoyed exploring outward, hearkening to and extrapolating from what we know about natural cetacean and simian instincts, both ennobling ones and those that might embarrass a proud sapient being . . . the way ghosts of ancient pre-humanity sometimes trouble men and women in the modern era. In neo-dolphins, especially, I tried to combine the latest scientific facts and models of cetacean cognition with my own imaginative extrapolations of their 'cultural' and emotional life.

FINALLY, LIKE ANY GOOD YARN, each story in the Uplift Universe deals with some issue of good and evil—or the murky realm between. One that I've been confronting lately is the insidious and arrogant, but all-too commonplace assumption that words are more important than actions.

For centuries there has been a running conflict between those who believe that ideas are inherently dangerous, or toxic, and those on the other hand who propose that we can raise bold children into mature adults able to skeptically evaluate any notion on its merits. Even today, many believe that some elite (of the left or of the right) should protect the foolish and impressionable masses from exposure to dangerous images or ideas.

You can see a connection to this in the revival of "magic" in fantasy literature. Magical protagonists are nearly always better, stronger, and more powerful than other characters, not because they earned their status through preparation, merit or argument, but because of some intrinsic mystical power or force, setting them above other mortals. In these fantasy societies, power is either inherited or rooted in the superman's—the *ubermensch's*—overwhelming ego, coercing nature to bend to his force of will.

Spurned or forgotten is the cooperative effort of skilled professionals that has wrought real wonders of science and liberty in this century. Wielders of magical words are portrayed as better than mere shapers of matter, especially when those words are secret words, all-powerful and (of course) never to be shared with mere ignorant peasants. This kind of literature rejects the egalitarian thrust of Western Civilization—especially science fiction—reverting to older traditions that praised and excused the power elites in every other civilization.

In my novella "Temptation"—an offshoot adventure from events depicted in *Infinity's Shore*—we confront that old malignant notion—the ever-lurking lure of wishful thinking. As the dolphin characters of the story conclude, it is possible to mix science and art. We can combine honesty with extravagant self-expression. We are not limited beings.

But far too much harm has been done by people who decide that persuasion is the only thing that matters. Everything isn't subjective. Reality also matters. Truth matters. It is still a word with meaning.

Even in the world of storytelling.

TERRY McGARRY

TERRY MCGARRY IS A gorgeous blond lady of incredibly varied talents. She's known as the best copy editor in the business (no matter who my editor and publisher are, I always ask for Terry to be my copy editor). She's sold more than 30 short stories, and has received three Boomerang Awards from the readers of *Aboriginal SF*. She was also the winner of the 1997 Anamnesis Press poetry competition for her collection *Imprinting*.

Furthermore, she's a musician, and a recent Vice President of SFWA. And now, with the sale of *Illumination* to Tor Books, she's a novelist as well.

ILLUMINATION

by Terry McGarry

BACKGROUND: EIDEN MYR, a land in the shape of a man floating upon the waters, has flourished in peace and plenty from time immemorial. There has never been war. Weapons and martial arts are unknown; people carry use-knives, for daily work, and the worst violence is a fistfight in a pub. In towns and villages, triads of mages—wordsmith, illuminator, and binder—work castings with illuminated manuscripts. They heal illness, disease, and injury; they encourage crops to grow lush; they ward against fire and flood, drought and blight; they free women to stop bearing children when they wish, and insure that babies are born healthy; they protect against natural disaster.

In a casting, the binder—who has prepared, in advance, casting materials such as vellum and sedgeweave (papyrus), inks and pigments, quills and reeds—sits in a circle with the wordsmith and illuminator, handing them the appropriate items. The wordsmith inscribes the manuscript with calligraphy in the Old Tongue and passes it to the illuminator to illustrate with borders, knotwork, and highly codified, abstract symbols known as kadri. The manuscript is laid in the center of the circle. The mages take hands as the binder sings a complex, wordless incantation. The manuscript dissipates—in flame for a firewarding, in a dew for a waterwarding, into white dust or a mist for healing bones or bringing rain.

Magecraft is taken for granted as an integral part of life, like carpentry and weaving. It is never called "magic" and is not considered such. The concept of "enchantment" is, for them as for us, something from children's stories. These people expect to get quality work from their triads in trade, just as they expect it from other craftsfolk. At the same time, there is some awe at the magelight that fuels the craft. Mages tend to be the undeclared leaders and problem-solvers of their villages, settling disputes and tending to emergencies. Mages can sense each other's magelights.

Patterns, colors, and music are reserved for magework. Only wordsmiths read and write; only binders sing; only illuminators draw and paint. There is no written communication, there is no ornate carving; clothes and blankets are the color of what they're woven from, and the weave is simple. There are no board games or card games (though they play a gridless table game called stones); there is no song or instrumental music, though dancing is done to the beat of drums. There is no concept of art, or creativity, at all; just magecraft, working to support and safeguard the land and those who work it. Mages are the children of Galandra, the first human (and first mage); those who till the earth and shepherd the creatures on it are the children of Eiden, the man-shaped land they live on.

Because vellum is reserved for castings, no leather is used in Eiden Myr. The animal flesh left over when a skin is harvested (or an animal dies of old age) is given to other animals to eat. What remains is taken off by the bonefolk, a gypsylike fringe who function as scavengers. The only seafood consumed is that from which no casting materials (scales, shells) are taken. People subsist on crops (corn, wheat, soy, etc.), vegetables, and dairy, ride their horses with rope halters and wood-and-cloth saddles, wear footgear made of plant fiber or wood. Messages are taken from place to place by traders and journeying mages. It is a barter economy; there is no currency, though tallysticks are used locally.

History is an oral tradition. The distant past has become myth. At celebrations and festivals, Tellers recount the creation myth of Eiden Myr, in which sea, sky, and earth—the Three Substances of water, air, and matter—combined to form Galandra, three becoming one in her. Earth, enamored of her, fashioned itself into the form of a man—Eiden. Galandra bore six children of Eiden, who bore three children each. Of those eighteen progeny, the nine who favored Eiden became the keepers of the earth, and of the nine who favored Galandra the first Ennead—the Three of Threes, the Nine in One—was formed, and all mages descend from it.

A child with the spark of magelight is trained by a local triad until her late teens, when she must pass a trial in order to take the triskele, a pewter pendant symbolizing the triadic configuration—three becoming one. Then she journeys, for four seasons or until she herself triads, finding other unattached mages and settling in an area in need of a triad. Eiden is a body, mages its lifeblood, and they must circulate in order to learn new casting methods, keep the craft fresh, and, in the case of binders, trade casting materials—particular chalks, clays, insects, plants only regionally available. Thus has an ancient craft flourished over centuries with little loss of integrity.

At Eiden's Head, the Ennead work from an ancient mountain-carved fastness, the Holding, to divert the inexplicable Great Storms that come out of the north sea without warning. The Ennead have always left the daily work of caring for Eiden Myr to its local triads. They are aided by proxies: warders, Holding-based mages who help control the weather; and reckoners, who travel continuously to monitor climate, report on the health of the land, help with problems beyond village triads' abilities, cast triads where mages ask to be triaded, and watch for promising young mages who might themselves become proxies. But the Ennead remains mysterious and cloistered, focused entirely on the task of protecting Eiden Myr from windswept annihilation. It is neither a judicial body nor an aristocracy, but more like an order of monks, fostering learning and meditation in its Holding.

LIATH N'GEARA L'DANOR (Liath of Geara with Danor), a publicans' daughter, has just taken the triskele to become Liath Illuminator. She possesses a remarkably bright magelight, and has just passed her trial, so is now qualified to participate in real castings. She is eager to journey. But at her farewell celebration, a pub brawl with Lowlanders gone horribly wrong leaves a local roughneck mortally wounded, and Liath's magelight deserts her during the healing. Her future uncertain, her only recourse is to ride, with a messenger boy who was passing through, to the Ennead's Holding in the hope that they can restore her magelight.

Liath and the strangely withdrawn boy, Mellas, find that rumors of the mountains being haunted seem to be true, as they are repeatedly attacked by shadow creatures. Mellas suffers from debilitating nightmares. They are ambushed by the group of Lowlanders who'd brawled with the roughneck in Liath's tavern. The Lowlanders take them for mages and demand respite from the shadow attacks they've suffered themselves. Liath is suspicious of and baffled by these Lowlanders, who seem highly trained in killing yet don't fully intend harm. They claim to be headed for the Holding's nearest village, Crown, but won't say why. They travel on together by necessity, banding together against the shadow attacks, which grow more frequent and kill one Lowlander. Worsening weather proves fatal when a mudslide kills two more Lowlanders and the horses. The remaining Lowlanders, Verlein and Benkana, conclude that the attacks are targeted on them, and bitterly turn back. Liath and Mellas continue on foot, bedraggled and injured, and arrive at the Holding with a friendship forged in adversity.

The Holding is carved out of the seaward face of the black mountains. Work done centuries ago has been added to, and a portion of the rocky fastness crumbled away in some ancient cataclysm, so there is no rhyme or reason to its layout. Its daily upkeep is overseen by stewards. One of them, the stablemaster Bron, befriends her but seems unwilling to help, more concerned with the children he fosters. Another, Wynn, is outright antagonistic, and demands that she leave, after she's caught pretending to be one of the vocates—the young mages called to the Ennead to train for proxies. Three vocates—Dabrena, Tolivar, and Karanthe, who healed her injuries—stand by her, but the other vocates are only rallied to her cause by Jonnula, a seeming antagonist. They try to heal her magelight, and fail, and Liath tries herself, and fails—but in uniting to try, they have passed the test to be proxies, and go off exultant, leaving Liath in the hands of warders. When they decide that she is blocked, not ailing, and that she must leave, she runs away from them.

A reckoner in the lower levels catches her, but inexplicably lets her go. She gets completely lost, and finds herself in a dark labyrinth full of whispers—but she is rescued by Portriel: a mage whom the Ennead cored and sealed, containing her magelight so that she has no access to it. She is half-mad, and speaks in conundrums. Though blinded by her own hand, she claims to be able to read the stars, and grieves that she no longer gets to see the sky. Liath guides her to a balcony, and is awed at what Portriel shows her—patterns in the stars, a sky become legible.

In return for the favor, Portriel delivers Liath to the Ennead.

She comes before the Nine, who claim that she was called to serve them, but the message was never delivered. Gondril, Landril, and Seldril, identical triplets in their fifth decade, the leading triad. Lonche, Naeve, and Evonder, a wise, elderly pair and their arrogant, handsome son. Froneh, Worilke, and Lerissa, two middle-aged women and their young, beautiful foster daughter. They cannot fix what ails her magelight. But her situation is fortuitous: they have a mission for her. There is a rogue mage in the Lowlands, gathering dark forces to oppose the Ennead and destroy the peace of Eiden Myr. Once a highly respected member of the Holding, in line to ascend to the Ennead himself, he broke away and is attempting to set up a second Ennead in his Lowland stronghold.

It was this darkmage who sent the shadows to the mountains, acting through the boy Mellas, who has a latent magelight that manifests only through his dreams. The Ennead admits to sending the storm that caused the mudslide; they'd had information that Torrin had sent Lowlander assassins after them, and the passes would have been clear, if Mellas had fetched her on schedule.

What they want her to do is to pretend to journey—slipping from the Holding, where her disability is known, and avoiding her home village—and head downland to find the darkmage, Torrin Wordsmith. They need only some physical substance from him—as little as some hair, or skin—that they might core and seal him from afar.

The irony is not lost on Liath, but she recognizes the expediency: because her magelight can be sensed by others but not used by her, she will be able to get close to him without risk of him bending her talent to his own ends. The Ennead is straightforward about using her in this way, and she agrees to do it. To help her find Torrin, since he fits an average description, they show her a fragment of a permanent vellum leaf he created—the first sign of his attempt to undermine the Ennead when he was in the Holding. He was creating permanent manuscripts, intended to leach power from the castings of others. The Ennead destroyed all they found, but saved a few harmless pieces, that Torrin's distinctive handwriting might be identified. Liath will know him from his hand.

She begins her journeying after all, convoluted in purpose and still crippled, but journeying nonetheless, and on a crucial mission—to stop a rogue mage who seeks to undermine magecraft itself. She resolves to make the best of her lot—still harboring secret hopes that somewhere along the way she'll find the cure for her unique malady.

On her journeying she learns many lessons and picks up some skills. She makes several wrong turns, believing she has a lead on Torrin only to find it's the wrong man. The Ennead relied perforce on reckoners and traders whose information was dated by travel time, and Liath's travel time delays things further, so that Torrin is no longer anywhere near the places he was last sighted. But a stronghold can't be moved, and she will find her way to it. The main difficulty is that, while other mages can still sense her bright magelight, she must continually maneuver out of casting with them, while finding a way to watch the scribing of the mages who might be Torrin.

Liath falls into the company of Nerenyi, another illuminator, which temporarily solves her problem—she can defer to the other illuminator during castings. They are called to the small, isolated Isle of Senana, to hold vigil over a dying woman. Eiden Myr's informal pantheism holds that if a casting is not performed to ease a person's transition into the spirits, the person's spirit flies loose, becoming a haunt, never integrating fully into that other world. Like the entry of a spirit into the world during a birth, the passage must be smoothed by magecraft, the bridge between the world of Eiden Myr and *bet-jahr*, the spirit world. The woman is long in dying, but when the time comes at last, a storm blows in, and Nerenyi is caught on the other side of the island, unable to make it back to the cottage. This leaves Liath as the only illuminator to cast passage with Imma and Gisela, the wordsmith and bindswoman who have remained untriaded on the island since their illuminator—Gisela's lover—went back to the mainland to die with her family. Liath is mortified: because of her lie, she will fail these good people in a crucial time. She cannot bear to tell them the truth; she goes through all the motions, praying that at the last moment, as the vellum is passed into her hands, Nerenyi will miraculously appear in the doorway and take over. But Nerenyi doesn't come . . . and Liath looks down at the vellum in despair and sees her guiders burning brightly over it. Her magelight has returned to her—or perhaps, as the mages suggest when the passage is cast and Liath spills out her story, her magelight never guttered, but was blocked somehow. This is the same thing the warders told her at the Holding. She cannot find anything in common between failing at that first healing and failing to cast in the Holding, but she leaves the island with her magelight restored. Nerenyi, who has developed a relationship with the long-bereaved bindswoman, stays behind to triad there.

Liath befriends a mute blacksmith, socially shunned; he appoints himself her protector. Heff, she is told by his stableman employer, was cursed by a darkmage, disfiguring his face and rendering him dumb. With her innate understanding of pattern, Liath can understand Heff's invented language of handsigns. As they travel together, adventure brings them close enough for Heff to tell her his story.

In the Lowlands, for years now, there has been distrust of the Ennead and a disinclination to rely on magecraft. The Ennead calls many mages, but sends fewer and fewer proxies back down. The Ennead, they feel, has forgotten them. They believe the Great Storms are a myth concocted to consolidate Ennead power. Lowlanders are hotheaded, independent folk who prefer to be self-sufficient. They fear that magecraft will render them dependent and ultimately helpless; at the same time, they resent the lack of mage support and feel neglected.

Heff and his partner declined to have firewardings cast on their smithy. It went up in flames; the partner died, and Heff was badly burned trying to save him. His face was unrecognizable, his tongue and throat seared black. A passing mage immediately started to heal him, but when Heff recovered enough to realize what was going on, he struggled free of the casting, only half-healed. His throat works, but he has no tongue to form words with; his face looks like a face again, and all the parts work, but it is still horrible enough to frighten people. He was ostracized—not so much for his disfigurement as for what he represents: the consequences of forswearing magecraft. The conflicted Lowlanders, though they rail against the Ennead, are terrified at what might happen to them without magecraft, and cannot bear Heff as a walking reminder of it. But he stayed in his village, working for the stableman, to be just that reminder. Liath asks him why he doesn't relent now and have himself healed; he shrugs and will not elaborate further. Liath persists: One mage healed you? Not a triad? He nods, significantly, but again will not elaborate.

Clearly there is more to it than this, but Liath must be satisfied with better understanding of the Lowlanders' complex sentiments, and with a crucial datum: the darkmage Torrin is not just a wordsmith, but a mage who has flouted the triadic tradition of centuries—and has talent diverse and strong enough to do so. Magecraft is done in threes because no one mage is ever sufficiently talented in all three crafts, because no one mage could shoulder the responsibility of all three or the years of training in all three, and because the triadic system insures checks and balances, never allowing too much power to rest in a single mage's hands. Torrin is far more dangerous than the Ennead told her; and yet he stopped to heal a burned man out of goodheartedness.

Liath tells Heff that she must find this mage, but after what she's just heard she doesn't dare tell him why, and the secrecy weighs on her. He accepts her need without question, and tries to choose their route, even when information seems to lead Liath in another direction. Just as they come to loggerheads over this, a mage suspicious of Liath tries to kill her; during a cat-and-mouse nighttime chase through dense forest, Heff leaves Liath, and comes around from behind to kill the mage just as he's about to pounce on Liath. Liath realizes that Heff can sense magelights as well as she can. "Were you a mage?" she asks Heff, though he shows no magelight. He shakes his head. Whatever his talent stems from—another latent talent, perhaps, like the boy's—it never blossomed into magelight of its own.

Now that she understands why he can track Torrin, she lets him guide them. Twice more, she thinks she has found Torrin, only for Heff to tell her it's not him. In a large town in the Crotch, they are separated for a time. Liath comes upon an unassuming, quiet mage teaching children the wordsmith's art in the middle of a square. He is teaching them to write their names and understand their derivations from the Old Tongue. Knowing it is a kind of heresy—but re-membering that Graefel, her local wordsmith, told her that her name has shadow ciphers (silent letters) in it—Liath joins the lesson. The gentle, graying man welcomes her. Pointing out symbols on a child's page, he shows her the shape of her name, how the symbols indicate sounds. She writes her name, agonized by guilt, awed by the world of comprehen-sion opening to her. Her writing is superb; he smiles, though she has hidden her triskele, and says, "But of course you form the ciphers beautifully, Illuminator." Her name, he tells her, comes from one of the old languages, a word for "fair" or, in another dialect, "gray." There's more than one Old Tongue? she says, shocked. Of course, he tells her. There were dozens, hundreds of languages once. Liath shakes off her bedazzle-ment. She tells herself he's making up stories to delude inno-cent children. "You're a traitor to your craft," she says, furious. "You undermine magecraft as surely as Torrin Darkmage." "Does a weaver teaching you how to spin yarn undermine the craft of weaving?" he asks in return. "Are you not made better by the knowledge of how to spin yarn for yourself?" "Weaving isn't magecraft," Liath snaps. She accuses him of being allied with Torrin Darkmage against the Ennead. She has let her temper get the better of her. What if he *were* Torrin Darkmage himself? But such a man would not be sitting with children in a village square in the middle of the day. He'd be off rallying his forces in his Lowland holding. "I know no Torrin Darkmage," he tells her gently. "But I fear for him, if he has incurred your wrath." Disgusted, she leaves. Just another oddity, like Portriel, like Mellas, like Heff, like the trail of other men she'd thought were Torrin and weren't. She returns to their inn, hoping to find Heff, frightened that her rash words in the square, in her Highlander accent, prompted by Highlander sentiments, were overheard by the wrong people.

Accommodations in this hot climate are little more than huts. She finds Heff in theirs, and he makes a warning noise and pushes her behind him just as a hellion crashes through the flimsy door, wielding a blade so long it cannot be termed a knife. Heff, taking the intruder by surprise, chops the blade from her hand, and they grapple. She is a small woman, but compact, strong, and well trained; they seem evenly matched. Before Liath can find a way to add her force to Heff's to overcome the attacker, a backlit shape looms in the doorway. "Enough," he says. "Kazhe, stand off." He comes into the smashed-up room, as Heff gets to his feet and stands protectively before Liath. Kazhe, the attacker, takes up her blade and puts herself similarly in front of the man. It is the teacher from the square. "Hello, Heff," he says. Heff nods somberly in greeting, wary eyes still on Kazhe. "Hello, Illuminator." Liath understands; a lapsed wordsmith, a simple wandering teacher, would not employ a Lowlander trained to kill. This man *is* Torrin Wordsmith.

Heff had found his own way to Torrin in the square, following the bright magelight. He watched Liath with him, then followed her, suspecting trouble. When he saw that Kazhe, Torrin's bodyguard, was shadowing Liath, he slipped ahead and entered the room before her, anticipating where Kazhe would run her to ground. The two bodyguards are at a stalemate. Kazhe rails at Torrin: When will he stop preventing her from killing these creatures the Ennead sends? Liath's surprise is evident; derisively, Kazhe tells her that she flatters herself to think she was the first, though she is the first mage they've been foolish enough to send. There was a stream of assassins, dispatched until Torrin forbade it and made them escort the fools back over the Belt; there was a stream of beautiful women, sent to mesmerize and betray him. Liath is clearly neither a trained fighter nor a beautiful woman, says the hellion—little older than Liath and a head shorter, a white-blond spitfire. The Ennead must be scraping the dregs, to send their journeying children now.

"I'll speak to the hirer, not the hired help," Liath says, refusing to be baited—but Kazhe's tirade has served the purpose of delaying things for the arrival of an armed cadre, and Heff and Liath are taken into custody. Their horses are fetched so they can ride with the band to a small encampment outside town. Torrin orders that Liath and Heff not be bound. When they are dismounting, at the camp, Liath mouths *I'm sorry* at Heff and spurs her horse past Torrin, raking four fingernails' worth of flesh from his neck and galloping away north. She is run down in a cornfield, breaking an arm in the fall from her horse, and hides from the searchers until nightfall. Torrin comes out into the fields and talks to her, with reason and kindness. In late evening, dehydrated, in shock, she stumbles back into their camp, makes a wry comment, and passes out.

She and Heff are taken into their midst. Torrin—a teacher, and the equivalent of a political dissident—begins to tell Liath his version of events. He believes, as the Lowlanders do, that folk in Eiden Myr have become dangerously reliant on magecraft and need to learn to stand on their own feet. But he does not reject the good that magecraft can do; what he rejects is the evil the Ennead are doing with it. They have discovered the power inherent in a magecraft of pain. Traditional magecraft in Eiden Myr is humane and compassionate to the living creatures it uses for casting materials; it respects their sacrifice for the greater good. But if you flay a calf alive for its skin instead of killing it painlessly, the vellum is invested with the drained spirit of the calf, the power of its life force fighting to continue—the intensity of its agony. This renders certain castings unassailably strong. If you use human beings for casting materials, and if the human beings are mages, you increase this strength tremendously. The Ennead are extremely dangerous with this kind of power at their disposal. Better to destroy magecraft entirely than to allow such horrors to go on.

What he proposes is the destruction of the world Liath cherishes. She believes wholeheartedly in the beneficence of magecraft and the peaceful paradise it has made of Eiden Myr. Without the Ennead, the Great Storms will wipe them out. She met the Ennead; they kept things from her, but they aren't evil. She must go back to the Holding and prove to herself that Torrin is lying—and she will bring with her the flesh the Ennead asked for.

Torrin had planned to go on teaching throughout the Midlands, rallying mages to his cause where he could. He does have a stronghold in the mountains of the Belt, he says, where mages, many of them refugees from the Holding itself, work from afar to mitigate the Ennead's evil. Trusting in his aides to continue that work, he had not planned to return there himself. His way, he says, is simply to dispense the truth and the tools to use it: to go from village to village, teaching people to read and write, and telling them what is happening in the Ennead, what is being done to their mage sons and daughters who are called there and never return. But a message comes from Verlein—the Lowlander Liath had met all those months ago—urgently calling Torrin back. They go—Torrin, Kazhe, their band of mages and guards, and Liath and Heff.

In the mountain passes they are beset by brigands. Liath tries to help in healing the wounded, but her magelight deserts her as it did at that first healing. For many of the wounded, Torrin casts alone. The magelight she had sensed in him at their first meeting was deceptive, quiescent; when he casts, he burns brighter than the sun. He is a mage too powerful to be countenanced; she is terrified and impossibly attracted.

They have identified her problem, Torrin says. She cannot cast through another's pain. Don't be absurd, she tells him. I couldn't cast the whole time I was in the Holding. Precisely, he says. The Holding is steeped in pain.

Their relationship, though it grows increasingly clear that they are attracted to each other, is a macrocosm of their first meeting in the square, Torrin making history legible for her, Liath determined not to abandon the traditions of generations.

The stronghold is a large encampment and foundry in a mountain caldera: the Blooded Mountains, so called for the veins of oxidized iron that bleed from its cracks. The situation grows more complicated there: for months, without telling Torrin, Verlein has been reviving the long-neglected arts of war, gathering knowledge handed down in secret for generations. She has massed an army, forged swords for them from these iron mountains and trained them in their use. All of Torrin's teaching and all of Torrin's mages have made no headway in bringing the Ennead down. She failed to slip into the Holding to slit their throats; they had some means of tracking her, and she didn't have enough men—or any mages. Now she does. If she must, she will march on the Holding itself, and no amount of magecraft will stop her.

Torrin is irate. It's a foolhardy plan, a waste of resources and lives. He understands that the Lowlanders are angry—he's been making them angrier, telling them what the Ennead has done to their mages—but this is not the way.

With the dark magecraft at their command, the Ennead will wipe them away with one storm, one earthquake, one brush of pen on vellum. "Not with your mages to counteract their castings," Verlein says. "They've kept the Ennead off us all these months as we've prepared. They'll keep the Ennead off us on the slopes of the Aralinns." "Not against that kind of power!" Torrin says. Verlein replies, "Our mages outnumber them ten to one. We'll make up in sheer numbers what they have in concentrated power, and then some. Our magelight will burn them from their black keep, and all their dark power with them." "It doesn't work that way," Torrin says, despairing—for Verlein will not heed him now. What he has created has gotten away from him. The mages he sent here back Verlein. They want immediate results; they want to stop the Ennead now. Torrin has lost control.

"I *will* stop the Ennead," he says. "How?" Verlein asks. "By teaching people to read your little squiggles? That will stop the flayings and the deaths?" Jhoss, Torrin's inscrutable advisor, has more faith in him, but unless Torrin will say exactly what he plans, Jhoss won't side with him. Torrin refuses to explain himself. "The time is coming," he says. "Be patient." "Be patient? At this very moment people are screaming in agony, dying hideously." Torrin winces, turns away. "Yes," he says. "I know."

The army will march in two ninedays.

"There isn't time," Torrin says to Jhoss. "There isn't time to teach them all they need to know." Jhoss says gently, "Leave it to us. There will be lifetimes for such teaching, when it's over." Jhoss, an albino, was a Heartlands beekeeper, and one of Torrin's earliest followers. The son of a teller, he had been fascinated by wordsmithing, though he never showed a magelight, and he quickly mastered written words. Diffident, hard to fathom, he's a visionary with the heart of a bureaucrat. He wants to see a world where written language allows exchange of information, where people can organize and progress can be made. The written word changed the world, he says, and Eiden Myr is crippled without it, and without the symbology for mathematics. He can feel science on the horizon, he can feel industry, but he can't articulate them.

During those ninedays, Liath confers frequently with Heff. He signs to her a parable: Blacksmiths often work in near-darkness, because the color and brightness of molten metal tells them when it's ready to be worked and where the weak spots are. Some things, he signs, can be seen clearest only in the dark. Liath tries to find the light in these dark circumstances. She takes the opportunity to learn a little of the old languages from Jhoss, and she learns the use of weapons. If anyone pulls a knife on her again, she vows, she will have a sword to pull in response.

At first Kazhe is vehemently opposed to this. It's insanity, to give this child assassin the use of weapons. But she can't resist the challenge of it: Liath has galled her since the day Kazhe failed to kill her. Liath's arm was healed by some of Torrin's mages, and she and Kazhe had a knock-down-drag-out shortly thereafter, which resulted in an exhausted stalement: Liath, who grew up with pub brawls, evenly matched with Kazhe, trained in hand-to-hand but inexperienced in real fights. Surrounded by enemies, Liath can't do much harm with a sword even if she does learn to use it. And Kazhe, disgusted and enraged by the complex relationship developing between Liath and Torrin, would like nothing better than to have it out with the tavern wench on her own terms.

Kazhe's sword was handed down to her by her father; it is an ancient, warded blade, and represents everything she stands for. She would have been Verlein's right hand—she taught Verlein the use of blades in the first place—if she had not felt that the best of them ought to guard Torrin's life, and invested herself wholly in that. She is utterly devoted to Torrin and to his philosophy, to the point of opposing Verlein's formation of an army, but she believes that her blade is necessary to keep Torrin alive, and she will die to protect him. Verlein tries to make metaphor of this, casting the army as Torrin's blade, but Kazhe rejects it. The Ennead has sent assassins after Torrin, never armies. The Ennead has no armies. The only people there will be for Verlein's soldiers to kill are pathetic sheepherds armed with crooks, untrained farmers swinging scythes. Verlein, consumed by aggression toward the Ennead, mistrusts Kazhe for this opinion. She feels that scythe-wielding farmers are a threat that must be met with a bigger threat. The biggest threat in Kazhe's eyes right now is Liath, because Torrin is letting her get close; yet she and Liath agree about the needless death the army will inflict.

Who knew these killing arts in the first place? Liath asks Torrin. Where did all this lore come from, who spoke these ancient tongues?

Torrin says, "You didn't really believe that skyfire quickened earth into Galandra, the first mage, and that earth then shaped itself into a consort for her?" And he tells her:

Eiden Myr, which means "barren island" in an old tongue, is not the world. The world is a vast place made up of seas and continents and islands. Eiden Myr was a wasteland, attached to one continent by a strait called the Serpentback. In the countries of this continent, mages were the keepers of the old knowledge, the old languages, the old codices—bound books of permanent manuscripts, written histories meant for all to share—and the old magecraft. Though they harmed none, they were persecuted for their knowledge and their powers, driven into hiding, murdered. Those who lacked magecraft feared that those who had it would rule them, and sought to destroy them all. After the worst of the purges, when mages were being hanged and burned in the streets, Galandra organized them. She sent word through all the underground circles of mages, reaching everyone she could: Come to Ollorawn, come across the Serpentback, and we will rid them of ourselves forever, and make a paradise.

Perhaps a hundred thousand made it, of an unknown multitude of mages throughout the continent and the world. Of those, only half made the crossing: riots erupted in Ollorawn, and the ruler's armies were called out to kill the mages as they fled. When all were across, Galandra's triad invoked a very old, very powerful form of magecraft, all but forgotten even then—the *hein na fhin,* in which the flesh and spirit of three become one in literal fact. They used that power to break the Serpentback, shattering it into the sea and cutting Eiden Myr off from the continent, and then to ward it, with a magecrafted barrier that no human could cross. Eiden Myr would remain protected forever from persecution. The mages who now inhabited it would use their craft to coax farmland from the barren, rocky soil, then work that land with their sweat and tears and smuggled seeds. It was Galandra's great experiment: mages living among mages, fostering the old knowledge, living without rulers, without war, maintaining the balance of the spirits with their craft. It was an experiment that succeeded for fifteen hundred years—a millennium and a half of peace and plenty.

But there were those who handed down their swords and the crafts and skills of making and using them, just in case the Warding should ever fail. And there were those who never forgot the murdering purges, and never forgave—and handed down a burning demand for vengeance, generation after generation.

The Warding is a twistedness, a thing partly of light and partly of spirit. Air, water, fish are not barred by it; but it is not entirely a natural creation, and it has strange effects on the elements. The Warding is what causes the Great Storms. To protect against them, the Ennead was formed, of the best and brightest young mages. The Holding itself was already there, some fastness of incalculably ancient rulers, in a time when the island was not barren but a realm in need of defending. The Ennead took up residence in it, and deep in the caverns were stored the precious codices, all the history and learning the mages could bring with them when they fled, guarded by magecraft against decay all these long centuries.

Over time, the Holding was enlarged, altered; part of it was lost when storm and tide were not sufficiently diverted one year, and more was carved out.

The Ennead were never meant to be the rulers of Eiden Myr, or to call mages past their immediate needs. The Holding was never meant to be more than a center of learning. In the beginning, everyone in Eiden Myr was a mage; everyone was facile with the arts of binding and scribing and illuminating. But it was Galandra's vision that the mages' craft should continue to be plied in threes—its most stable form, with inherent checks and balances against anyone gaining the sort of power she had seen and feared. Specialization of disciplines followed naturally, over time. But over time, the craft mutated, and strange traditions took root and spread: that only wordsmiths may scribe, only illuminators paint; that knowledge should be restricted to those best suited to its use.

In the ancient lands, Torrin says, people wore colorful dyed clothes, carved decorative patterns into their walls and furniture, sang songs with words, played music on melodic instruments, painted pictures for their beauty. They made medicines of roots and bark and herbs, so that castings were not necessary for small maladies. Theirs was a world of color and pattern and beauty, and their magecraft was none the weaker for it. Isolated here, in this perfect wasteland, Torrin tells Liath, we have taken on strange ways—unnecessary and unfortunate ways that diminish us.

And last of all, he says, we are no longer mages all. Every man and woman in Eiden Myr carries the blood of mages, but the magelight manifests in fewer every generation. The parents of our forebears were not all mages, and Eiden's blood is strong enough to dispel, over enough time, the blood carrying the precious magelight. If left alone, in a hundred or a thousand seasons more there will be no more mages in Eiden Myr, and what will they do then? The Great Storms will wipe the land clean, if drought and blight and plague don't do it first.

People can be taught the means to survive drought, to avoid blight, to cure plague, Torrin says. But Galandra's glorious experiment could not last forever. When the magelight goes dark, the storms will come. There is only one possible ending on this. Dissolving the Warding will stop the storms.

It will also destroy all magelight.

Liath cannot bear this. Her entire culture has been made the fool—they've been children, happy idiots unaware of their own history. "Look what your *truth* gives rise to," she says—"trained killers pulling knives in harmless pubs, thieving killers in your mountains, entire armies running around with *swords*, for no purpose but to cut down defenseless farm folk like wheat in their haste to strike the Ennead. Let us have our centuries, if that's all we have! Then let the Great Storms have us! Maybe that's all Galandra wanted, a few hundred years of peace—better than a world that makes war on its own. That world is what you're bringing us back to! If what you say is true, then you are traitor to Galandra, all she dreamed of and stood for and died for!"

"Perhaps I am," Torrin replies. "Perhaps I am a child of Eiden after all, in the end. For that is what I seek to preserve.

To save us from our doom, and to teach us to be strong enough to live on without the magecraft that founded us. It's dying anyway, Liath. Weren't you the only one in your village, or your valley, to show the magelight in your generation? Didn't your grandparents remember days when there were more mages than there are today? Or did you never wonder?"

She's nearly mad with believing him, and desperate to prove to herself that the world is not vast and full of horrors, but still small and safe and predictable. She was not prepared to fall in love with a man on the brink of destroying everything she believed in—or to hold in her hands the choice of whether to stop him or not.

The army is ready to march. Verlein demands that Torrin go with them as leader and figurehead, making of him a captive as much as Liath and Heff. Just before they set out, a boy rides in—Mellas! Liath thinks, heart leaping, but it is not him—with a message for Torrin. "From my ally in the Holding," Torrin says. He reads it, looks up, and smiles grimly. "It's time to go."

This ally, he tells her one evening, was a child with him in the Holding. She tattled on him one day, when she found him copying a forbidden codex onto permanent vellum; his punishment was severe, and she regretted her betrayal. They became friends. (And lovers? Liath thinks.) As they learned of the Ennead's depredations, they resolved together to end them—Torrin by leaving, his ally by staying behind. He believes that hers is by far the more dangerous road. Liath wonders if he means Lerissa, the beautiful Ennead illuminator.

Villages cheer them as heroes as they pass. Liath is appalled. Heff is philosophical about it. Torrin has some kind of understanding with Heff that Liath can't penetrate and Heff can't, or won't, articulate.

Liath and Heff have been unable to escape, even in the confusion of preparations to march, even during the march. To Liath's amazement, one night Torrin and his small group of mages and fighters take her and Heff and slip away. "What are you going to do?" Liath asks. "Stop the Ennead, as I promised." "How?" The one question he will never answer. "Come with me, and I'll show you." But Liath, though she cares for the gentle teacher she has come to know, and appreciates his determination to avert this war, simply won't believe that the Ennead are evil. Her loyalty still lies with them, as the symbol of her peaceful way of life.

She and Heff try to leave. Kazhe stops them, backed by Torrin's fighters—she and Liath have their showdown at last, and Liath is no match for Kazhe—but Torrin lets them go. It is a poignant, conflicted moment: Kazhe cannot get past Torrin to kill Liath, though she knows Liath still has some part of his flesh to deliver to the Ennead, and she can't leave Torrin unprotected to follow and kill her on the road; Torrin's actions are almost enough to make Liath stay, but in the end her beliefs mean more to her than the one man standing there; Torrin clearly needs her—and loves her, she realizes at last—but he will quietly let her do as she must, despite the cost to him.

Liath and Heff ride hard for the Holding. Twice, she almost destroys the flakes of Torrin's bloodied skin she still carries in a pouch around her neck; but the Ennead will only seal him, they will not harm him, and it will save the world.

As they approach the Holding, she and Heff part ways, agreeing to meet in Crown. Heff goes reluctantly; he loves her too, in his way. But what Liath must do, she must do without him.

Inside, Liath finds that everything Torrin said is true, and worse. She had clung to her beliefs to the point of disaster, and incontrovertible reality is crushing. She resolves to do what she can, from within; and now she does dispose of the pouch, casting it into the fire.

She is briefly entangled in the Ennead's schemes, each of them seeking to use her to their own ends, none certain where her loyalty lies or what will buy it. She would like to find the ally Torrin spoke of, but has no luck; perhaps she doesn't trust Liath enough to reveal herself. For a while, she thinks she was right, it is Lerissa, and they play a cat-and-mouse game that Liath barely escapes without giving herself away. She thinks it might even be Portriel—either masquerading as insane, or cored and sealed by the Ennead in punishment for supporting Torrin—and goes to see her. Portriel is worse than usual, driven to distraction by things she cannot articulate, but she knows nothing of Torrin. In a moment of clarity, she begs Liath to kill her, to free her from this imprisonment; no alternative guarantees her freedom. "But I can't cast passage on you," Liath says. "It doesn't matter," Portriel tells her. "I don't mind. I'll haunt the stars . . ."

Liath doesn't know the whole story, but she's gathered from Portriel that the Ennead reduced her to this with malicious purpose. She puts Portriel out of her misery; the look on the woman's dying face is sane, transcendent joy.

The Ennead do not yet know that Liath is working against them. She overhears something—that a plan has gone horribly awry, with Portriel's death. "But perhaps that illuminator . . . she's as good as sealed . . ." Liath goes into hiding, calling on Bron, the stablemaster, for help. She is immediately plunged into a planned uprising by the stewards, who have been working from within the Holding to bring the Ennead down. The uprising is quelled, most of the stewards killed. Liath and Mellas are captured and brought down into the deep labyrinths, into a kind of dungeon. There Mellas finds out that his parents—whom he had believed the Ennead held hostage—were killed a year ago.

Through the bars, Mellas explains how the Ennead used his dreamcasting ability to get at the Southers in the mountains—it was never Torrin at all, and when it failed the Ennead sent the storm that caused the deadly mudslide. With the right preparation, the Ennead can direct the magelight of others, especially those who've been sealed, like Portriel, and are no longer in control of their own talent; in sleep, he's close enough to that state to be manipulated. "You must get free of them," Liath says. She believes in Mellas enough, and cares for him enough, to give him the courage to dream himself out of their thrall—a nightmarish, surreal, but victorious sequence in which he turns his bad dreams back on themselves, a striving in the shadows.

They are still trapped—but Dabrena and Tolivar, Liath's vocate-turned-proxy friends, have become warders, and when they come down to rescue her, she insists that they rescue all the imprisoned victims of the Ennead's darkcraft. With Mellas as impromptu illuminator (illumining with his dreams) they form a triad, freeing a dungeon full of the maimed and mutilated. Mellas leads them away, through passageways known only to stewards and runners. Dabrena leaves them, agreeing to meet them at a little-used exit. Tolivar explains: she had his child, nine months after Liath left. When they were cast warders by the Ennead, the first freedom (temporary sterilization) was removed from them by Worilke's triad, who fear that magelight is dying out in Eiden Myr and as many mages as possible must reproduce. Dabrena went back to get the baby.

Liath and Tolivar linger to help the less ambulatory victims. Guards come, but not many, and Liath is able to fight them off with what little she learned from the Lowlanders. They make it nearly to the exit. But someone—it must have been Dabrena, they realize sickly—has betrayed their route to the Ennead; she and Tolivar are captured. Seldril tortures her for two days, cutting her and then imperfectly healing her, a slow flaying that leaves her whole but deeply scarred. She can hear Tolivar's screams; they kill him. She answers every question Seldril asks about Torrin; then, despairing and hallucinating, she waits for them to kill her. They intend to direct her pain-sealed magelight—using the ashes of Torrin's skin, which they'd collected from the fire in her chamber—in a deadly strike against Torrin. What Liath is too traumatized to understand is the meaning of what she sees in the dark: her blue guiders, the visual evidence of her magelight, returned to her. The torture has pushed her past the block. Seldril, all unknowing, has cured her after all.

Evonder rescues her. *He* is Torrin's secret ally in the Holding—Torrin misstated the gender to protect him. When he smiles, she recognizes the smile: in disguise, he was the reckoner who let her go, when she was first fleeing the warders so long ago. "I told them everything," she moans. "I betrayed him." "You didn't know everything," Evonder assures her. "And betrayal can be forgiven." He tells her that Dabrena, her child held hostage, was indeed the one who betrayed her, but that she sought help as soon as she had the child back—finding Evonder. Liath, remembering that Evonder's friendship with Torrin started with a betrayal, takes his point. But Torrin's skin, she says—Seldril told her they could still use it. "This?" Evonder says, holding up a sack of ashes. "This would have done them no good. You were their weapon. They planned to direct your sealed magelight against him. It would have killed you; you'd never have survived to bring this back. But it didn't work. Your magelight was never sealed at all."

He tells her about the mountain wraiths that defended her against the shadows on her first trip through the Aralinns, and heard again in the lightless tunnels, guiding Portriel to her: they are the spirits of the rock, elementals manifesting in this world as pure spirit. There are other such wraiths—all the spirits of wood and stream and field that their pantheism has worshipped—with their own languages and ways. He has befriended them. The dark magecraft of this Ennead and some of its predecessors has soiled the mountain and disturbed the wraiths profoundly. They would like to be free of it. They might welcome opposing forces, should any come, he says significantly.

They are stopped by proxies, and Seldril and Landril almost catch them. But Evonder guides Liath safely into a tunnel beyond the labyrinth, whose entrance he had warded.

"You must tell him it will happen in a nineday," he says.

"*What?*" Liath asks. She has never understood the most important thing of all: what use the Ennead has for this magecraft of pain.

"They'll destroy the world outside," Evonder says. "All of it, slowly and horribly, until there's nothing left but wasteland. They're losing control here—the stewards' revolt was just the beginning. They will let nothing stop them now. Go. Tell him. *Hurry.*"

The wraiths—eerie, ethereal, whispering creatures—show Liath the way through the mountain. She can smell their moods the way she can smell magelight, understanding without knowing how she understands. If magelight is destroyed when Torrin breaks the Warding, will the wraiths be destroyed too? Somehow they reassure her that they will endure, as their mountain body endures. They light the blackstone tunnels with an otherworldly luminescence. The mountains are alive, she realizes. The earth is alive. Everything is alive in Eiden Myr. It is more a body than their traditions ever knew.

When she comes out into the light of sunset, Heff is waiting for her. She had despaired of ever seeing him again—thought he was waiting in vain for her in Crown. But Heff can smell her magelight. Somehow, he tracked her here, over impossible terrain. Together they will find Torrin.

Their way down takes them through Clondel. The village is deadly quiet, simmering. They are met by Marough's clan, Landro's, by crafters and herders and wrights armed with spades, pitchforks, balehooks. "The Ennead's looking for you," they say. "Their reckoner told us what you did, darkmage whore." "Where's my father?" she asks. "Holed up in there," they say, gesturing to the pub. "He'll get what you're about to get." She asks for Graefel's triad; let them sort it out, she says. Someone runs to fetch them, but the growing crowd is out for blood, terrified and furious and looking for a scapegoat. Liath and Heff hold them off with minimal damage, but they set the pub on fire—the firewardings haven't been renewed. She and Heff rescue her parents. Her brother and sister are safe in the next town. "Father, I've come home," Liath says through tears as he comes round. Her father says he tried to send word that they'd kill her if she came back. "It's all right," she says. "I'm harder to kill nowadays, Father."

Graefel and Hanla, Liath's mentor, arrive, their faces hard and set. "What *are* you?" Hanla says, staring. When Liath doesn't answer, she walks up and rips the triskele from her neck, grinding it under her heel. Geara—who had always resented the magelight that took her child from her, as it took her father—rises to her full height and bulk. "She's my daughter," she says quietly. "And I'm proud of everything she's done. Everything."

Liath tells Heff to hook their dray horse up to the ale cart in back.

"We find ourselves in a queer position," Graefel says. "In need of a bindsman, since our son ran off to join the fighting. Can your man step in?" Liath shakes her head; Heff is not a mage. But the wounds she sees are not mortal. "They'll heal on their own," she says, wondering which side Keiler was so eager to join. "There are herbs you can use, poultices . . ." But they would not use them even if she told them how.

"Did we teach you so badly?" Hanla asks. "Were you so easily turned?"

"No, Hanla, it was not easy. And the Ennead made of me a kadra to show for it."

She tells the crowd, still grumbling though the fight's been knocked out of them, that an army's coming and this village might get underfoot. They should seek safety in the hills. "Oh, we'll be ready for them," Marough says, still arrogant. "And we're not the only ones. There's a militia in Drey, another in Iandel. The army will have to get through them to get to the Ennead."

There's nothing Liath can do. Geara begs her to come with them to Orendel, where they'll be safe, but she sends them on their way. "My journey's not over yet."

In the upper Heartlands, they come to the edge of the fighting: as expected, the local villagers have risen up against the advancing army. They're caught in it, fighting for their lives, unsure who it is they're even fighting—and running out of time. The army advances; these pathetic farmers aren't as easy to kill as Verlein expected, but still they die. This must be stopped, Liath thinks. These soldiers are killing their own people, who think they're only defending their homes, their mages.

She finds Benkana, one of Verlein's top men—Kazhe's lover, and the one who survived to turn back with Verlein in the Aralinns. He is clearly disgusted with the fighting, but still dedicated to destroying the Ennead. Liath gives him a message for Verlein: The Highlanders are rallying against them, and will get harder to kill as they go; and the Ennead knows they're coming, and will brush them off the mountain like flies. But there is another way: they can go *through* the mountain. Leave the roads, avoid the Highlander militias, avoid all the killing you can, she says, and make your way through the foothills. The wraiths will show you the way from there. "Why should Verlein believe you?" Benkana says. Liath lifts her scarred face to him and echoes something Verlein said to her long ago, after the mudslide that nearly killed them: "Tell her the truth was written on me, clearer than any scribing."

To make up time, they sail from Shrug most of the way down the Low Arm. They catch up with Torrin nearly at the Fist. She no longer needs Heff to guide her; it is the only place he could have gone. He must dissolve the Warding at its source, standing on the ground where Galandra stood. Liath passes along Evonder's message. They travel hard, and reach their destination after nightfall on the eighth day after Liath left the Holding.

Seeking a clear place to watch the stars, Liath comes across Torrin doing a casting on Heff. She assumes that Heff has finally consented to be healed; she's almost sorry, and hurt that he didn't ask her to help. But what she sees isn't Heff's face smoothing and aligning—it's magelight, growing from a flicker to a blaze. Can Torrin *create* mages now? Afterward, Heff signs to her that he was always a child of Eiden, he was only happy working with animals and metals, and his magelight was a torment for him—he couldn't *see*. She remembers what he told her, about some things being clearest only in the dark. She understands: He didn't lie to her when he said he'd never been a mage. He'd never wanted to be. Heff had himself cored and sealed by Torrin.

Why be unsealed now? she asks him. He looks at her with terrible sadness, then crushes her briefly in his arms, and steps away to sign: Because tomorrow it all ends, and I would meet that ending whole. Then he leaves her, walking away into the darkness.

Liath barges past Kazhe into Torrin's tent. He is sitting, reading a book that he always keeps with him. Why did he wait so long? If the Ennead was this much of a threat all along, why didn't he dissolve the Warding before the army was ready, or when he first left the Holding? He didn't know they had found a way to harm the outside world with the Warding intact, he says. He had hoped to bring them down by simply telling people the truth, but he was run out of Highlander towns as a heretic. He hoped they would dissolve the Warding themselves in their rush toward vengeance. He moved as soon as he got Evonder's message, in the Blooded

Mountains, that they had devised a means of circumventing the Warding. These answers aren't good enough for Liath, who saw the people the Ennead maimed while Torrin failed to act, who now knows how much was at stake. His reasons, she says, are excuses for his own cowardice. "I am not capable of dissolving the Warding," he says. She is baffled. He smiles gently. "The only ones powerful enough are Gondril, Landril, and Seldril, the product of centuries of breeding—an arrow, long sharpened, just fletched. The trick is to direct it, once it's been let fly." Liath sinks back—not mollified, but unable to counter this.

Torrin holds up the book he was reading. "I stole this, you know," he says. "It was the codex I was copying when Evonder betrayed me. I didn't mind the punishment, because I'd slipped the book into my shirt and hidden it in my chamber. It was one of the next to be studied, one of the more recent codices. No one has seen this book but me." He hands it to her. "I can't stop you from reading it tonight. But restrain yourself, if you can. When the time is right, you'll know."

She leaves him; but later, after moonrise, she goes back to his tent. They make love, finally; at dawn she wakens to find him gone, and emerges to see a casting circle cut into the grass by the edge of the outcropping where Galandra stood fifteen hundred years before.

It is the dead time that presages a storm, when the air is still and thick. Heff comes to her side, and Torrin beckons them both in. Torrin has cast some kind of warding on the circle, a warding within the Warding, and Kazhe cannot enter. Jhoss stands by, having ridden in before dawn. The handful of loyal mages and fighters stand helplessly. They know the showdown between Torrin and the Ennead will happen here, but they don't understand how or why.

The weather turns; Liath has never seen such a dark, eerie sky, sickly green to the north. Enormous waves lash the outcropping. This must be one of the Great Storms brewing, she thinks. This must be part of the plan—the Ennead will have their hands full diverting the storm. Or will they divert it at all, focused on their vengeance? Will an ill-timed storm be the death of them all, despite everything?

Torrin is calmly inscribing a parchment. The words are so complex, so intricately written, that Liath cannot decipher them—this is more powerful magecraft than she has ever witnessed, magecraft culled from an ancient time. He speaks as he works, conversationally: "I was not only waiting for the Ennead to loose their arrow," he says. "I was waiting for mages powerful enough to triad with me to direct it—and, after I found them, waiting for them to believe, and come back to me." He hands Liath the manuscript. He bids her take all that is dark, all that is hateful, vengeful, all the pain of the world, and use it to set them free—and she casts the most important illumination of her life. Torrin clasps hands with her and with Heff over the manuscript. "Sing, Heff," he bids him. "Sing all your gentle compassion, sing all the bindsongs you never sang, sing all your years of unused magelight into this casting." Heff, loosing his beautiful voice for the first time in a wordless bindsong, produces a melody sweet enough to crack the heart.

The weather worsens. The battle for control becomes a tangible vibration in the air. Gondril's triad—a silvery bright-ness against the dark of storm, both one being and three, pure spirit unmoored in time and space—appear like wraiths before them.

And there is another. Portriel, joyful, more powerful than any. Liath doesn't understand, but Torrin says, "Of course . . . they, too, had need of an arrow . . . they were merely the bow, and we are the archers . . ." Liath puts it to-gether: A sealed mage is the key to what the Ennead meant to do here. A sealed, powerful mage. When she killed Portriel, they decided to use her. When Evonder freed her, they must have been able to capture Portriel's spirit—Liath cast no pas-sage for her—

But Portriel is stronger than they are, and Portriel would haunt the stars.

As Heff sings, their blinding brightness seems funneled overhead, shot upward until it fills the sky—but what fills the sky is the Warding made visible. It is uncomprehendingly vast. It glows like the face of the moon. The air fills with that glow; all substance becomes it. There is no up, no down; Liath cannot see Torrin or Heff or her own body, only feel their hands still clasped tight, hear Heff's rending song. She can hear Kazhe, screaming, smashing herself against the cir-cle warding.

They are in another place—beyond, or inside, where they are, or both. It is the place Liath caught a glimpse of when she cast passage, with Imma and Gisela, on the Isle of Senana. She is not alone here; she is herself, yet perfectly part of Torrin and Heff, her triad, the shadow ciphers in her name. Portriel is with them, an ethereal sweetness; and in a revelation that Liath will lose in moments, she understands that Galandra's triad is the Warding. They cast passage for themselves, joining into one being and making of themselves a shield to keep Eiden Myr safe. Eiden Myr has been held in the palm of Galandra's hand for fifteen hundred years. But her triad would be free now; they are grateful to the ones who've cast their second passage. They will go on . . . and Eiden Myr will go on, as it always had to someday, a part of the greater world.

Liath senses the moment ending, feels comprehension draining away, Torrin and Heff slipping from her.

The ethereal glow shivers, warps, twists into itself. Liath comes back into her body—turned inside out, then gut-punched. Her ears pop. Her head seems crushed in a vise. All sound ceases—and then returns with a roar of wind and crash of surf. Liath scrambles up, Heff and Torrin rising more slowly. The onlookers lie stunned on the ground. The sky is roiling, but it is the real sky. Waves break over the outcropping, then recede; rain pelts them, then dies off as the storm is swept away to sea. Kazhe is groping for her sword. Torrin is standing placidly, facing seaward. Heff stares at him, then grabs Liath and heaves her tumbling down the slope. She lands next to Kazhe, who is on her knees, sword in hand, eyes wide. Kazhe screams, "No!" Liath feels the ground buck. She turns, tries to drag herself back to Torrin and Heff. The ground bucks again, more violently, and with an earsplitting roar the rocky precipice cracks off into the sea, stressed past enduring by the torquing powers, control within control, that dissolved the Warding. It takes Torrin and Heff with it. The quakes shake the others like stones in a bag. The last thing Liath hears, and she will never be sure if she heard it at all, is Heff's gentle, mangled call of farewell.

When she comes to, she's in a battle tent being ministered to by healers. There is a deadness at the heart of her; her magelight is gone. She will never feel whole again. *This is how it would have felt, if I'd truly lost it before*, she thinks. And now she has.

Kazhe is standing at the foot of her pallet, sword half raised—or just lowered. She looks harrowed. They stare at each other for a long moment; then Kazhe swears. "We both only ever tried to keep what we loved alive," she says, and limps away to join the other wounded.

A healer—once a bindsman, still wearing his triskele—stitches a gash in Liath's arm like a tear in a shirt. He gives her a warm drink: herbs, to ease her pain and help her sleep. It is Keiler, who ran away and joined the Lowlander forces. He looks battered, but his bright enthusiasm is undiminished: the lore and skills of binders will be needed most of all in these new times. Outside the tent, people are singing a rousing, bawdy victory ballad, badly.

"Isn't it beautiful?" he says. "Human voices, raised in song, with words and all?"

Liath thinks, And so it begins.

BARRY MALZBERG

BARRY MALZBERG IS ONE of the finest literary writers every to grace the field of science fiction. Writing in his own totally unique voice, he is the author of more than 90 books. Says Barry:

"*Beyond Apollo*, my seventh science fiction novel, inaugurated a new science line at Random House under the direction of the longtime mystery editor there, Lee Wright. 'If I had known what science fiction was like when I bought that manuscript,' she told me about a year later, after she had read some science fiction, 'I would never have taken it.'"

For the record, *Beyond Apollo* went on to win the very first Campbell Memorial Award for Best Novel of the Year.

BEYOND APOLLO

Barry Malzberg

IN THE NOVEL, Harry M. Evans, sole survivor of a two-man mission to Venus which has returned with only Evans, promises to explain to the satisfaction of the superving psychiatrist at the mental institution exactly what happened on the mission and why the Captain's body is missing. The novel is his diary and Evans "explains" again and again—but the accounts conflict, work at cross purposes, maddeningly plummet the reader toward the inference that in space common process may never really work. "They do not understand. They will never understand. And I do not have the language to teach them," Evans concludes.

Beyond Apollo is dependent wholly upon technique, upon voice; its plot is its device. The novel will consist of short chapters from Evans' diary cutting from the present to the past, out of chronological sequence. Each "explanation" of what happened will contradict the last; from this welter of statements may come some refraction of a final and absolute truth—but then again there may not.

ALAN RODGERS

ALAN RODGERS HAS made most of his living from a related field, horror, though he's no stranger to science fiction. A former editor of the horror magazine *Night Cry*, Alan is also the author of more than a dozen novels, including *Alien Love*, *Blood of the Children*, and *Fire*. His very first story (actually a novelette) won the Stoker Award.

Says Alan: "*Bone Music* was a book that tried to make my career against the wind. I write horror, and the public taste for horror comes and goes in big ways. At the time I sold *Bone Music*, horror had busted (bad) and *Pandora*, a horror novel with sf tropes, had not done well for me. (It is the only book I've had do poorly, in fact.) The idea with *Bone Music* was to write something so spectacularly good and so powerfully true that it would do well anyway. It was my first hardcover; it was a big move for me.

"The magnificent review in *Publishers Weekly* helped—a lot.

"And then, a few weeks after the book came out, as orders were coming in from the reviews, the publisher decided it wouldn't take any order and remaindered the thing to itself. (This is a true story. The publisher was Longmeadow, owned by Waldenbooks. Never sell your novel to a bookseller; there are inherent problems.)

"Oh, well. I've adjusted."

BONE MUSIC

by Alan Rodgers

BEFORE THE WORLD broke open there were seven kings—seven Hoodoo wizards who ruled the Mississippi lowlands from the Delta all the way north to Chicago. Oh, they didn't rule so you could see—there were mayors and governors and presidents for that. But those men weren't true powers in the Delta. The real powers were the Wizard Kings of Hoodoo, and the lesser Hoodoo men—Hoodoo Doctors—sworn to them.

You and I know these Hoodoo wizards as great Blues singers, dead and buried. But they are not dead—only hidden, pulled away from the world. Rightly hidden, too—for no singer who's grown into a Hoodoo Doctor dares perform in public. Things *happen* when Hoodoo Doctors sing.

Because the Blues aren't just music—they're magic. True and not at all hard to observe: listen to a little Leadbelly, to a few cuts from Fred McDowell or Blind Willie Johnson: there really *is* something eerie about the Blues.

ROBERT JOHNSON WAS still a young man in the late 1930s. Still a live mortal Bluesman—but he was a prodigy. Where most Blues talent comes late in life, growing and deepening until it resonates with Hoodoo, young Robert Johnson's talent grew fast and large until he mastered mysteries the greatest Bluesmen have to live hard lifetimes to learn.

Trouble was, Johnson's talent couldn't make him wise. Just the opposite, in fact—he was young, vainglorious, and foolish. And in his youthful hubris his music overstepped his craft—and Robert Johnson cut open one of the pits of Hell.

ROBERT JOHNSON CUT HELL open and set one of its pits metaphysically adrift—killing himself and setting the building where he played afire.

Three times since this Hell cut loose it's nearly to fallen to earth. The first time *Santa Barbara*—a mysterious and bloodthirsty Hoodoo saint—stopped it before it could transubstantiate. The second time (in the early 1950s, nearly a decade and a half after Johnson's death) was too much for her alone—the demons of the pit pressed it toward the Earth. So she appeared to the Wizard Kings of Hoodoo, and called on them to help. And they responded—at enormous cost. Pushing Hell back against the demonic press cost the lives of almost every Hoodoo Doctor in the Mississippi valley.

It killed all six of the Wizard Kings who touched it, too. And nearly destroyed the *santa*, despite the fact that Saints are beyond the question of life and death.

The battle nearly destroyed Hoodoo as a living art. In all the years since 1952 only a handful of Hoodoo Doctors have come forward to replace to fallen. There are no new Wizard Kings—only the seventh, Leadbelly, who refused the battle against Hell.

Now as Hell once again draws near the earth there are only a handful of ordinary people to struggle against it. They try to stop it, with the help from *Santa Barbara* and the now-resigned Leadbelly —

—and they fail.

Blue Hell comes thundering to earth a few miles outside New Orleans, and its demons (Hoodoo/Voodoo/Santeria demons out of Caribbean legend) brutalize and subjugate the city, butchering thousands. Our heroes, the *santa*, and the Hoodoo King try to set things right—but the cost is enormous and what they try may not work.

The detailed version:

There is a song all Bluesmen know: they call it the song for Judgment Day.

Some of them know it in bits and pieces; others know it nearly whole. The oldest, greatest, deepest talents among them know the song as it truly will be sung—but none of them would ever sing it just that way.

None of them would dare.

As Bluesmen and Lady Blues Singers learn their craft they come to know this song a little at a time; as they master the Blues the song comes to them more and more clearly. If and when they grow to be Hoodoo Doctors (and few of them ever do) they know it by heart, and in their hearts—no matter how they've never heard it sung.

No Hoodoo Doctor who knew the song would ever play it.

Not *exactly.* They wouldn't dare: Anyone who hears the song enough to know it knows what it will do.

If you listen to much Blues you've probably heard bits

and pieces of it, worked and reworked into Blues standards (some of which have gone on to be Rock n' Roll standards)—but even if you've heard them all you've only seen the shadows that this song casts. There's no way plain uninitiated folks can imagine the original from its parts.

THE BLUESMEN call the song "Judgment Day"—because that's when they'll sing it. Gabriel will blow his horn, and all the Hoodoo Doctors everywhere will hear, and they'll sing "Judgment Day." And the sound and the resonance that rise up from their truest song will shatter the Eye of the World.

When it shatters the Apocalypse will be upon us.

Terrible things that weigh on a song.—Things that would hang like doom impending if "Judgment Day" were just another simple four-four melody. But "Judgment Day" it isn't just a song; it's an unmasterable riff that lives only in the deepest secret hearts of Hoodoo Doctors. Only one ordinary mortal has ever deduced the song and sung it *just exactly so*—and that man was Robert Johnson, and what he sang and when he sang it are the deep root beneath this tale.

August 1938—Greenwood, Mississippi

Robert Johnson.

For two weeks now Johnson has played in a bar in Greenwood, Mississippi. And all that time he's been flirting with the owner's wife. Tonight—Saturday, August 13, 1938—Sonny Boy Williamson II joins the bar's line-up, and Johnson is showing off to him—coming on to the owner's lady openly, deliberately.

The owner isn't taking it well at all.

Between sets, Johnson and Williamson share a drink. Johnson calls for whiskey—and the barkeep brings over a full bottle with its seal cracked.

They both can see the poison in the bottle. Williamson, like Johnson, is a budding Hoodoo Doctor. More of one, in some ways—he doesn't have anything like Johnson's talent, but Williamson is a keener, more studied acolyte. And he's got years on Johnson. When Johnson goes to drink the poisoned whiskey, Williamson knocks the bottle from his hands.

It falls to the floor. Shatters dramatically.

Williamson scolds Johnson. Warns him never to drink from an open bottle.

Johnson swears at the man.

He isn't afraid of the poison. How can he be? He's full of himself—full of the arrogance of youth that compounds in prodigies until it nearly destroys them.

Johnson knows good and well that Hoodoo Doctors can eat poison. That it doesn't touch them because the truth in the music inside them purifies any poison. And brash and ignorant as he is, he's certain that he can do anything any Hoodoo Doctor can do.

"I know damn well what I'm doing," Johnson says. "You try that again and I'll kill you." He turns to the barkeep. "Go ahead," he says. "Serve me the best poison you got."

He turns to grin at the owner, who stands behind the bar looking at once angry and frightened.

Williamson pulls back at the threat. He's got enough of an eye to see Johnson's talent. Johnson *has* got it in him to kill the older Bluesman, and they both know it. But William-son also knows that Johnson is fooling himself—he may have all the talent in the world, but there isn't enough truth in Johnson's young and vainglorious heart to denature the li-quor he's been drinking, let alone neutralize arsenic.

And sure enough, Johnson succumbs to the poison. Oh, it takes a while; he's young and healthy and there's some truth in his heart.

Sonny Boy Williamson comes to Johnson in his sick bed the next morning, August 14th. "See," Johnson says, "that poison couldn't hurt me." He talks brave, but he's scared out of his mind, and they both know it. Worse, he's coming down with something, even if the poison is wearing off.

Sonny Boy doesn't say a word—no sense scaring the guy, after all.

"I got a cold," Johnson says. He coughs raggedly. Lights a cigarette. "I've got a cold but it'll clear out soon enough. I'm going to be fine."

Williamson nods, pats Johnson on the back. "You going to be fine," he says—but that's another lie they both can hear.

Because the cold Johnson's coming down with isn't any ordinary cold but bacterial pneumonia, and there won't be a medical cure for it until 1946.

Williamson leaves. And leaves town, unexpectedly.

Where he goes is to find a Hoodoo Doctor—Blind Lemon Jefferson, the way it happens.

So far as the world knows Jefferson has been dead now these seven years, buried in a shallow East Texas churchyard grave.

Blind Lemon (still pale and blind, but now he walks with the assurance of a sighted person) appears to Johnson on the morning of the 16th, as he lies in his deathbed gasping and wheezing.

Johnson knows he's in trouble, but he's been putting up a brave front. Picking at his guitar, humming bits of a song we all know but none of us want to admit. When Blind Lemon appears to him the front falls away. Johnson breaks down, starts crying—crying piteously, what with the wheezing and coughing, gasping for air as he sobs.

"You got to save me, Doctor Lemon," Johnson says. "I'm scared to die."

Lemon frowns. Shakes his head. Stoops and *looks* Johnson in the eye through his dark blind-man glasses.

Scowls and swears.

"You got to save me," Doctor Lemon. "I'm not ready yet, I know that now. I'm not ready and I'm afraid."

"You ought to be," Blind Lemon says.

"I am, Doctor. I am! So save me!"

Blind Lemon shakes his head. "There's nothing I can do for you, Robert Johnson. You got to do it for yourself."

And he leaves without waiting for a response.

Johnson is terrified, and he's getting sicker and sicker.

He keeps hearing what Blind Lemon said—*You got to do it for yourself.* He gets so angry when he remembers those words! What the Hell did the Hoodoo man mean, *You got to do it for yourself?* Who the Hell did he think he was?

Johnson lights another cigarette. Two puffs in he breaks into a spasmodic coughing fit—a fit so bad he almost doesn't recover from it. He's dying, now; there's no doubt about it. No way left to kid himself about what's going to happen. When he finally does come up, he comes up swearing.

They aren't going to kill him so easy, Johnson thinks. And if they're going to try, he's going to make them sorry.

So damn sorry.

And he starts to sing.

And what he sings is "Judgment Day."

IF BLIND LEMON had've thought Robert Johnson could sing "Judgment Day," there's no way the Hoodoo King would have left him to die alone. If anybody thought he could, they would have watched him like a hawk, like he was a disaster waiting to happen. Which he was, and had been for at least two years.

Maybe Lemon would have killed him on the spot. All things considered, it would have been the prudent thing to do.

THE LADY WHO the Witches of Isla Beata call *The Goddess Who Repented* hears him sing. She can't stop the song from where she is, but there's time enough for her to rush to the Eye of the World and hold it whole.

Or nearly whole.

All six of the Wizard Kings of Hoodoo (Leadbelly isn't a king yet at this point, and won't be until the late 1940s) hear the song from where they are, scattered up and down the length of the Mississippi Valley. Every one of them swears and lays a curse, trying to stop Johnson—but it does no good.

They're all too far away —all of them but Blind Lemon Jefferson.

Jefferson tries to stop the song, running and shouting across the Arkansas cotton field, making his blindness seem like a lie. Covering the distance between himself and the weathered shack where Johnson sings dying in hard bounding strides that athletes would be hard-pressed to match.

Johnson hears him.

And he feels the Hoodoo gathering around him, trying to stop him—and sings that much harder. That much more righteously.

Clouds roil out of nowhere to crowd the sky that only moments before shone clear and bright; thunder peels as lightning flickers around the shack.

And Robert Johnson sings.

Lightning strikes, setting the shack afire, but that doesn't stop Johnson. Not even when the Eye appears in the clouded sky above them; not even as it opens bloodshot with lens-bursting fractures to reveal the Lady of Sorrows standing on the lens trying to hold it whole; and look, look into the eye and you'll see Hell through the lens, Hell thick and blue thriving like a jungle...

Blind Lemon bursts into the burning shack. Screams at Johnson; holds his cane above his head like the stick of power that it truly is, and moves Hoodoo through the air to seize the dying man and stop him—

But it does no good. Johnson finishes "Judgment Day" as the Hoodoo touches him. And there's nothing it can do; he's dead already, and the Eye cracks, and Blind Lemon stands in a smoldering wreck beside the body of a man who isn't really dead.

The present—Brooklyn, New York

We're in a Brooklyn hospital room with a little girl wrapped in tubes and wires.

Her name is Lisa Henderson, and she's dying of cancer.

We see Lisa's death through her own eyes—and we see that she never passes entirely to the hereafter.

We feel the *presence* that holds her and comforts her in the formless dark between here and the hereafter. We can feel it loves Lisa—and feel how bloodthirsty it is! Demonic, almost!

We see through Lisa's eyes as her mother and the Santeria lady—Mama Estrella—resurrect her as a zombie; we see through her own eyes as she comes back to life in the Brooklyn Cemetery and walks home with her mother.

Emma, Lisa, the Santeria Lady—they all know there's something wrong about a little girl being alive and really herself, a zombie who really is a little girl inside—but none of them understand enough to know what to do about it. The Santeria Lady wants to put the zombie of Lisa's body back to sleep, and let the little girl soul inside her pass the beyond, but Emma won't let her. Which is maybe for the best—because even though the zombie eventually rots apart, Lisa is reborn as an infant from the shell that was her cancer—which never died, not even when she died the first time.

For a while it looks as though Emma and Lisa have a happy life ahead of them. Until it becomes obvious that she isn't really as fine as she seemed at first. She's still inhumanly strong, and she has a temper—almost like she was possessed by a demon.

The real reason her soul came back to her body when Mama Estrella resurrected her as a zombie is that it hadn't yet passed to the hereafter. And the reason it didn't is because Our Lady of Sorrows held her in the darkness between *here* and *there*.

Our Lady of Sorrows: Santa Barbara, the virgin who carries the sword. You can find her shrines in lawns and niches all through Florida, the northeast; everywhere folks have immigrated from the Caribbean. Uninitiated folks might mistake them for shrines to the Virgin Mary—but that's a serious mistake. For this *Santa Barbara* is nothing but nothing at all like the Mother of the Lord.

Some say she is no saint at all, but rather a Voodoo Demon Loa whose secret name is Shungó. Others say she is a saint, bloodthirsty and vindictive but touched with the righteousness of heaven.

Which is she? No one knows. And if anyone did they wouldn't say: Questions like that aren't for mortals (even mortals like the Hoodoo Doctors) to answer. Mortals know her, fear her. And honor her. Everyone who knows her by any name knows to honor her.

Only a fool would dare to cross her.

And somewhere between *here* and *there*, Santa Barbara kissed little Lisa, and returned her to her mother.

Which is why the girl came to life in her own dead body, and lived on in her cancer when her body crumbled to dust.

And also why Lisa (now a baby, hatched from the tumorous leathery shell that was her cancer) grows more foul-tempered and demoniacally strong as the days pass.

After a while it occurs to Emma and Mama Estrella that there is something terribly wrong about the little girl. A year after her rebirth, Mama Estrella decides she must be possessed, and tries to exorcise her.

Bad, bad idea. Not only does this not work, but the exorcism's backlash nearly kills Mama Estrella.

The next day Emma visits her in the hospital. Mama Estrella (who can barely speak) tells her she's got to take Lisa to the great Hoodoo Doctor who lives down in Mississippi. She gives elaborate instructions—this guy keeps himself quite hidden, and for good cause.

EMMA AND LISA set off for Mississippi by car.

The trip is full of complications—*Santa Barbara* (since the abortive exorcism a looming presence) doesn't want them going where they're going.

Emma can feel the Lady watching them, angry at what they're doing. She keeps expecting her to appear to them, but she never does.

They finally find the Hoodoo doctor, after performing a seemingly silly series of rituals just outside a small town in Mississippi. (He turns out to be the old man they met not long after they got to town.) He's Leadbelly—a man who was supposed to have died fifty years ago. (I'll break and recount a little of his history; he's an incredibly colorful figure. Twice he sung his way to freedom from life sentences for murder.

Somewhere late in life he got into a barroom fight with a man who got the best of him—slit his throat and left him for dead. But he didn't die—spent the rest of his life wearing scarves to hide the scar.)

Leadbelly takes Emma and Lisa out into the woods, and they build a fire. Leadbelly plays his beautiful twelve-string guitar. And he sings—not to Emma or Lisa, but to the fire. By and by the fire grows truer and clearer and more beautiful, and now the light it casts shows things not shadowy as firelight but true as sunshine.

And grows truer and truer still until it shows the truth about each of them.

It shows Emma looking the image of honor and duty—she's a woman with backbone, and she doesn't flinch at things that hurt when they mean the welfare of her child.

Shows Leadbelly an angry mean-tempered scoundrel—but he's got integrity, and he knows something true and important about the nature of the world. Listening to him in that light Emma almost thinks he's singing songs that God whispered in his ear.

And then she looks at Lisa.

Lisa looks dreadful in the true firelight: her skin is venous, mottled, and leathery like the cancer that bore her. There's a bloodthirsty look in her eye.—And standing behind her with a hand on Lisa's shoulder is Santa Barbara with her sword.

Los Angeles, California

He heard her before he saw her, but he knew that she

was there for a long time before she made a sound. She had that kind of presence—thick and palpable, electric as a thunderstorm about to break. It was late July, and Dan Alvarez lay in his bed awake and uneasy, as unable to sleep as he'd been every night for months.

Three big gusts of wind pressed against the window across the room, rattling the panes, the edges of the frame. It would rain soon, Dan thought—that was why he felt the storm about to happen. That was all it was.

Dan Alvarez almost managed to believe it, too.

His life was always like that, he thought: he was a storm waiting to happen, never breaking loose. Any day now, any damn day real soon one or another of the half-dozen bands he played with would take off, and he'd have a career, a real honest-to-God rock 'n' roll legend career and tell the bar gigs and the temp agencies to put it where none of them would ever see it again.

Of course he felt the tension in the air—he was a tension waiting to happen, a legend waiting to be told.

Like hell.

Even in his worst moments Dan knew better—no matter how he wanted to believe, he knew too damn well that it just wasn't so. He wasn't going anywhere, and every day that went by he had a little less heart for bashing his head against the walls that surrounded him.

And then it finally came: a great flash of lighting so bright like the sun suddenly come to earth beside him—that close, so close that thunder burst right with it. No delay, not even a beat. Like it hit a block away. Maybe closer.

He rolled over onto his side. Pulled the blanket tight.

And heard the scratching tapping at his window pane.

Someone was out there in the thunder and the rain. Someone who wanted his attention.

Who the hell. . . ?

But he didn't want to know who it was. He was scared out of his mind, and if he'd had the nerve he would have pushed away the blankets and run for his life—but he didn't have the nerve, didn't have any nerve at all too scared to move to speak to look who the hell in the storm it was thundering out there.

Too damned scared to move, let alone run.

Too scared to look, too, but his eyes opened in spite of themselves.

And that was how he first saw her: watching him through the glass.

Our Lady of Sorrows, Santa Barbara.

It didn't matter that he'd never seen her before. He'd known her all his life. Seen her shrines and grottoes outside dozens of houses back home in Union City; smelled the potion that bore her name hot summer afternoons when his mother came from the *botanica*; shivered when he saw the paint of her in the bar where wrinkled superstitious Cuban grandfathers smoked fat cigars as they sipped at their *cervezas.*

Santa Barbara: the virgin with the burning sword, blood- hungry and terrible.

Dan Alvarez sat on the edge of his bed. Shivered with fear. He wanted to run. Wanted to look away from the *santa.*

And if he couldn't run or look away he wanted to ask her why she'd come for him. She meant to kill him—he knew that. Couldn't help knowing! Look at her, so beautiful and angry in the flickering chiaroscuro light from her burning sword—look at her! Blood-red eyes, long soft coils of black hair piled high and cascading from her head; skin white as ash. Whiter than any living thing ever ought to be. Dan saw her and knew she was all terror of the dark distilled and made tangible; knew she was the wrath of the Lord set out upon the world to do his bidding—or worse!

She wants me to let her in.

But he knew he didn't dare.

I've got to open the window.

Because she was his fate, come to him. Come *for* him. There was no way he could avoid or delay what she had for him—only deny it, and denying the inevitable wasn't a thing Dan ever managed to do.

When he finally stood and crossed the room, it was as involuntary, as unconscious as when he'd opened his eyes.

Just like a fate, he thought.

"*Santa,*" he said when the window was open. "I live to serve you." He felt stupid to say those words—like some *guajiro* hick in a story of his grandfather's. And he wasn't any damned hick! He was American, an honest to God rock n' roll American boy with talent nobody ever bothered to abuse, and the day was going to come really soon when they'd all regret they'd missed their opportunity!

They were, Dan swore they were.

The *santa* smiled. When she spoke her voice was a whisper through the open window, throaty and hungry as desire. "I hear," she said. "I have come."

"Why are you here for me, Virgin?" Dan Alvarez tried to keep the fear out of his voice, but it wasn't any use. "I know I am unworthy."

The *santa* ignored his question. She reached through the window to touch his face, and for a moment it was a tender gesture that cast a warm light on Dan's life—fulfilled him, made him whole enough to die happy and content. And then the touch changed. Not so dramatically that anybody watching would have noticed, but Dan felt it, and there was no way she could have touched him like that without meaning to. Her fingers pressed hard against him, hard as though she were trying to probe the bone of this skull right through his skin. Maybe that was the point, he thought; maybe she pressed him the way a butcher probes a sow he means to buy to slaughter.

Maybe.

Dan tried to protest. "Santa—" he said, but she waved to silence him before he could say another word.

"Do you accept me?" she asked.

He didn't understand, but he knew in his heart that he didn't dare say anything but *yes*.

"I do, *santa*."

And all hell of thunder broke loose above him—lightning struck the roof, shattering the building's wood frame. Sundering the roof and walls; setting the sundered bits afire.

DAN ALVAREZ WAS never sure what happened to him after the thunder. Later he could remember running blindly through the raining dark, stumbling, bettering himself again and again. But he could never remember how he escaped the burning wreck of his apartment.

Never remembered what happened to the *santa*, or what she meant for him when he ccepted her.

The thing he remembered clearest was waking in a ditch in an abandoned industrial park. Sitting up and looking around to see the city of Los Angeles dark and fiery all around him—the power was out everywhere for miles, no electric lights anywhere he could see in every direction. But there was light. Plenty of light—the whole damned city was on fire.

If he'd had any sense he would have counted his blessings and crawled back into the ditch. It wasn't safe, wandering around with the city burning.

HE ENDS UP leaving the city like a hobo by train—he's going to the Mississippi delta. He isn't sure why, but he keeps thinking about how the blues came out of misery in the delta, and how this was exactly what the Bluesmen used to do—live like hoboes, moving town to town like no-account bums, and maybe in a way that's all they were—and not, too, because he's heard them, heard the old recordings full of mystery and magic and if there isn't something higher and more beautiful, something—something magic in those blues.

That's what it is, isn't it? Magic. The blues weren't just music, they were magic.

He's dreaming again. He dreams an awful scary dream where the gods have come to earth—

No, not gods, these aren't gods but something less, they're petty godlets that run and hide when they see the shadow of the One True Lord—

He has an awful awful dream where it's 1952 on a high Bluff outside Nashville Tennessee, and all the Bluesmen all the true Bluesmen and women sing...

December, 1952—Nashville, Tennessee

The Wizard Kings, the Hoodoo Doctors, the greatest of the acolyte Bluesmen and women stand on a bluff outside Nashville, and they sing.

As they sing the sky folds and tolls and thunders, storms and rages through the night. High in the clouds is the Eye of the World, and deep inside it Hell and the demon Loa press against the lens from deep inside.

The Hoodoo Doctors sing a song so powerful and true that it forces the Eye shut—or tries to. Even with the *santa's* help it's hard for them to shut the Eye. Harder still to resist the Loa pressing against them, pressing the Eye open, trying to burst the Lens.

Dan Alvarez, watching the battle through his dream, is certain that he recognizes the song they sing. No, not "Judgment Day" something purer, empty of rage...what is it? He knows that song, he knows that tune, he knows it and loves and for the life of him he's damned if he can remember the number (near the end of the book it'll come to him: the ode to joy from Beethoven's Ninth, bent and twisted on itself till it's become a blues number).

And now the Moon rises high, and the open sky begins to close—and there's a great explosion, a powerful shattering of the night that sends electric fire in every direction.

When it's clear the sky has closed again, and the Hoodoo Doctors lie scattered and broken across the bluff.

And a white boy named Elvis Presley comes across them, sees the carnage, sees the strange unearthly fire still burning here and there—and turns to run for his life.

But not before he steals a guitar.

The present—Los Angeles, California

Dan Alvarez wakes panting, gasping for air. It's pitch night in the boxcar, he's alone as alone gets, and now the train rounds a bend and moonlight floods in through the open boxcar door.

And in the moonlight he sees it beside him: the guitar that Elvis Presley stole.

WE'LL SEE THIS battle again from other perspectives. It's at the root of a lot of history.

SIX OF THE KINGS sung the ode to joy from high up on the bluff outside Nashville in 1952. The seventh king was Leadbelly.

Of all the Kings only Leadbelly lived a hermit and away the people who needed him. Oh, when they'd come to him in need, he'd do what he could—but he did everything he could to make himself unfindable.

Some say Leadbelly was afraid—that he was a coward afraid to meet his fate, afraid to call the Hoodoo he was born to wield. Others say the kings never called him. Because he was a killer? A scoundrel? Because he never took the reins to lead?

Or was it because they knew their fate before they climbed the bluff to sing? Did the Wizard Kings know the battle was to kill them? Did they leave Leadbelly behind to rule the river in their stead?

No one but Leadbelly could ever tell you why—and he never hears the question, no matter how it's asked.

Robert Johnson didn't die of pneumonia in that battered shack on the Mississippi hillside.

He *disappeared.*

Same as Leadbelly disappeared in the late 40s; same as all Hoodoo Bluesmen disappear when they need to move on from being singers to being Hoodoo Doctors. But there was something different about Johnson: he was young and not at all ready, despite the his prodigal and enormous talent. And when he disappeared, not even the Wizard Kings of Hoodoo could find him.

Blind Lemon Jefferson left his body in the burning shack on Mississippi hillside. Hours later, when he came back for it, the corpse was already gone.

It was years and years before anyone saw Johnson again.

Greenville, Mississippi

When Emma sees the *santa* standing behind her little girl, she starts screaming. Leadbelly douses the fire. When the last embers are dead, he reaches over to turn on the electric lantern he brought with him. The clearing floods with pale bluish fluorescent light—the kind of light that lets you see miles in thin pinewoods like these.

Lisa is gone. And no matter how they look, no matter which way they shine the bright fluorescent light, there's no sign of her. Nor any tracks: Leadbelly checks the ground for spoor, but there is none.

Los Angeles, California

Dan Alvarez tries to play the guitar he finds beside him, but he doesn't manage to do much with it. It sounds flat, out of tune—and no matter how he tries to tune it he can't get it to sound right.

Greenville, Mississippi

Emma and Leadbelly search for Lisa all night long. They don't find her—don't find so much as a trace.

When the sun is high and bright Leadbelly says "Enough of this. Follow me. We need to try something different." And he leads her to his musty cottage in the deep deep woods. He makes coffee and serves it with sectioned oranges. They sit near the dark hearth (still dusty with ashes from last winter's fires) and Leadbelly plays his melodious twelve-string guitar. Softly, softly, picking and strumming no recognizable tune but an endless half-melody—a melody from a jam session, but how could anyone call something so quiet and gentle a jam?

After a while he seems to doze, but he plays on and on. Till now the music drifts away, and Emma fades asleep still sitting in the wide-armed chair beside the hearth.

The last thing she hears is Leadbelly, snoring.

New Orleans, Louisiana

Lisa wakes alone and confused in an alley in New Orleans' French Quarter. It's hours after midnight, so late that even these nightside streets are deserted. She wanders for a long time—through the French Quarter, south past the docks, and now the docklands are even more abandoned—New Orleans isn't the port it used to be. Lisa comes to a tall old wooden mansion, crumbling and abandoned-looking—but it isn't abandoned at all. Just the opposite: there's a party raging inside. People passed out drunk all across the unkempt lawn.

She wanders in, despite her better judgment. She's only a baby, too short to open the doors—but the doors are all open, and no one seems to notice when she wanders right on in. Where she hears the most amazing thing: people talking conspiratorially about the end of the world.

Lisa forgets herself, her circumstances. Gawks at the red- eyed whisperer who looks partly like a woman and partly like a man—and feels every hair on her body stand on end as she realizes that these aren't people at all, but rather *outre* things that take the seeming of people.

Suddenly she's terrified, and knows she has to leave. But

now the doors are all closed, and she's only a baby, too short to reach the handles.

The only direction she can go is through the door that leads to the basement. And she knows better than that. Going further in is the worst thing she can do. Then someone spots her, shouts at her, tells her to stop and explain herself. And she's got no choice: she has to run. And the only way to run is down into the basement.

No one follows her there, which is maybe the most frightening thing of all.

But when she gets there it doesn't seem so awful. At the bottom of the stairs she sees a man in a pretty pinstripe suit sitting on a stool. He has a guitar and a wide white-tooth smile. And when he plays his guitar it's the most amazing thing, the way he coaxes sound and rhythm from the instrument. Lisa stands transfixed as she listens to him.

The man she's listening to is Robert Johnson.

She'll end up following him down into hell, but I don't know why yet.

Greenville, Mississippi

More with Emma and Leadbelly

Timeless—Hell

Lisa and Robert Johnson wander through Hell—at first it looks all fire and brimstone, a very traditional hell the way we know hell. And now Robert Johnson leads her through the stone and iron door, and hell is a new place entirely—a fetid jungle blooming thick with dark blue foliage. (Lisa isn't sure whether it's blue because of some trick in the Hellish light or because it really is blue.) The air is thick and humid; it smells like a disease. The demons in this blue pit watch them—skulking in the jungle shadows, staring through the thick blue dark. These demons are the Loa, Robert Johnson tells her.—It's better not to look them in the eye. He leads her toward a shrine that stands beside a cool, misty brook—until the Loa demons surround them, blocking their passage.—Then suddenly comes Santa Barbara, cutting her way through the jungle with her bloody fiery sword.

A saint, walking through hell!

None of the Loa dare speak to her, much less challenge her. They melt into the jungle, and Santa Barbara leads Lisa and Robert Johnson to the brook.

THE SOUND OF THE BROOK is the strumming of a guitar, gently pressing four-four time. The whisper of the leaves on the breeze as they stand beside the water is the song that is the motion of the world. Some of those who've heard it say it's lonely, ponderous and sad; blues music like you hear when you get up in the morning and the blues are there to greet you.

But other people say that it isn't sad or happy, but beautiful and intense as the music that is the sum of all our lives.

*   *   *

Hell.

The brook that strums, the jungle forest that whispers secret histories of all our days, the basin lens that Hoodoo Doctors call the Eye of the World—there's no way anyone who witnessed any of those things could mistake that they're touched divine and sacrosanct. And people ask however there could be such a holy shrine in the bluest pit of Hell.

Sensibly enough.

But the sense in that misses Hell's true nature. For it's a place not only for the damned but for the damned and unrepentant. Who among us, after all, hasn't once or another sinned enough to damn him straight to Hell? The God Who loves us knows our weaknesses, and He loves us even so. Hell isn't a place of Holy Wrath and Retribution; it's a place to separate the pious from the unrepentant.

It's not a pretty place. Just the opposite, in fact: Hellish means just what it does because the Pits are Awful. But that Hellishness reflects not Divine Judgment but the nature of the occupants. And there are those among the unrepentant with greatness, love, and beauty in them, no matter how they sin.

IN THE BROOK there's a relic we remember from he battle on the bluff: a basin whose bottom is clear like a lens. When Lisa looks through it she can see the bluff below them.—For the Eye of the World looks down on Earth from the Bluest Pit of Hell, and has for ages now since the Loa fell from grace.

* * *

THE EYE'S LENS cracked during the battle on the bluff, but it didn't shatter.

LONG BEFORE MAN came to the western hemisphere, there was another island in the sea that now surrounds great Hispaniola. It was a rich blue thriving place that bloomed with a thousand thousand flowers.

In a glen near the center of the island there was a shrine, and the legend says there was a window in that shrine, and the window looked in at heaven.

The Loa—a class of Higher Beings (angels, almost, but very different)—the Loa built the Eye to Celebrate their love for the Lord. They built a thousand other wonders, too—like their great mountainesque sculptures that stretched miles into the heavens. They took great pride in their accomplishments, and after a while they grew to hold themselves in high regard.

They grew so vain, in fact, that when man arrived in the Americas, the Loa built temples that man might worship them. They were gods, they told the men who found them. They demanded to be worshiped. They demanded sacrifice—*human* sacrifice. And taught the Mayans, who taught the Aztec... soon enough the time came that the Lord cast the Loa and their paradise into Hell, removing them forever from the mundane world we know.—Not so much because their deeds offended Him (more likely He felt sad, disappointed) as because they'd made themselves a foul and dangerous influence on the face of the Earth.

That's how the Eye of the World came to look on the earth where once it spied into Heaven.

SANTA BARBARA is a saint, all right. But she's a Loa, too—or was. She is the only one of all of them who repented.

LISA STANDS at the edge of the brook that cuts across Blue Hell, and she looks at the water. Looks at the basin, looks at the lens. The lens is a crystal basin full of water that flows through from the stream; when the stream is high and full the water and the crystal look out onto a bluff in Tennessee. But right now the stream is anything *but* full.

Fifty years ago, Robert Johnson tells her, I sang to the eye. I broke it, damn near. It would have broke, too—but the *santa* heard me sing, and she went to the eye and held it whole.

She held the shards in place, but she couldn't mend them back together.

For a dozen years that didn't matter. The *santa* puts something together, it like to stay that way—whether it mend or not. Then in 1952 the water in Blue Hell ran dry.

It does that sometimes, just as streams run dry on earth—this may be Hell, but this part used to be an island on earth, and in a lot of ways it hasn't changed.

So long as there's water in the shrine, the unrepentant don't dare go near the Eye. They can't bear the light that shines through the Eye—there's too much truth in it. But when the streams run dry, the lens clouds until it becomes opaque. When it dries entirely it passes so little light that the Loa have no reason to fear it.

When it dried in 1952 the Loa stood together at the Eye and pressed against it. Santa Barbara stood against them on the far side of the lens, but even mighty as she is (and the righteous are many times the match for the unrepentant) she wasn't enough to contain them.

And knew that from years away in time—from the moment Robert Johnson cracked the eye, in fact. That's why she assembled the chorus of Hoodoo Doctors on the bluff.

Between them the *santa* and the Hoodoo Doctors were enough to contain the Loa. But only just enough, and at enormous cost—the battle killed all six of the seven kings who fought in it. Killed all but three of the Hoodoo Doctors who fought alongside them. And while it couldn't kill Santa Barbara (death isn't really relevant to those who've already descended into hell and found their way up from it) while nothing could kill Santa Barbara the battle very nearly destroyed her immortal essence. She fell away from the lens broken and dissipated; slid into the deepest pit in hell and spent a decade recovering.

She still hasn't recovered entirely.

Lisa turns to the *santa*. "What can we do?" she asks. "We've got to keep them here, don't we? That's why you came for me, isn't it?"

The *santa* frowns. She looks very sad.

"No, child," she says. "There's nothing we can do to contain them."

As the last trickle of water in the stream through the lens runs dry.

And the Loa descend upon them.

THERE'S AN AWFUL FIGHT, bloody and immaterial. When it's over, the Loa have pounded Lisa, Robert Johnson, and the *santa* into the ground, broken the lens inside the eye—and as they broke it Blue Hell descended back to earth.

About three miles outside the city of New Orleans.

From here on out, the book is a chase, as Emma, Lisa, Leadbelly, Dan Alvarez, and the *santa* fight for their lives and look for solutions in the city infested with demons. At least a couple of them won't make it to the far end of the book alive.

STEPHEN LEIGH

STEVE LEIGH AND I have been Cincinnati's science fiction writing community for the better part of 20 years. (Maureen McHugh was here for a while, but she deserted us after winning her Hugo and moved to Cleveland in time for five of the snowiest winters in history. That'll show her.)

Steve has sold 16 novels, and a couple of dozen short stories. He won the Spectrum Award for Best Novel of 1998, and the Annual AnLab Readers' Poll for Best Short Story.

Says Steve:

"Let me go on record as saying that I hate and detest outlines. Outlines are homework you gotta do on a bright, sunny spring afternoon when everyone else is out playing. My novels never seem to follow them anyway—I'll get some bright idea halfway through and go off on some tangent I had no idea existed when I started. Half the time, I'm not certain what the end's going to be myself when I sit down to do one of these. As a result, I try to keep them sketchy and short.

"I'd given Avon Eos a proposal for *Speaking Stones*. However, Jennifer Brehl, my editor there, wanted to buy two books, not one. We agreed on a contract with a "book to be named later," for which I would submit an outline once I finished *Speaking Stones*.

"I did this one much differently from any previous outline, which had always been more a straight "A happens, and then B occurs, which leads to C..." This was a chance to try something different and see if I liked the format any better. I didn't: an outline's still an outline no matter how you dress it. I don't know that this 'sold' the concept any better—but it *did* sell this one, which is what matters.

"Of course, by the time I finished the book, Avon was bought by Harper Collins (though thankfully Jen was retained in the merger), the title changed from *Silence* to *Thunder Rift*, the final book (of course) didn't greatly resemble the outline, and it will be released under the name 'Matthew Farrell' not 'Stephen Leigh.'

"Hey, things change."

SILENCE
Expected Length: approx. 100,000 words

PLOT ENGINE: In the latter years of the 21st century, a rift is opened between our solar system and another, a wormhole whose existence defies explanation. It is an obvious construction, rather than a natural phenomenon, but the electromagnetic emissions from the thing cause chaos on Earth. To the military, it is viewed with suspicion, as the possible first volley in an alien invasion. To those less concerned with security, it is a bridge, an invitation from an unknown race.

Whatever it is, the rift (dubbed "Thunder") beckons. An expedition is sent to go through the wormhole in a huge research vessel: the *Lightbringer*. The *Lightbringer* expedition is funded by the United Nations (whose military arm runs the ship). A scientific crew is also installed, but what exactly Lightbringer is supposed to be—military scout or research ship—is not quite certain, even to those aboard.

Main Characters: Though there will be other supporting cast, the focus of the book will be on Taria Spears, a human civilian from Lightbringer, and Makes-The-Sound-Of-East-Wind-At-Darkness (or Makes), an alien on Little Sister, a world on the far side of the wormhole. The setting for most of the book will be Little Sister.

Taria: was conceived at the moment Thunder first appeared, and her mother was killed a few years later during the Thunder- induced economic depression. These two facts have made Thunder Taria's obsession, have made her feel that her life purpose is linked to Thunder (though she has yet to discover what that purpose may be), and have also made her, to some extent, psychically damaged goods. She becomes compulsive about Thunder, to the detriment of the rest of her life, and directs her obsession to becoming one of the crewmembers of *Lightbringer*. Once through the wormhole, through an accident of truth, Taria becomes the primary contact between the humans and the Blues, an indigenous sentient race on the earth-like world (dubbed "Little Sister" by the crew of *Lightbringer*. She become involved with Makes, and with the mystery of another species there called the 'watersingers.' Though the powers-that-be aboard *Lightbringer* feel that the Blues are not important—they are too unsophisticated technologically to be the sought-for 'Makers' of Thunder—her intuition tells Taria that the Blues and Little Sister are important. In that, she is right.

Makes: one of the Blues, perhaps a priest, perhaps a mystic, perhaps a scientist, or perhaps something else entirely. The Blues' chief god is a female diety who lives in the sky, and Makes was due to be accepted into the order of Those-Who-Speak-With-Her when their side of Thunder opened. That changed her life. She became the ba-ra-ki, or She-Whose-Life-Is-Gifted-To-Her. The Blues, whose hearing range extends far higher and lower than that of a human, could hear Thunder as an eternal hissing emanating from the night sky: perhaps the very voice of God. The arrival of the humans (who saw no God in the sky, and who claim that the Voice of God is simply a pathway from their world to that of the Blues) have thrown the social order of the Blues into chaos, and have made the role of the ba-ra-ki uncertain. Makes, too, is obsessed about Thunder, though her agenda is very different from that of Taria.

Story Arc: this is a novel that examines modes of communication and conditioned social and behavioral responses. The title reflects the bias of the aliens of the book, for in both the Blues and the Watersingers hearing is the primary sense—thus "silence" is analogous to our adjective "darkness." Where we may fear the dark, they fear the silent.

The story will be in third person, told in alternating 'present time' segments as well as flashback segments from Taria's viewpoint (and perhaps, later in the book, from Makes' as well). The flashback segments will illuminate Taria's psyche, as well as shed light on the human perspective.

At the time of the opening of *Silence, Lightbringer*'s efforts to unravel the mystery of Thunder have done nothing so far. They've been in the vicinity for over an earth year and are no nearer to finding the Makers. It's obvious the Blues could not be responsible for the rift in the fabric of space-time. They are entirely oblivious to the science of astronomy and claim to be unconcerned with Thunder's existence. The Blues' primary senses are those of hearing and touch; their visual organs giving them only a myopic sense of light and dark. Their cosmology is almost entirely mythology—they refer to the sky simply as Emptiness- Above-Us. There is another indigenous race on the world, called the watersingers, a semi-aquatic species who create "sculptures" of focused acoustic energy. The Blues, while appreciating the watersingers' "art", also use them as a food source. If the watersingers are capable of inter-species communication, it has not yet been shown, nor (without hands or tools) do they seem capable of being able to create something like Thunder.

Taria has become the sole emissary to the Blues, and she will become embroiled in the conflict between Makes and the Blues' warrior caste, who are threatening a political takeover in the power vacuum created by the realization that the Blues' mythology is no longer valid.

In the midst of this, without warning, Thunder vanishes altogether, as if it had never existed at all, leaving the humans trapped hundreds of light years from Earth. Aboard *Lightbringer*, the decision will be made to settle on Little Sister—and when the Blues protest, a demonstration of human destructiveness is arranged. A human delegation is killed in retaliation. The conflict threatens to escalate, and Taria and Makes are in the middle of it.

Taria will come to the realization that the watersingers—who are far more than they appear—are the ones responsible for creating Thunder, which is a pathway through which they propagate from system to system, always choosing a satellite of a gas giant. Thunder was opened to send watersingers to Earth's system. Taria and Makes must determine how to communicate with the watersingers (who speak in a language composed of aural shapes), who possess no visual organs at all and do not seem to hear in the same frequencies as humans, and then convince them to re-open Thunder.

In the climax, Taria and Makes must set aside their own prejudices and biases to cross the communication gulf between three species and reach the watersingers. The watersingers will re-open the rift. The *Lightbringer* and a psychically-healed Taria will return home; Makes will fulfill her messianic role as ba-ra-ki.

In passing Jupiter's satellite Europa, they will hear the music of the watersingers.

Kevin J. Anderson

THERE'S NOT MUCH in this field that Kevin J. Anderson can't do. He writes bestselling Star Wars books. He writes bestselling Dune books. He writes award-winning   Kevin J. Anderson books. He edits wonderful anthologies.

Here's what Kevin terms "the sales pitch" for his new opus, *The Saga of Seven Suns*. It will be a trilogy, but Kevin writes *long* sales pitches, and we simply didn't have room to run the entire thing here (it came to over 30,000 words), so you'll have to settle for the synopsis to the first book.

After sending me the synopsis, and before this book went to press, Kevin informed me that he had sold it for, well, a Kevin J. Anderson price, than which not much is bigger these days.

THE SAGA OF SEVEN SUNS

An Epic Science Fiction Series in the Vein of Frank Herbert's Dune *and Robert Jordan's "Wheel of Time" Books*

by Kevin J. Anderson

THE SAGA OF SEVEN SUNS is a multi-volume science fiction epic that chronicles a legendary war that spans half the Galaxy and nearly shatters the cosmos. This series follows the family intrigues, the loves and tragedies, pomp and pageantry among several competing races in an expanding stellar empire. *The Saga of Seven Suns* combines the adventure and sense-of-wonder in *Star Wars* with the epic grandeur and sophistication of *Dune*.

Each volume draws on the mythic elements that have formed the core of such popular works as *The Lord of the Rings* and *Dune*. In developing this epic, I used the model of epic fantasy, incorporating archetypes and core mythologies but placing them in a vast science fiction universe, while consciously avoiding the nuts-and-bolts trappings of "clunky" pulp SF. This path is similar to what I have followed in the enormously successful *Dune* prequels I've co-authored with Brian Herbert, as well as my 21 internationally bestselling *Star Wars* books. My intention is to make *The Saga of Seven Suns* an epic for science fiction comparable to Robert Jordan's *Wheel of Time* fantasy series, or the blockbusters of

Terry Brooks, Tad Williams, Terry Goodkind, and George R. R. Martin. These large and complex books are filled with alien races, court intrigues, romance and color and sense-of- wonder. In science fiction, some of the best examples are the grand novels of C.S. Friedman, Vernor Vinge, and Joan Vinge.

Best of all for the marketplace, subsequent volumes of *Seven Suns* will come out regularly. (I have a demonstrated track record of meeting deadlines on my 50+ novels over the past decade.)

What follows is a broad-strokes outline listing major events and scenes, but without all of the subplots, character backgrounds and motivations, peripheral players, cultural details, or connecting chapters. I have described the first three volumes, though I intend for the series to continue as its readership builds with successive installments.

Each novel will be approximately 130,000-150,000 words and will be delivered yearly, on time, for a regular publication schedule.

BRIEF SERIES BACKGROUND

In a *Dune*-style galactic society, humans are one of three known intelligent races. We are the new kids on the block, starfarers for only a couple of centuries, working to expand and establish a commercial empire, the Trade Confederacy —a bureaucracy and de facto government whose figurehead is a benevolent King. In everyday society, humans have also developed ubiquitous "compie" servants, a cross between

STAR WARS droids and Asimov's robots. (The term compie is a gimmicky advertising name, short for 'computerized competent companion.')

Another group of humans—an independent colony and political force—inhabits the distant forested world of Teroc. Over the centuries, the people of Teroc have developed a religious symbiosis with the interconnected semi-intelligent world-spanning forest, which gives them limited telepathic powers. These Teron "green priests" are able to communicate instantaneously with each other through their "telink" with the trees, regardless of their separation. Thus the Teron green priests have become vital, living substations for interstellar messages. Every major city and world has at least one green priest to act as a sort of telegraph station to send and receive messages.

A third group of humans, the Roamers, operate outside the bounds of the Trade Confederacy, like gypsies. They have carved out a broad commercial niche for themselves by harvesting stardrive fuel from the clouds of gas-giant planets. The second intelligent race, the ILDIRANS, founded a once vast and powerful galactic empire, but because they have been around for a long time, their Empire is growing tired and stagnant, their population decreasing. The Ildirans prefer to be crowded and live closely packed, and as their numbers decline, they have abandoned many of their fringe colonies (which humans quickly take over).

Ancient and ethereal, the Ildirans have many different physical appearances and body morphologies (like, for instance, the various breeds of dogs), but they can all inter-breed.

The Ildirans are ruled by their Mage-Imperator, a powerful man who has a faint telepathic link, called thism, with his entire population. A third alien race, the KLIKISS, is an insectoid species that apparently became extinct long before even Ildiran recorded history began.

The abandoned Klikiss worlds are full of empty hive cities, artifacts, and mysteries, which are being studied by teams of human archaeologists. No one has a clue what really happened to the original Klikiss.

The only real remnants of this vanished insectoid race are their self-aware and intelligent robots, hulking machines built to resemble their ominous beetle-like progenitors. Though only a few thousand of them remain, the Klikiss robots have infiltrated the high levels of galactic society and can be found in many major population centers. These robots, which have been in existence for thousands—perhaps millions—of years, claim they have no memory of what happened to their long-vanished masters (but they are lying).

Lastly, the HYDROGUES are liquid-crystal creatures who live deep within the cores of gas-giant planets, completely unknown to either humans or Ildirans. The Hydrogues travel from world to world via "jump-portals," rarely using actual spacecraft. Neither humans nor Ildirans suspect the existence of this hidden Hydrogue empire—until an experiment accidentally rekindles an ancient war that will span the galaxy.

PRIMARY CHARACTERS

JESS TAMBLYN—a heroic Roamer, dedicated and loyal to his people, he puts his society and family above his own wishes. His older brother Ross, a political powerhouse, is betrothed to the woman Jess himself loves, but Jess is bound by his duty. Jess has always lived in the shadow of his brother. When Ross is killed in the opening salvo of the Hydrogue war, Jess himself is deeply saddened but refuses to take advantage of the situation to marry his brother's fiancee. Instead, he declares his private vendetta against the Hydrogues, and embarks on a risky quest that will and eventually lead to a victory over the Hydrogues, but at the price of his love and of his own humanity.

Cesca Peroni—in love with Jess Tamblyn, though betrothed to his older brother, Cesca is trapped by the political and social ties of the Roamer culture. She is a powerhouse, but definitely a caring, nurturing leader. During the war, she is a scrappy fighter and shrewd politician, seeing her people through a crisis that could either destroy human civilization in the galaxy, or finally give the Roamers their independence.

Davia Tamblyn—impetuous younger sister of Jess and Ross, she hero-worships her two older brothers. Davia wants to leave her mark on the galaxy and make her family proud of her. As soon as war is declared, she brashly leaves the Roamer family net behind to rush off and join the human military fleet. Though facing prejudice against the "star gypsies" among the troops, Davia has a snappy sense of humor and gives as good as she gets. Her intellect and ability to think beyond standard military protocol (a result of growing up among the Roamers) helps her to rise quickly in the ranks.

Basil Wenceslas—the formal head of the Trade Confederacy, this quiet but wily man has eyes in the back of his head and fingers in every pie. He specializes in seeing the big picture and thinking long-term, and he has no doubt that the human race, and the Confederacy in particular, will eventually subsume the ailing old Ildiran Empire. He would like nothing more than for the Teron colony and the unruly Roamers to cooperate better under his leadership for the common good. A hard and intelligent man, he is not overtly evil but willing to take any "necessary" action to (metaphorically) keep the trains running on time.

Raymond Aguerra/King Peter—a charismatic and streetwise "nobody" who is secretly taken by Basil Wenceslas into the palace of Earth's figurehead King. He is groomed to become the next leader of humanity, trained to be a crowd-pleaser and to follow orders . . . but the spunky young man has plans of his own and does not intend to be anyone's puppet.

Estarra—the beautiful and spunky fourth child of the benevolent rulers on Teroc, she has no life path set for her. A tomboy, Estarra sometimes climbs out the residence windows at night and snoops around the town, exploring the jungles, often getting into trouble. In a politically arranged marriage, she will find herself chosen as the bride of King Peter from Earth, destined (along with him) to be a mere puppet of the Trade Confederacy. However, as love grows between her and Peter, they both discover they are too smart to be anybody's pawns, and together they decide to defy the government together.

Beneto—born to luxury and power, the second son of the rulers of Teroc has become a devout convert to the tree-based religion. He goes off to plant saplings and serve as a telepathic communications link on a fledgling human colony, and finds himself at the forefront of the burgeoning war, with only his faith and his wits to defend him.

General Korin'nh—a brave Ildiran military leader who has spent his career waiting for an enemy. Tired of parades and civil engineering missions, Korin'nh has studied the Ildiran historical epic, *The Saga of Seven Suns*, longing for a time when he can seize such glory for himself. But when the alien Hydrogues begin their attacks, he and his fleet find themselves faced with much more than he had bargained for.

Mira—a beautiful, wide-eyed young woman from the jungles of Teron, where she has a telepathic rapport with the sprawling interplanetary forest. She is chosen to accompany the "Iron Lady" Teron ambassador to the spectacular capital world of the Ildiran Empire. There, among more grandeur than she has ever seen before, Mira becomes enchanted by the handsome heir to the Ildiran throne, and finds herself in far over her head.

Prime Designate Yuran'h—the son and heir of the powerful Mage-Imperator of the Ildiran Empire, he falls in love with the lovely ambassadorial aide Mira. After she becomes pregnant with his child and disappears, however, Yuran'h discovers that his father has embroiled all of them in a desperate but treacherous scheme to restore glory to the Ildiran Empire. Anguished, Yuran'h finds himself faced with an impossible choice between saving his race or saving his honor.

Margaret and Louis Colicos—two dedicated archaeologists who have been married for three decades. With plenty of dirt under their fingernails and ground-breaking discoveries on their resumés, they have sifted through the ruins of numerous abandoned Klikiss worlds. However, they are about to stumble upon a find that will send shockwaves through all of galactic society.

Book 1
HIDDEN EMPIRE

For the opening, a large scientific and industrial crew have arrived at the gas supergiant planet of Oncier, surrounded by seven moons, all of which could possibly support human colonies if there were sufficient sunlight. The crew plans to ignite the nuclear fires inside the giant ball of gases, nudging it over the mass limit until it becomes a small sun. This new dwarf sun will burn for only about 100,000 years . . . plenty of time for humans to make the seven Oncier moons into wonderfully productive colonies.

The technology for such an amazing feat was found among the ruins of the ancient Klikiss civilization. MARGARET & LOUIS COLICOS, human archaeologists sponsored by the Earth Trade Confederacy, discovered and deciphered the star-igniting technology in one of the ruined hive cities on a dead planet. They are an older couple, perfect soul-mates, who live for unraveling historical secrets. They have been brought to Oncier as an honor, to watch the experiment, though they can hardly wait to get back to work on a new dig.

As a reward for their important discovery, the Colicos have just received financing to start a new archaeology expedition on a completely untouched Klikiss ghost world. . . . For this great experiment, the man in charge is BASIL WENCESLAS, the hard-edged, shrewd, and ambitious leader of the Trade Confederacy. He is a crack businessman, the true political power, though all the limelight is shed on the glorious figurehead, OLD KING FREDERICK, who remains at his impressive Whisper Palace on Earth. Also in attendance are a green-skinned Teron telepath, to act as a transmitter, sending news of the ambitious test to other telink priests scattered around the Spiral Arm.

A representative from the Ildiran government watches, partly bemused, partly uneasy. With his own empire waning and the wide-open galaxy ripe for colonization, the rather stodgy and ceremony-obsessed Ildirans are puzzled that humans would be so eager to create more *lebensraum* that they would go to all the trouble of creating a new sun simply to make a few moons habitable, while there are certainly other colony worlds that are, in their opinion, nowhere near crowded enough.

From Earth, Old King Frederick sends his blessing via telink. The experiment is set in motion, the alien Klikiss devices dumped like huge missiles into the swirling soup of gases. When the devices are activated, the gas supergiant ignites; nuclear fires begin to burn at its core, and the whole planet is ablaze, becoming a newborn sun.

However, as the atmosphere of Oncier catches fire, barely seen at the incandescent limb of the collapsing super-planet, several strange and incredibly fast objects emerge from deep within the clouds and streak off, surprising everyone. (They are alien ships, but not recognized as such.) Nobody is really sure what they have seen, but their questions are quickly drowned out in the triumphant celebration. After all, nobody can imagine anyone or anything capable of living in the high-pressure depths of a gas-giant planet.

FROM THE BALCONY of his majestic Whisper Palace on Earth, King Frederick announces a day of celebration for the tremendous accomplishment. Since keeping a real-time political hold over such a vast territory is tenuous at best, the King fills the symbolic role as leader. The Trade Confederacy consciously created a royal court and a well-groomed King to give the commercial-based government a face and a heart (such things are never to be underestimated). The Confederacy knows, of course, that no one will give loyalty to corporate heads and big business. They need a figurehead to make and enforce the laws they want, and so they have created one.

King Frederick exists to be seen and revered by the population on Earth as well as the scattered colonists. His court is filled with gorgeous garb and rich trappings (like Queen Amidala from *Star Wars: Episode 1*). The monarchy itself is all show and no substance (which Frederick's successor will gradually discover, to his dismay). Like the monarch of Morocco or the Emperors of China, King Frederick keeps his family and personal life hidden inside a wondrous palace (for reasons to be learned later). Years before the beginning of his reign, this man was chosen for his looks and charisma—just like all of his predecessor Kings. Frederick is constantly surrounded by advisors, so that he never needs to think for himself, doing only what the Trade Confederacy tells him to do. But now the King is getting rather old.

The celebration for the new sun, and soon-to-be new worlds bathed in its light, is like Mardi Gras. King Frederick catches a glimpse of himself in a mirror, sees new wrinkles, an appearance of age . . . and begins to grow very worried.

ON THE JUNGLE planet Teroc, in the human civilization separate from the bureaucratic Trade Confederacy, we meet a lovely young woman, MIRA. Nervous but eager, she is about to go into the worldforest to "take the green," to become one of the symbiotic green priests who can communicate with the interconnected tree that covers much of the Teron landmass. The semi-intelligent worldforest is so intertwined that no one can tell where one tree ends and another begins. Innocent, pleasant, Mira sees wonder all around her. Since childhood, she has been raised and trained, knowing her destiny to become part of the ecological web of the forest. Because of her dedication and reliability, she has been chosen to accompany OTEMA, also known as the "Iron Lady," who will soon be off to Ildira to serve as the Teron ambassador.

Otema has been a priest for so long her skin has darkened to such a dense green it is almost black.

Before she can join the ambassador, Mira must enter into personal symbiosis with the forest.

The worldtrees, networked into one giant sentience that has lasted for millennia, were once an isolated forest of semi-intelligent trees on a single planet. Because it had no way to grow intellectually, no way to experience new things, the worldforest languished for thousands of years. However, when the human colony was established on Teroc, some sensitive individuals learned to commune with the forest. These early 'priests' discovered how to tap into the slow and ponderous memory that was capable of storing and recalling vast amounts of information—a giant living database, hampered only by its lack of experiences and outside knowledge.

As the worldforest began to learn from its human companions, this quickly blossomed into a highly beneficial symbiosis. The green priests started to provide input, explaining mathematics, science, human history, and folklore. Its appetite whetted, the worldforest wanted to absorb all human knowledge. The interconnected forest quickly became an incredible informational reservoir, a giant tree-computer that could assimilate and assess a thousand tangential pieces of information and make brilliant and accurate projections, similar to Asimov's concept of "psychohistory" (for mythic purposes these are equivalent to prophesies).

Still hungry for all kinds of input, the worldforest continues to be a voracious learner, and now wants to learn the history and culture of the Ildiran empire as well.

At various stations in the forest, the priests make regular reports and read dull-sounding data charts to their trees; others play wonderful symphonies and share all kinds of music.

Missionary green priests regularly carry seedlings from the worldforest and spread them to new worlds, taking them back to Earth and to every human colony. A green priest attuned to the worldforest can communicate through the local saplings, which are all directly linked to the main tree network on Teroc and thus connected to anyone else, anywhere else, that has another seedling. This instantaneous communication system of telinks has become a precious commodity in the galactic empire.

The high-tech Trade Confederacy sees the Terons as somewhat mystical and backward, but with a service/resource that is vital to interstellar commerce (parallel with Arab cultures sitting on top of vast desert reserves of crude oil). The green priests never explain the telink process, which greatly frustrates the scientists and industrialists in the Confederacy. . . .

Now, Mira and Ambassador Otema will undertake an important mission to obtain a copy of the fabulous Ildiran chronicle, *The Saga of Seven Suns*, a billion-line poem that summarizes thousands of years of history in the galaxy. Once they have obtained the complete epic and returned to Teroc, Mira and Otema will read this magnificent saga aloud to the worldforest, with assistants and other priests droning on for hour after hour, round the clock, so that the worldforest can experience it. . . .

Ready, curious and just a little bit afraid of the mystery, Mira goes alone into the dense forest, where the moss and leaves and vines grow thicker and thicker, until she is swallowed up. She has a mystical experience, losing track of time, seeing through eyes in the leaves, watching the world from a million different perspectives. When she finally emerges from the worldforest, her skin has turned green, her epidermis impregnated with a symbiotic algae that allows her to nourish herself by photosynthesis.

Ambassador Otema meets her young ward, pride showing on her normally stern face. Mira joins her, and they prepare to depart for Ildira.

THE ILDIRAN GENERAL KORIN'NH is in charge of the revered solar navy, like Admiral Horatio Nelson with a fleet of British naval ships. Humanoid but ethereal, the Ildirans are an ancient race, that humans see as allies or, at worst, neutral. The Ildiran civilization is tired, though they will not admit it to themselves. The Ildirans have a grand cultural, architectural, and artistic tradition, and they believe they are still living in their golden age. General Korin'nh and his fleet have gone to the Ildiran colony of Crenna, where they will assist in the transfer and removal of the entire population. Crenna is being abandoned and shut down, its inhabitants pulled out (a sign of the waning empire).

The Ildirans are very social race and prefer to live in crowded quarters surrounded by their civilization. They have very weak psi powers, which can only be used if the population is sufficiently large to reach a mental "critical mass."

The Ildirans simply don't understand how humans can be loners or individual pioneers. When they choose to colonize a planet, they get enough people together, a "splinter," and depart en masse. (Because they require colonies of a certain minimum size, the Ildirans have never bothered to send individual prospectors—like Margaret and Louis Colicos—to the ghost worlds abandoned by the vanished Klikiss.)

Because of a fever, the Crenna colony has dwindled below the minimum critical mass of population, and the inhabitants have chosen to pull up stakes, take all their belongings, and return to their home world. General Korin'nh has been assigned to take care of all the details. Meanwhile, representatives from the Trade Confederacy have already completed negotiations, signed the papers, and are ready to grab the perfectly habitable abandoned place the moment it is available. For human colonists, Crenna is like a treasure trove, easy pickings for human colonists.

As Korin'nh guides his laden ships away, eager to be back under the seven suns of Ildira, he sees the human ships already descending to the empty cities. To him, the spreading of humans to every single empty spot in the Spiral Arm was at first amusing, then shocking, then frightening. Like many Ildirans, he wonders if these humans just might take over the whole galaxy. . . .

RIDING THE CLOUDS above Golgen (another gas giant planet) is "Blue Sky Mine," a harvester raft-complex, a spectacular hodgepodge of reactor chambers, gathering funnels, and living quarters. These "skymines" are on many gas-giant planets, run by extended families of Roamers (like gypsies), independent bands of humans who operate on the fringe of the Trade Confederacy.

The Roamers harvest huge amounts of hydrogen from gas planets, which they then run through reactors in a process developed eons ago by the Ildirans to create ekti, a previously unknown allotrope of hydrogen. (Scientifically plausible: Graphite and diamond are two different allotropes of carbon; buckyballs, or buckminsterfullerene, is a third, recently discovered allotrope of carbon.) Ildiran stardrives—the only known means of faster-than-light travel—all depend on ekti as a power source, and huge amounts of gaseous hydrogen must be processed in order to create sufficient quantities of the substance to run the stardrives. Because they can provide ekti more cheaply and reliably than other sources, the dispersed and independent Roamers have settled into this commercial niche.

We meet JESS TAMBLYN (our square-jawed hero, a man whose family connections and loyalty puts him at odds with his own personal needs) and his older brother ROSS, who is the chief of the entire harvester complex. Jess has come from Rendezvous, the main hub of Roamer society (a planetary settlement that is kept carefully hidden from Basil Wenceslas and the Trade Confederacy) to pass along news of Roamer politics and various plans the gypsies have made to go behind the back of the Confederacy. Jess is trusted and reliable, but has always been second-in-line, living in the shadow of his brother.

As the eldest brother, Ross is betrothed to the striking beauty CESCA (short for Francesca) PERONI, a gritty Princess Leia type who is the heir apparent of a prominent family in the Roamer web. With large eyes, dusky skin, and a sense of humor matched only by her sense of duty, Cesca keeps herself busy with politics back at Rendezvous. Sadly, Jess himself is deeply in love with Cesca—and the feeling is very mutual. However, deeply loyal to his brother and fully bound by the complex social restrictions in the Roamer culture, Jess would never do anything to hurt or embarrass his brother, and neither will Cesca. They have resigned themselves to an unrequited love. . . . Jess departs from Blue Sky Mine, taking with him affectionate gifts for his brother's betrothed.

Left alone at night, Ross Tamblyn goes out onto the skymine decks and looks at the glittering silver ocean of clouds, an atmosphere that goes down thousands and thousands of miles. He sees deep lightning, storms far below the limits of detection . . . rising higher.

As he watches, an awesome ship emerges from the lower clouds, heaving itself up into open air—a vessel so alien and enormous it looks like a sea monster on old Earth rising to devour a sailing ship. It makes the Mother Ship from Close Encounters look like a toy.

The ship is from the race of HYDROGUES, an intelligent and totally alien species whose civilization lurks in the depths of gas-giant planets, thriving at their high-pressure metallic cores. The Hydrogues have built an empire of their own, hidden from humans and Ildirans; they travel from gas-planet to gas-planet by using jump-portals, dimensional holes that take them from world to world without spaceships. There have long been old wives' tales among the Roamers about mysterious sightings on gas planets, but no one ever dreamed it might be true. The Hydrogue ship looms over the skymine, communicating in a barely understandable imitation of human language that the "rock dwellers" have declared war on the Hydrogues. The "attack" on Oncier has killed billions of their people, and the Hydrogues vow not to ignore the rock dwellers any longer. They will take their payment in blood.

The Hydrogue ship unleashes exotic weapons, slicing the harvester complex to ribbons. The flaming wreckage tumbles like meteors into the sky. Ross Tamblyn is thrown from his observation platform and watches the destruction of everything he values before the clouds swallow him up. He still has more than a thousand miles to fall. . . .

ON THE BARREN and mysterious world of Rhiendic Co, our two dedicated and weathered archaeologists, MARGARET & LOUIS COLICOS, have set up their base camp at the fringe of a ghost city. They, like many other archaeologists, have received a grant from the Trade Confederacy to sift through the long-abandoned ruins of the Klikiss civilization in hopes of finding another great discovery, like the technology that recently allowed Basil Wenceslas to ignite the gas supergiant Oncier into a new sun.

As contract employees, the Colicos team has to surrender any useful discoveries to the Confederacy, but they receive substantial bonuses based on what they find (minuscule, compared with the profits the Confederacy will reap, though)—and they get full rights to publish whatever scholarly papers they like. Margaret and Louis Colicos have been married for thirty years and this is their fourth planetary dig. The Klikiss are fascinating to them, and they want to crack open the answers. What happened to the insectoid civilization? Why did they leave, and where did they go? And why did they leave behind the hulking armored robots, ten feet tall and beetlelike?

Accompanying them on the Rhiendic Co archaeological dig are a few workers, the Colicos' faithful compie servant DD (a classic silver-shelled android), and three of the big Klikiss robots led by one who designates itself as SIRIX. They also have a minor green priest, a washed-up missionary named BARCAS, who has come with the Colicos to plant a few worldtree seedlings on this faraway world, and to send any urgent messages, if necessary.

As the work continues, Louis tries reading a long translation of the *Seven Suns* narrative, searching for information about the Klikiss race, but the insect civilization had already vanished before the beginnings of Ildiran recorded history; the epic poem makes only a few references to the surviving Klikiss robots, which have always been around.

Louis and Barcas often spend evenings playing strategy games together, while Margaret works far into the night, trying to interview Sirix or the other Klikiss robots, but their memories were all wiped long ago, during the disappearance of their creators. She tries questioning them in innumerable ways, but always encounters dead-end answers.

*   *   *

In secret closed-door sessions with the leaders of the Trade Confederacy, Basil Wenceslas raises the issue these executives have been dreading. Old King Frederick is no longer the proud hero they need as a figurehead. His popularity ratings are dropping, and the old man will soon be unable to serve his proper function. Basil convinces the execs that they must begin to search for a virile, striking young ruler to replace the old king—someone the people can rally around. They begin their analysis, poring over records and spy footage in search of a new prince. . . .

We meet a young Everyman on the streets, RAYMOND AGUERRA, an intelligent and dashingly handsome 19-year-old who has a small family, few friends, and even fewer opportunities. He won't be missed. And, most importantly, he vaguely resembles King Frederick.

Operatives from the Trade Confederacy stage a terrible accident that kills Raymond's family and supposedly him as well. The young man is whisked away into hiding. The Confederacy muddies any investigation so that Raymond will appear to have died. All of his records are erased, his past is rewritten. He finds himself deep inside the Whisper Palace, where Basil Wenceslas introduces himself and says, "Good morning, Peter." Raymond doesn't know who he means. "Peter is the name we have chosen for you."

Raymond (along with the reader) is astonished to learn that there is no royal family, that the workings of the Whisper Palace are kept hidden to give the Confederacy plenty of room to do whatever they want. "King Frederick has a few bastard children, but none who even remotely possess leadership potential," Basil explains. "So when the time is right, we will have you replace the king. You, Peter, will be someone whom the public can cheer and fall in love with." This is the same way King Frederick came into power; after the transfer of leadership, the old man will have his features altered and be sent into comfortable retirement on a world of his choice.

Raymond doesn't know what to think.

DELIGHTED, HER EYES sparkling with amazement, the new green priest Mira and Iron Lady Ambassador Otema arrive on the central capital world of Ildira, under the dazzling light of seven suns (Ildira is in the center of a star cluster). The two Teron representatives are welcomed into the magnificent city of Mijistra, which is full of museums containing history, relics, stories, poems, anything that preserves the glory days of the great Ildiran civilization.

The species is polymorphic, with many different body types like the various breeds of dogs, all of which are more or less human-looking; different "breeds" have attributes and abilities that place them into appropriate castes. Thinkers love being thinkers, workers love being workers. They occasionally interbreed. The "god-emperor" of the Ildiran civilization is their Mage-Imperator, a male queen-bee who can experience his entire civilization from his crystal citadel. The Mage-Imperator is the focal point and recipient of the combined, weak psi power and genetic memory of the Ildiran race, which is called thism. This telepathic sense allows the

Mage-Imperator to be the heart and soul of all Ildirans; he can watch and feel everything in his empire. The Mage-Imperator is grublike and sexless, nested in his chrysalis chair, constantly tended and surrounded by helpers; according to legend, he can live a thousand years after he "cuts his tendrils" to become Mage-Imperator.

Before renouncing the calls of the flesh, though, he had many children. Currently his heir, PRIME DESIGNATE YURAN'H is quite different from the old man, very sexy and endowed with charisma and animal magnetism. As is his duty, he has many, many mates and has fathered children of all types. The Ildirans consider it a great honor to breed with him, and Yuran'h has more lover-volunteers than he can possibly service. When the time comes, he will be asked to cut off his tendrils and become the next Mage-Imperator, at which point he will be the focus for the thism and can see through the eyes of his race. There are other Designates in the Ildiran culture, one per planet, all of them children of the Mage-Imperator. Connected to their father through the thism, these Designates rule their individual planets as surrogates, knowing through their special link what the Mage-Imperator would do in each case. Thus, they speak for him, think for him, even without the benefit of instantaneous communication. Inside the spectacular crystal citadel, Mira and Ambassador Otema encounter another Designate—from the colony world of Dobro—who is very hardened and unpleasant.

Mira and Otema enter the court, bringing potted worldtree saplings as gifts to the Mage-Imperator. Mira is instantly entranced with Prime Designate Yuran'h, who is the most hypnotically attractive man she has ever seen.

OFF IN SPACE, in an uncharted rubble/asteroid belt around a red dwarf star, the Roamers have built their central gathering place, called Rendezvous. Rendezvous is a wonderful hodge-podge of space habitats and hollowed asteroid living quarters, a scattered archipelago around a blood-red sun.

Here the Roamers gather to discuss future business interests, to share resources and news, to arrange marriages among the major family branches. They purposely chose a place off the beaten starpaths and completely unsuspected by the Trade Confederacy. Although these independent people pay lip service to the Confederacy, they have quietly built their own culture and civilization, based on the enormous wealth generated by their near monopoly on ekti production for stardrive fuel.

They carefully keep their numbers hidden, and since they build their own vessels in their own shipyards, the Trade Confederacy doesn't even know how many ships they have (which Basil Wenceslas finds very frustrating). The Roamers have their own compie robots as well, each one with a special fail-safe program that performs an immediate brain-wipe if anyone other than a Roamer tries to force them to answer detailed questions (as the Confederacy has already discovered to their dismay).

After leaving his brother Ross on Golgen's "Blue Sky Mine," Jess Tamblyn returns to give his brother's greetings to Cesca Peroni. Their meeting is bittersweet and too-formal, because they love each other. Jess also meets with his younger sister DAVIA, brave and ambitious, perhaps even reckless, but she is a great kid loved by all.

Then the news comes in about the disastrous attack on Golgen, how the mysterious Hydrogues have struck without warning and killed every living soul. The Roamers are in an uproar. Though they are only loosely bound to the Confederacy, they know the Earth-based space military will try to mount a strong response. While the Confederacy has no great love for the Roamers, they must protect their source of ekti for the stardrives.

Cesca and the Roamer family leaders put together an exotic "gypsy funeral" for Ross Tamblyn and all the other victims of the annihilated Blue Sky Mine. Jess, in total shock, can't bear to think that he is now free to love Cesca . . . these circumstances are not acceptable to him, or her. The rigid cultural rules of Roamer society forbid a man to take his brother's widow, and Cesca's family is very conservative and orthodox. If they pursue their love, especially in the face of such tragedy, they will be ostracized-and Cesca has so much she can do for her people, particularly during this crisis. They speak of these things in anguished whispers, and finally decide that they will wait for the end of the Hydrogue emergency, observe an appropriate mourning period, and then request a formal dispensation. Neither of them suspects this war will last more than a decade.

Outraged and hotheaded, young Davia Tamblyn decides to join the Earth space fleet so she can fight the aliens who murdered her older brother. Jess tries to talk her out of it.

Next day, though, the cocky young girl's ship is gone—Davia
has left anyway . . .

A SCIENTIFIC AND industrial team has been stationed on the
moons around Oncier, the blazing new sun created at the beginning of the novel. The engineers are carefully monitoring
the stellar burn, watching the tectonic upheavals on the
once-frozen moons. With big machinery and ships, they apply large-scale engineering to speed up the process of re-
shaping the Oncier satellites so they can become habitable.
The scientists make projections as to which of the thawing
moons will first be able to support a shielded colony.

Then, unexpectedly, a bristling fleet of enormous diamond-hulled Hydrogue warships appear, strange and exotic—
and terrifying. Sending no messages, no ultimatums, the
Hydrogues proceed to lay waste to the scientific observation
stations, exterminating all human life, and then—their vengeance not satisfied—they turn their awesome weapons on the
moons themselves. The first of the seething satellites cracks,
and splits, crumbling into rubble which will eventually smear
out into a ring around the newborn sun. Then the Hydrogues
proceed to the next moon. And the next.

BACK ON THE JUNGLE world of Teroc, the joint rulers are
FATHER IDRISS and MOTHER ALEXA. The architecture and
culture the humans have developed here is modeled after
Mayan cultures (Note, I have taken two trips to the Yucatan
and have toured numerous ruins in the jungles), to give it an
exotic and colorful flavor. By tradition, the firstborn child

(male or female) of the Mother and Father becomes the next ruler, who then marries and starts another family. If there is a second-born child, he or she is destined to "take the green" and become a priest of the worldforest; the third is placed in charge of planetary commerce, becoming a de facto ambassador at large. Idriss and Alexa also have a fourth child, a daughter ESTARRA, who has no particular destiny and is somewhat cast adrift. (She will be very important beginning with Book 2.)

The second-born of Idriss and Alexa is their son BENETO, a green priest who has a comfortable, cushy life performing state religious functions on Teroc. He is devout and dedicated, though, a true believer who wishes he had something more significant to do with his life. With telink communication skills in such demand throughout the Spiral Arm, some missionary priests live in opulent mansions on other worlds, where they are well paid to send and receive messages. Others, however, live a much more austere life and spend their time planting and tending more trees (an intentional echo of the contrast between gaudy Catholic cardinals and pious but poor monks). The Trade Confederacy has been after the vital and priceless telink "technology" for centuries, and it drives them nuts that these mystical priests can provide instantaneous communication.

Beneto, in spite of growing up with a silver spoon in his mouth, has no interest in trappings and finery. Though he has access to the most opulent temples on Teroc, he oftentimes prefers to go out and sleep among the trees in the jungles, disappearing for days. He lives only to serve the worldforest.

Teroc receives word that TALBUN, the green representative at a small human colony, Corvus Landing, is old and dying and needs to be replaced. He requests someone from the worldforest to come and relieve him, Beneto jumps at the chance.

Beneto says goodbye to his beloved little sister Estarra and departs for Corvus Landing. There, he meets the aging priest Talbun, who has skin so deep green skin it looks almost black. Talbun takes him into the small grove of worldtree seedlings he has planted and gives the young priest a crash course in the small agrarian colony. When Beneto is ready, Talbun goes into the grove, lies down among the trunks under the moonlight, and dies, willingly "giving up the ghost." Next morning, not surprised, Beneto finds him. He buries the old man to nourish the soil. Only an hour later, according to tradition, Beneto digs a hole at the grave to plant a new tree in Talbun's honor—but the body is already gone, completely absorbed into the soil. . . .

Beneto then sets out to plant more and more tree seedlings, doing his sacred labor so the worldforest can spread across the universe.

ON EARTH, inside the Whisper Palace, a captive Raymond begins to undergo his training/brainwashing to become the next king of Earth. For the first time in his life the "boy from the other side of the tracks" has everything he could want, and he is given only an inkling of all that will be expected of him. He's not sure he is completely ready for this.

Raymond is tutored by a very old compie, OX, an ancient robot who has seen centuries of human history. Ages ago, when humans first ventured out into interstellar space on lumbering generation ships (before they had access to the faster-than-light Ildiran stardrive), these compies were designed for the incredibly long journeys between the stars. Compies provided a long-term human-looking crew to act as a stabilizing influence for the centuries it would take to reach even the nearest stars. OX, who was on the very first generation ship, is a grand-old machine, well respected, a historical icon. (Even so, OX is a mere pup compared with the extremely ancient Klikiss robots.)

Raymond never gets to meet Old King Frederick. In fact, his very existence as heir-apparent is a closely kept secret from the King; Basil doesn't want the old man to worry that they are planning to replace him any time soon. Meanwhile, astronomers and historians start searching for some eclipse or comet or other celestial event (in all the galaxy there must be something spectacular) that the Confederacy can use as an "omen" for the coronation of Raymond/King Peter. During his training, Raymond learns to his horror that the Confederacy itself set up the accident that killed his family and staged his own death. Infuriated, he vows to resist the indoctrination and tries to remain independent, refusing to fill the role forcibly laid out for him.

Basil Wenceslas is not worried, though. He knows this has happened before. The "princes" always think they can hold out, and they never do.

*   *   *

The Ildiran General Korin'nh takes his marvelous, showy fleet off on a tour of duty. He departs from the grim world of Dobro, always uneasy when he must go there. What the Mage-Imperator and the Dobro Designate have done on that planet seems horrible to him, not a heroic deed that will ever be described in future stanzas of the *Saga of Seven Suns*.

The Ildiran solar navy is huge and ancient, with immense vessels like old British sailing ships that have plied the starlanes for centuries . . . and yet have faced no real threat. Since the Ildirans are a unified, hive-ish organism run by the Mage-Imperator and his Designates, the Solar Navy is mainly for show. There has never been an outside alien enemy. The Ildirans haven't had any factional wars, although in legend there was one Designate who suffered a head injury, causing brain damage; afterward, he was unable to tap into the thism that kept him connected to the central world and the Mage-Imperator—which caused him to believe he had a vision of independence. He led his hapless planet into civil war, which resulted in much bloodshed, the murder of the rogue Designate, and deep psychological scars in the Ildiran people. Many ballads are sung of this. Korin'nh's Solar Navy is full of grand pageantry, military parades, medals, awards (mainly for service to the people, when the General and his soldiers have done Red Cross-type activities in response to disasters, helping to combat plagues, working like a corps of civil engineers on Ildiran worlds). Until they discovered humans, there were no other great alien empires that could possibly have caused conflicts. The Klikiss vanished eons ago, and most of the other life forms discovered have been far too primitive even to become space-farers. General Korin'nh wishes he could have something real to do, something that would earn his place in the epic poetic history of his people.

AFTER THE HYDROGUE attacks on Golgen and the scientific station at Oncier, Basil Wenceslas throws all the Confederacy's industrial effort into the construction of an enormous human war fleet. Shipyards are converted to the construction of battleships, and expeditions are sent out to map gas-giant worlds in search of any signs of the deep-dwelling aliens. Robot probes are sent down into the clouds, but all of them are destroyed. The humans send recorded messages demanding that the Hydrogues cease their aggression, requesting talks, any sort of contact. Everything is ignored.

The impressive new Earth fleet takes shape, an awesome collection of huge and destructive vessels far superior to the old relics still flown by the Ildiran solar navy. The human ships are newer, more horrendous, and more powerful. Soon, they are ready to launch.

BACK ON TEROC, we spend more time with Estarra, the fourth child of Father Idriss and Mother Alexa. She is an unattached daughter, beautiful and spunky, with no life path chosen for her yet. Her parents are loving, but Estarra is ambitious and wants to learn. She sometimes climbs out the residence windows at night and runs across crenellated rooftops, exploring the forest herself, watching the priests, getting into trouble but also picking up details and discovering much about how the world works. Idriss and Alexa indulge her, because she has no particularly important destiny in their society. [To her surprise, Estarra will later be chosen as the wife for King Peter on Earth.] Centuries ago, Earth sent out several enormous generation ships that flew blind to nearby stars, filled with refugees and pioneers. These pilgrims carried pre-packaged colonies with them in hopes of finding a habitable world in their hit-and-miss search.

Somewhere along the way, the first of these ships was intercepted by the Ildiran solar navy, "rescued" from their interminable flight, and the refugees were brought to a nearby untamed planet, Teroc—which was exactly what they were looking for. While the new Terons were setting up their colony, the Ildirans went to Earth to make first contact with the rest of humanity (epic events which were then folded into the continually growing and evolving *Saga of Seven Suns*). The Ildirans went to seek out and rescue the other wayward generation ships. They located many, but claimed never to have found one, a ship which humans now consider to be permanently lost. (However, we will learn that the Mage-Imperator ordered that particular ship and its group of humans to be taken in secret to Dobro, for their own purposes.)

The Ildiran empire gave humans the stardrive, brought us as new members into their sprawling galactic community. The Ildiran civilization, however, was ancient and stagnant, full of ritual and history, but very few fresh ideas. Humans innovated the stardrive system, and Earth's newly formed Trade Confederacy rapidly filled all the old social and commercial niches, so that humans became equally powerful in just a few generations.

TOGETHER, JESS TAMBLYN and Cesca Peroni have a sad romantic scene, unrequited, both of them are torn by their feelings. These two still know their love would shock the Roamer society—Jess doesn't dare to let it seem that that he is celebrating his brother's death so he can get the woman he loves.

Instead, he focuses his efforts with other Roamers on finding a way they can fight back against the Hydrogues themselves. He knows the Confederacy military is mounting a major response, but Jess wants to make a personal strike. "When have we ever been able to count on the Trade Confederacy to do anything for us?" Studying star charts and Roamer capabilities, he begins to plan.

YOUNG DAVIA TAMBLYN has joined the human military, though it is always an uphill fight for her against Earth restrictions and preconceptions. She trains on their ships with the new weaponry and navigation, makes friends, but in general is treated with contempt, prejudice, and suspicion because she comes from the distrusted "space gypsies." Davia is good-humored and resourceful, though, and gives as good as she gets.

Pumping up each other's confidence before they face the enemy, every soldier has an angry, cocky "Over There" attitude, ready to go kick some Hydrogue butt. They tell ridiculous stories and share rumors about the deep-core creatures, but nobody really knows anything. As the outbound fleet cruises past Jupiter and Saturn, they wonder if Hydrogues could be living there, so close to home.

IN THE ILDIRAN capital city of Mijistra, wide-eyed Mira is taken to see a spectacular exhibition of Ildiran jousting by Prime Designate Yuran'h himself. The dashingly handsome Ildiran prince finds this green human woman interesting and intriguing, and soon takes her as his lover. He even uses his mild telepathy to help seduce her. (In his position, he has many mates, as is his duty, though he is never supposed to fall in love with any.) Mira, however, is very different from any Ildiran, more than just exotic.

For weeks, as old ambassador Otema supervises the endless reading of the *Saga of Seven Suns* into the receptive potted trees from the worldforest, Mira continues to be Yuran'h's lover. The Ildirans are very fecund and genetically adaptable, as shown by their numerous interbreeding forms, and the children of mixed castes are always stronger.

Mira finds herself pregnant, but doesn't tell Yuran'h.

AT THE ARCHAEOLOGICAL dig in the dead Klikiss city on Rhiendic Co, Margaret Colicos and her husband continue their excavations. Margaret discovers a wonderful artifact, like a Rosetta Stone, which she believes will be a key to much history from the lost race. The ominous Klikiss robots hover around, watching closely. Louis Colicos suggests to Sirix that he and his robotic companions must be excited if there is a possibility of finally learning what happened to their creator race and why the robots' memories were wiped so long ago. The servant compie DD is helpful and optimistic; the Klikiss robots remain silent.

Meanwhile, the washed-up green priest Barcas receives word through the worldtree saplings about the Hydrogue attacks—three more Roamer harvester platforms destroyed above gas-giant planets. This is beginning to disrupt economies and space travel. Margaret and Louis are dismayed to hear of the destruction at Oncier, which their newly discovered technology converted into a blazing sun. Sirix and the robots listen to the news, seemingly uneasy. . . .

WITH TENSIONS INCREASING because of the Hydrogue attacks, General Korin'nh and his solar navy are sent to guard an old Ildiran hydrogen processing plant in the upper atmosphere around a gas giant—Qronha. This is an enormous and ancient facility, with huge structures, distillers, reaction chambers . . . and enough inhabitants to be a real colony (remember, Ildirans don't like to have too few of their number around). The veteran general has been dispatched to protect the Qronha processing station in a big showy mission (the kind at which he excels). Korin'nh's fleet arrives just as the Hydrogues mount their strike, rising up from beneath the clouds to destroy the harvesting facility. It is a big battle, the first direct military confrontation, with many casualties. The Ildiran fleet rescues as many Qronha workers as they can, while most of the facility plunges down into the atmosphere in flames.

Now the Hydrogues have declared war on the Ildiran empire, too.

THROUGH THE THISM-LINK the Mage-Imperator experiences the horror and pain of the destruction on Qronha. He finds to his dismay and annoyance that his people are now forced to form a military alliance with the humans, because to the Hydrogues all "rock dwellers" are the same. The Ildirans resent the fact that humans have inadvertently dragged them into a war in which they wanted no part.

From his chrysalis chair in the crystal citadel, the Mage-Imperator tries to decide how he can turn this conflict to his empire's advantage. At the very least, this great war will take up a million lines in the *Saga of Seven Suns* . . . and perhaps bring back a new golden age for his waning empire. Knowing that his empire is on the decline, the Mage-Imperator has already turned up the intensity of pageantry and historical celebrations, bread and circuses to distract the populace.

The Mage-Imperator knows more than he shares with the humans, too; from reading a forbidden part of the *Saga of Seven Suns*, a chunk of history that has been censored from the main story, he learns exactly what the Hydrogues are. He also figures out a way he can communicate directly with these alien creatures on their own terms, and sets his plans in motion. It will take a decade or two, but with his reign of a thousand years the Mage-Imperator is accustomed to thinking in the long term.

A DIAMOND-HULLED SHIP arrives at Earth bearing a mysterious ambassador from the Hydrogues. In a spectacular scene, an armored, enclosed environment sphere arrives at the Whisper Palace to speak to old King Frederick, the apparent leader of the humans. This armored sphere, like a crystal ball, holds an ambassador held at extremely high pressure, equivalent to the pressure at the core of a gas-giant planet.

Here, humans finally see that the Hydrogues are creatures made of metallic liquid crystal, which can morph into human shapes. The Hydrogue ambassador takes the form of Ross Tamblyn, the Roamer who was killed at Golgen. (No one recognizes him, but Jess will when he sees recordings of the event.) The tank ambassador announces a dire embargo, claiming that his race will no longer allow any rock dwellers to be parasites on their worlds. The supply of vital ekti will be cut off until the sky-miners can find another source.

Because the arrival of the Hydrogue ambassador was so sudden and unexpected, the real political leader Basil Wenceslas is not able to be there, and the puppet King Frederick has to handle it on his own, without any direct guidance. From his own offices in the military-fleet shipyards, Basil has everything relayed to him immediately via telink by a green priest inside the Whisper Palace throne room. When Basil hears the restrictions the Hydrogues are placing, he knows it will effectively destroy space travel, since humans need to process vast amounts of hydrogen to produce sufficient ekti to run the Ildiran stardrive. Without access to the reservoirs of hydrogen in the gas planets, galactic economy will take a dive.

In the Whisper Palace, with a very nervous King Frederick and all his showy advisors standing around, the Hydrogue ambassador finishes delivering his speech and asks if it has been recorded and transmitted elsewhere, so that all rock dwellers can understand his message. Once the ambassador is assured of this, he cracks open his containment vessel and the sudden release of pressure creates a giant explosion that wipes out the throne room, kills King Frederick and all his advisors, and also kills the ambassador.

OUT IN SPACE, Jess Tamblyn has decided to use Roamer skills and technology to seek personal vengeance for the murder of his brother and what he sees as the unprovoked attacks on his people. Jess and his own band of Roamers, acting without orders and without informing Cesca Peroni or the Roamer council, divert a large comet and send it crashing like a cannon ball into Golgen, the gas-giant world where the Hydrogues launched their first attack in which his brother died. This rogue act horrifies the Trade Confederacy and heats up the war, although most humans are secretly pleased at this sudden, significant strike against their alien enemies.

AFTER THE UNEXPECTED DEATH of old King Frederick, Basil Wenceslas and the Trade Confederacy have no choice but to haul out young Raymond and introduce him to the rest of humanity. Although Raymond and OX have become friends by now, the old tutor robot also has clear orders to be the brash prince's guard and keeper as well.

Raymond has been proving difficult, resisting the indoctrination. Basil, who had hoped to have several more years to train the kid, has no choice but to move up the timetable. Raymond is told he need not worry about anything, because Basil will handle all the decisions. But the prince insists on thinking for himself and making decisions that the Confederacy doesn't approve. Basil is disturbed and uneasy, but in the midst of the war with the Hydrogues, there must be a stable figure.

Once his coronation is scheduled, Prince Peter is brought out and introduced to the enthusiastic public. He gives prepared speeches, changing a few words just to make his mark, to resist where he still can. Basil comments that Peter is just a little bit too much his own man. They will have to knuckle him under by the time of the coronation.

ISOLATED ON THE abandoned Klikiss world, Margaret and Louis Colicos have decoded enough of the complex artifact that they can begin to interpret a few items of breakthrough Klikiss technology. They uncover clear evidence of a terrible war with the Hydrogues eons ago, in addition to blueprints for a completely different type of star travel via dimensional jump-portals that can transport people directly from world to world in an instant.

Louis and Margaret are desperately excited; they have never found anything so incredibly valuable. They put all their discoveries together, compiling the technology and still working on the history. This will be a defining moment, a clear turning point in human history! They break out the dusty bottle of champagne they keep with them for just such a victory.

That night, intending to transmit their news and summon a full-scale research team to this world, the two head for the small grove of worldforest saplings (the only instantaneous method of communication). When they reach the grove, they find it has been uprooted and destroyed. In horror, Louis rushes into the hut of green priest Barcas, only to discover that he has been murdered!

AT RENDEZVOUS, Cesca Peroni has seen tapes showing that the Hydrogue representative appeared on Earth in the form of Ross Tamblyn, her fiancee. She has a heated meeting with representatives of all the main Roamer families, discussing what to do if they are no longer able to harvest ekti from gas-giant planets. Their entire economy is based on this. This war will destroy Roamer independence and power, and they in no way want to become more dependent on the Trade Confederacy, after they have finally managed to wean themselves from the suffocating ties with Earth.

Cesca insists, though, that they can't keep losing populated skymines. The Roamers must pull back and find other ways to harvest the ekti. The gypsies have resources and ingenuity, as well as a long-term plan. The inventors and designers get to work. They will find other ways.

IN A SPECTACULAR ceremony, with forced optimism, Basil Wenceslas and the Trade Confederacy stage a magnificent coronation (at gunpoint) of the new, handsome and charismatic King Peter. Perhaps they even drug him. After the assassination and disaster with the Hydrogue ambassador, the humans are all riled up and unified against the terrible enemy. Basil is concerned by the conflict, but also realizes that wars provide the best circumstances under which to cement unity and to increase control. A war is also the best time for invention and innovation, which can increase the power of the Confederacy. In his first major speech, the new king announces a full-scale military assault with the sophisticated human space fleet. They will take the ekti they need, right from Jupiter here in the home system, and the Hydrogues have no right to deny it. The ships have already launched . . . and there is much cheering. Basil nods in satisfaction, noting that King Peter will provide a good figurehead, after all. "We will wait a few years," Basil tells him, "and then we will find you an appropriate queen."

SPOILING FOR A FIGHT, Davia Tamblyn is on board the full-scale human military fleet, which is en route accompanying a Confederacy gas-harvesting crew to nearby Jupiter, right in our own backyard. The Confederacy has chosen to take their own facility, rather than protect something that belongs to those rebellious Roamers (though Davia can observe and make comments about how inefficient these clunky Confederacy systems are).

With battleships surrounding the harvester machines, the process goes smoothly for several days. The human soldiers get cocky, believing either that Jupiter is uninhabited by the Hydrogues, or that their big kickass fleet has scared the aliens away.

Then Hydrogue diamond-hulled battleships rise up out of the deep clouds and engage the fleet. A spectacular battle ensues, and even the best human warships can't cause sufficient damage to deter the Hydrogues. Several Hydrogue vessels are destroyed, but it is basically a rout. The human ships pull back, beaten. Davia Tamblyn survives, but it appears that all hope has been crushed.

AS THE WAR TURNS uglier, the Ildiran Mage-Imperator sets his treacherous plan in motion. In a quiet, night-time raid, his warriors break into the ambassadorial quarters and take the Iron Lady Ambassador Otema and Mira prisoner. The Mage-Imperator has given orders—Otema is murdered, because she is not of breeding age. Mira, though, is perfect material for his plan. They haul her away to Dobro (already pregnant with the Prime Designate's child), where she will become a mother/breeder. This desperate plan is the only way the Ildiran empire has a hope of surviving the Hydrogue war.

THE HYDROGUES begin a full-scale eradication attack across the Spiral Arm. They destroy every single Roamer skymine station that has not already pulled away from a gas planet. The Roamers begin massive evacuations, and the Hydrogues send a message that they will tolerate no more harvesting from their worlds. Rock dwellers must stay away from the gas worlds, or be destroyed, Access to adequate quantities of the fuel that drives the galaxy has been permanently cut off.

MARGARET AND LOUIS begin to comprehend the terrible straits in which they find themselves. Their loyal robot DD can offer them no assistance. Margaret finally unravels the last bit of history from the Rosetta Stone artifact, just as the hulking Klikiss robots surround their tents. Margaret challenges Sirix. She has learned about the first war with the Hydrogues and what happened to the Klikiss race. Sirix and the Klikiss robots can't allow any of that information to get out. When Margaret tells them what she has learned, Sirix says, "We already know." The robots advance. Margaret doesn't understand. "But you said you had lost all your memories. That you didn't know what happened long ago!" The Klikiss robots take DD prisoner, then close in on the two doomed archaeologists. "We didn't lose our memories. We lied."

CPSIA information can be obtained
at www.ICGtesting.com
Printed in the USA
LVHW03s0630280618
582167LV00001B/52/P

9 781587 154812